Simplified Digital Automation with Microprocessors

Simplified Digital Automation with Microprocessors

JAMES T. ARNOLD

Varian Associates
Palo Alto, California

ACADEMIC PRESS   New York   San Francisco   London   1979

A Subsidiary of Harcourt Brace Jovanovich, Publishers

ACADEMIC PRESS, INC.
111 Fifth Avenue, New York, New York 10003

United Kingdom Edition published by
ACADEMIC PRESS, INC. (LONDON) LTD.
24/28 Oval Road, London NW1 7DX

Library of Congress Cataloging in Publication Data

Arnold, James T
  Simplified digital automation with micro—
processors.

  1. Digital control systems. 2. Microprocessors.
I. Title.
TJ216.A76   629.8'95   78—51242
ISBN 0—12—063750—2

PRINTED IN THE UNITED STATES OF AMERICA

79 80 81 82 83 84 85 9 8 7 6 5 4 3 2 1

Contents

Preface

I have written this book in the hope that it will be useful to readers who are not already familiar with computer technology. The text strives to provide the reader with a workable understanding of the utilization of simple digital circuits as building blocks in structures that by virtue of the programmable operation of the microprocessor can in fact lead to very powerful systems. I have stressed the point of view, through a number of examples, that a limited access to this power can solve a variety of problems in a timely and economical way.

The trend in the application of microprocessors is toward greater sophistication and, in many cases, elegance which mark professional maturity. This is certainly to the good. The potential performance of these remarkable devices requires complex and competent management if that potential is to contribute to solving complex problems. It seems to me, nevertheless, that there is still a place for an approach to microprocessors and their application by imaginative nonexperts.

The neophyte approaching microprocessor and digital applications may be expert in other fields. Use of any device to solve problems really requires a deep insight into the discipline in which those problems lie. Frequently the individual possessed of such insight in a field other than the application of digital circuits and microprocessors will best be able to define the structures that will lead to effective solutions. The beginner with neither the time nor perhaps the inclination to become a microprocessor or microcomputer expert can still derive benefits and economies by being aware, and taking advantage, of the facility offered by microprocessors.

The approach to system designs taken in this book does not attempt elegance or completeness in its treatment of the very capable devices which lie at the center of automated systems. The satisfaction in the approach I have taken will be found in the successful implementation of systems that use just what they require from microprocessors to automate their procedures.

With these prefatory remarks, this book is directed to the adventurous individual willing to step outside of a familiar field to take advantage of a new and versatile tool and use a part of the capability it offers for economical automation.

It has been exciting to explore the application of microprocessors to simple systems that use only a fraction of their full capability. I have been encouraged by my colleagues and helped by many individuals who deserve much of the credit for this work. To Professor Raymond E. Dessy, who is an acknowledged expert in the application of computers to the automation of instruments, I owe special thanks for correction of errors and many helpful suggestions.

I would like also to acknowledge the help of the Technical Publications Department of Varian Associates and its supervisor, Mr. Frank Jean, for many hours of help in the preparation of the manuscript.

Most importantly, I must cite my wonderful family, whose loving encouragement and enthusiastic support have made it possible for me to complete this work.

**Simplified Digital
Automation
with Microprocessors**

I

Automation, an Introduction

Automation—the step-by-step control and execution of processes without a one-to-one, step-by-step intervention of a human operator—and its application have a very long history. No attempt will be made here to present that history. A few examples, serving as illustrations, will be sufficient to introduce both the subject and the concept.

In this introduction, the systems to be considered will be limited to a class in which the results of the automated processes are predictable and are consequent to the specific design of the systems. Within this class, in order to be the subject of automation, an enterprise must be one that has a well-defined objective as well as a plan by which that objective can be reached. The plan may be conceptualized in terms of a progression of events that includes the objective. The progression need not be serial in time, although it is usually convenient to represent it as a serial sequence. This sequence is made up of a linked chain of events, each of which falls into the definition of predictability by the rules of premise and consequence.

Since automation implies the execution of a process without step-by-step human intervention, it necessarily involves the use of devices and mechanisms that are adapted to carry out the steps of the automated process. Organization of the devices and mechanisms is the sphere of the designer of the system. It is the designer who must define the objective of the enterprise to be automated and who must then order the progression of events to occur in a system in such a way that a desired result is reached.

The actual processes to be automated may be simple or complex. They may be lodged in a very wide range of activity, and their sophistication can be as great as the designer's skills and patience will allow.

I-1 OPEN AND CLOSED LOOPS

The plan of an automated operation that leads to a predictable result implies control of its progression of events without intervention of a human operator. The sources of this control allow classification of automated systems into two generic categories, namely, *open-loop* and *closed-loop systems.*

An open-loop system is one in which the progression of events traverses a predetermined series of steps, however complex that series may be, from an initial point to a concluding point, without reference to the result of the process executed by the system or to the result of any step in the progression.

A closed-loop system is one in which the control of a process is automatically mediated in a prescribed manner, at least in part, by some reference to the result of the process executed or to the result of one or more steps in the progression of events comprising the process. The mediated control sequence in closed-loop systems can be quite simple; it is the dependence of the control sequence on the results of the process that distinguishes it from an open-loop system.

The terms *open loop* and *closed loop* have their origins in electronic technology, although the concepts antedate the development of electronics. There is no absolute basis for preference of one category or the other. The application of the control system in an automated process will indicate most frequently the desirability or necessity to choose one or the other.

To illustrate the two categories of automated systems, examples are shown.

Figure I-1 illustrates an open-loop control system. In this example, a series of four valves is operated by the lobe of a rotating cam. The valves are numbered in sequence V_1, V_2, V_3, and V_4. The cam rotates with its shaft in a prescribed (clockwise) direction, and its lobe L engages the toggles of the valves in the succession V_1, V_2, V_3, V_4, V_1, V_2, V_3, V_4, V_1 . . . . As long as the cam shaft turns, this sequence is

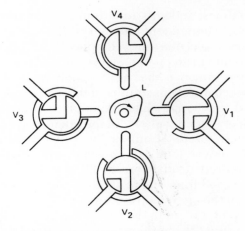

Figure I-1 Automatic valve sequencer.

preserved. It should be noted particularly that the results of the process are not independent of the manner in which the open-loop control system operates. For example, no mention has been made of the rate of rotation of the cam or of the uniformity of its rotational speed. However, the operation of the system is in no way dependent on the results of opening or closing valves.

In order that the system be useful, it may be necessary to provide for the rotation to be started and stopped and for its rotational rate to be regulated. These provisions can be derived from an outside reference, for example, an accurate clock. So long as they are in no way dependent on the results of the valve operation, the system remains an open-loop system. (The intercession of a human operator acting on his cognizance of the results to modify the sequence does not alter the definition of this system as an open-loop system. His action in such a case is not a part of the automated sequence.)

Open-loop control systems can be refined to an arbitrary precision. In the instance described, for example, the rate of rotation can be very precisely regulated so that operation of the valves occurs at very precisely determined intervals. Moreover, the valves themselves can be constructed with great precision so that their flow rates are very close to the designer's requirements. In addition, open-loop systems can be designed with considerable complexity. The system of valves and cam could be provided with an arbitrary predetermined plan or program of starts and stops, each with different rates of rotation introduced at different specified times, and still adhere to the definition that the program of steps is not dependent on any result.

In spite of the precision and complexity of operation that the designer can provide in an open-loop system, there are important constraints on its performance that are implicit in its definition, quite apart from the mechanical constraints of the explicit design. In the example described above, one objective might be to transfer a quantity of liquid to each of four containers. In the open-loop system, the quantity of liquid can be predetermined. The property of quantity is preserved by the system so long as a constant supply condition is maintained. If the desired result were to fill a succession of containers whose capacity varied from one to another, the constraints of the definition imposed on the open-loop system would prevent it from satisfying the requirement, except in the trivial way of overfilling every container and discarding the overflow. The property of filling a container of arbitrary volume cannot be provided in the open-loop system, unless additional information relating the required volume is furnished prior to the result and unless the mechanism is adapted to accept and act on this information.

Quite apart from the constraints imposed on an open-loop control system by its definition, there are the explicit constraints imposed by the actual mechanical design. In the example of Fig. I-1, for instance, the sequence of valve operation must always be from one valve to its nearest neighbor. The sequence . . . , V_2, V_4, . . . is not possible. Moreover, with the prescribed sense of rotation of the cam lobe, operation of the valves is cyclical and includes only the sequence in which the designating subscripts of the valves increase until the largest is passed, whereat the cycle begins again with the lowest. Thus, the sequence . . . V_3, V_2 . . . is not possible.

It should be emphasized that the constraints mentioned in the paragraph above are not implicit in the definition of open-loop systems. They are explicit mechanical constraints arising from the designer's choice of mechanisms. If inverted or alternate sequences in valve operation had been required, the designer could have used different mechanisms to accomplish the desired result.

A closed-loop system is distinguished from an open-loop system by the incorporation of (1) a sensing mechanism to monitor a result of its operation and (2) a means to use this information automatically to modify the operation of the system. A closed-loop system may include a number of open-loop steps in which the operation proceeds without reference to the result. Figure I-2 illustrates a simple closed-loop system. In this system a container C is filled to a level h. The provision

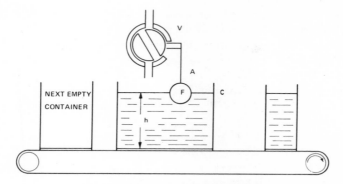

Figure I-2 Valve control with feedback.

that is made to satisfy the requirement of filling the container to the specified level lies in the mechanisms of the float F and its linkage A, which operate to close the valve V when the level of the liquid reaches the height h regardless of any differences in container volume that may obtain.

To be useful, the system of Fig. I-2 may include some open-loop steps. These might be to position an empty container below the valve-delivery point prior to filling, to start the filling operation, to override the float mechanism and hold the valve closed after the filling step has been completed, and to displace the filled container to make room for presentation of the next empty container. Within reasonable bounds, all of these steps may be taken without any reference to the result of any operation in the cycle. However, the property of filling a container of arbitrary volume requires that the system include the sensing device (float) and the mechanism (linkage to valve toggle) by which the information sensed is automatically conveyed to modify the result (stop flow when the container is filled to the level h).

I-2 AN ADDITIONAL EXAMPLE

Automation has found considerable use in industry to reduce the labor and cost in fabricating a variety of items. Figure I-3 shows an automated contouring mill in a representative schematic way. The function of this system is to carve a surface $Z(x, y)$ on a billet of material, using the motor-driven cutter C. This system could be operated en-

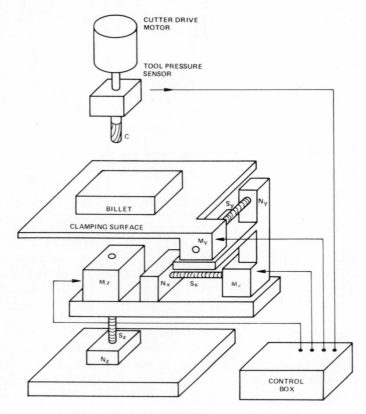

Figure I-3 Automated contouring machine.

tirely as an open-loop system. However, for further illustration, its description will include a closed-loop step.

Three mechanisms that are similar to each other are included in the system to provide calibrated motion of a clamping surface in the three mutually perpendicular directions x, y, and z. These mechanisms are made up of precise jack screws S_x, S_y, S_z that engage nuts N_x, N_y, N_z to provide motion in the three respective directions when they turn. They are actuated by motors M_x, M_y, M_z that are capable of turning in precise uniform increments that are small enough to satisfy the requirements of the contour of the desired surface $Z(x, y)$ in response to electrical signals from a control box.

Included in the cutter-drive arrangement is a tool pressure sensor that responds to the force required to advance the cutter in the billet. The information from this sensor is delivered to the control box as an electrical signal. The function of this part of the system is to furnish a closed-loop means to modify the operation, which in this case is to reduce the rate of advance of the cutter and thereby prevent overstress of the cutter blades.

Several modes of operation are possible within the explicit mechanical constraints of the system described above. The choice of mode will be made on the basis of its suitability to the specific surface contour $Z(x, y)$ to be generated. In one mode, with the cutter clear of the billet, the screws S_x and S_y will be advanced to establish a cutter position X_k, Y_k above the work, and then the screw S_z will be advanced to the position Z_k, during which time the cutter will remove material from the billet, leaving the final level Z_k expressed on the work. These steps will be repeated for each point X_k, Y_k, Z_k on the prescribed surface $Z(x, y)$ until all points have been cut to conform to its contour.

In another mode, the screws S_x and S_z may be operated with S_y fixed so as to generate the profile $Z(x)$ for a fixed value of y. In this operation the cutter removes material from the billet to leave this profile of the required contour expressed in its surface. As each profile is completed, screw S_y is advanced by a small increment, and a new profile is generated by the motions of S_x and S_z. This operation is repeated until the entire surface is cut in a series of profiles conforming to the surface $Z(x, y)$.

In any mode of operation, if the tool pressure sensor indicates excessive stress on the tool blades, an electrical signal is delivered to the control box, which responds by reducing the rate of tool advance.

Clearly, a variety of modes can be devised to operate the system for a desired result. In order to implement a mode, the control box must issue an appropriate set of (electrical) signals to the drive motors and must be prepared to respond to information from the tool pressure sensor. The plan of attack to generate a contour must be predetermined and introduced into the control box in a program of steps. A frequently used means for introducing and storing these steps is the punched paper tape. Each step of the system operation is encoded in a pattern of holes punched in a narrow strip of paper (tape). Within the control box, a set of electrical contacts senses the presence or absence of holes and, through a decoding matrix, interprets each encoded step to operate, in this case, the drive motors M_x, M_y, M_z.

The generation of encoded tapes is the province of a programmer. The use of tapes for control provides the means by which the system becomes a general purpose tool, that is, a surface contour mill that can generate any one of a class of surfaces $Z(x, y)$ subject to the commands residing in the encoded tape provided by the tape programmer. A section of tape with hypothetical commands is illustrated in Fig. I-4. The

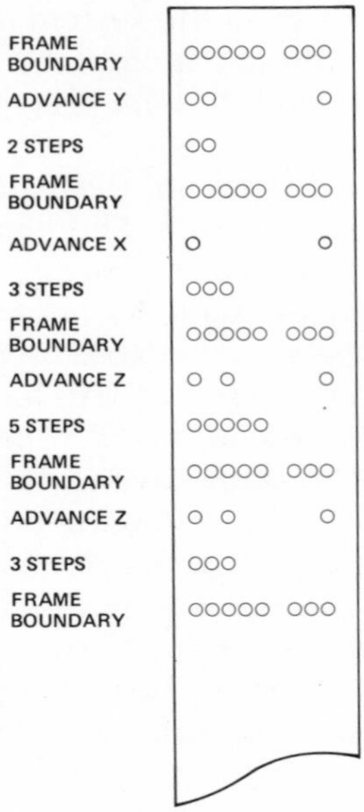

FRAME BOUNDARY	OOOOO OOO
ADVANCE Y	OO O
2 STEPS	OO
FRAME BOUNDARY	OOOOO OOO
ADVANCE X	O O
3 STEPS	OOO
FRAME BOUNDARY	OOOOO OOO
ADVANCE Z	O O O
5 STEPS	OOOOO
FRAME BOUNDARY	OOOOO OOO
ADVANCE Z	O O O
3 STEPS	OOO
FRAME BOUNDARY	OOOOO OOO

Figure I-4 Crudely coded punched paper tape.

tape reads from top to bottom and encodes commands required for a section of the profiling mode of operation. Each encoded command is structured according to a specific prescribed pattern within a command or instruction frame. The frame boundaries are indicated by a recognizable pattern of holes. Interpretation of the coded commands is indicated in the figure.

To generate a control tape, the programmer first may list the steps to be executed, (in this case the y, x, and z motion commands defining the required profile) and then may encode each step as a pattern of punched holes in successive frames on the tape. It should be noted that the code illustrated is quite inefficient. Much more compact codes can be devised. Moreover, a variety of programming aids have been developed to assist the programmer in establishing the required sequence of commands, and automatic encoding and tape-punching machines have been devised to generate the actual encoded paper tapes.

I-3 THE AUTOMATED WORLD

As a result of human inventiveness, the application of automation has grown steadily through the recorded history of man. The recent development of electronic control technology has caused a major spurt in the growth of automation in the industrialized parts of the world. Simple and familiar automation such as that found in home appliances, traffic signals, elevators, and the like is being followed by automated factory assembly stations, automated railway and aircraft control, and even automated landing of spacecraft on distant planets.

Whereas earlier automated systems relied on control devices that were often mechanical in nature and were capable of processing no more than a few simple commands per second, systems based on recent electronic technology can process millions of commands per second. It is this vastly expanded processing capability that has made possible automated systems of a sophistication and complexity that, in some cases, mimic human intelligence and, in many cases, far exceed human capabilities for speed and accuracy in handling information and guiding processes.

In spite of their impressive capabilities, automated systems rely for their operation on only a few simple types of logical steps that link identifiable conditions. They rely for their operation on such elementary statements as

Proceed from step N to step N + 1
Add increment U to quantity V
If quantity V is greater than quantity W go to step M
If condition C is true go to step L
Condition A true together with condition B true implies condition
    C true
Condition A true or condition B true implies condition C true
Condition A true when condition B is false implies condition C
    true

It is the speed with which modern electronic systems can process such simple logical steps and the skill and artistry expressed by the system's designer and programmer that give these systems the enormous capability found today.

The application of this capability began in endeavors whose importance could justify very substantial expenditures of effort and could support very large costs. Electronic technology has developed in the last few years to the point at which the lowered costs of the devices permits the automation of almost any activity. The twenty-dollar microprocessor available today has the control capability of the $2-million system of the 1950s or the $20-thousand system of the early 1960s. Application of this low-cost technology will become more and more pervasive with time. For the most part automation will operate to reduce the human attention and labor necessary to carry out a host of routine tasks.

EXERCISES

1. Devise a turnstile system that will admit visitors for an entrance fee and will render a count of the visitors admitted.

2. Design a punched paper-tape code to command four separate operations in which each operation shall be governed to proceed at integer rates varying between −15 and +15.

3. Design a system that will open your bedroom window in the morning unless it is raining.

4. Design a pottery-kiln control system able to fire clays in accordance with a temperature cycle as follows:

0–75 min: Temperature rises uniformly from 20 to 800°C
75–135 min: Hold temperature at 800°C
135–240 min: Increase temperature to 1050°C
240–600 min: Reduce temperature uniformly to 20°C

II

The Digital Approach to Information and Processes

The management of information and processes is facilitated by languages in which words are symbols that represent elements of the information or process in question. In spoken or written languages, the words, in general, are assigned unique connotations. In contrast to words, members of the set of real numbers can be assigned arbitrary connotations. These numbers, by their assignment, constitute a language that can be designed to satisfy special requirements. Often this is accomplished with great compactness and efficiency. One such assignment, of course, is quantitation, wherein the number defines the property of quantity only, and additional words are required to complete other elements of information. However, other connotations may be assigned to members of a number set in a particular enterprise, and, if the assignment and the rules of usage are properly carried out, the "language" can be used to accommodate the requirements of that enterprise.

The usefulness of number languages lies partly in the fact that there exists a universally accepted set of precise rules for number manipulation that is rooted in mathematics. These rules can be used advantageously to facilitate logical and precise expression of the elements of information and processes required in the enterprise. Moreover, since the information and process steps must pass through a mechanism or device in an automated system, the regularity of the number set is adapted to the design of uncomplicated mechanisms and devices.

Without limiting the range of expression, it is possible and convenient to simplify the symbology further by using the set of integers, rather than the entire set of real numbers, in constructing languages to represent elements of information or processes. This simplification further reduces the complexity of mechanisms and devices required to implement an automated system. Of course, the detailed characteristics of mechanisms and devices used will depend on the number system employed.

For all but a few readers, comments on number systems extending beyond the most general remarks may seem unrewarding and dry when taken out of the context of preparation for the more interesting sections which deal with the application of digital logic. The paragraphs which follow should be approached simply with the aim of grasping binary arithmetic. The presentation begins with examples drawn from familiar decimal arithmetic and proceeds to the conceptually simple but less familiar arithmetic of binary numbers. The very formal constructions of Boolean logic are implicit in digital applications and are useful in the most professional approach to digital logic. However, most simple applications can be devised and understood on an intuitive basis once the fundamentals of binary numbers are firmly grasped.

Number systems in common use rely for their expression on digits that can be combined to form numbers. The important attributes identifying the meaning of a digit within a given number system are *place* and *value*. When these two attributes are specified for each digit making up a number, the number itself is specified. The number system used defines a discrete range of values that a digit can assume. The Arabic numeral system assigns ten possible values or *states*, 0–9, to designate the value of a digit. A number in the decimal number system using Arabic numerals then can be expressed as a combination of digits as follows:

in the first place: state five
in the second place: state three
in the third place: state six

In shorthand notation this is 536, and, of course, the meaning of these two notations is the sum of five hundreds, three tens, and six units. The compactness and precision of the digital expression is evidenced by the fact that the number can be represented by the three written symbols 536.

II-1 THE REGISTER

A mechanism can be devised to express an integer number. This important device is called a register. One familiar example of a register comprises an ordered set of wheels, each wheel being capable of turning to one of ten positions. The ordering of the wheels establishes the attribute of place. The ten positions to which each wheel may be turned represent the field from which the second attribute, state, may be determined. The turning of a wheel to successive positions exposes faces inscribed with Arabic numerals from 0 to 9 that identify its state. Figure II-1 shows a typical three-digit decimal register showing the fifth state in the highest place, the third state in the middle place, and the sixth state in the lowest place. This setting represents the number 536.

Registers may be used to store numbers. They may be manipulated in specified ways to modify numbers. The familiar mechanical adding machine makes an addition to a digit by rotating its digit wheel through a number of steps prescribed by the addend of the addition (with provision made to take account of an overflow state beyond state 9).

The register is the most commonly used mechanism or device found in any digitally automated system. The system itself is adapted to bring information to registers, to transfer information from register to register, to modify information in a register in some prescribed way, and to deliver information from registers to a destination.

II-2 NUMBER SYSTEMS OTHER THAN DECIMAL: THE BINARY SYSTEM

The decimal system is a compact and convenient one for numeration. Other systems using, for example, 12 states per digit or 5 states per digit have been used, but only in rare instances. Of course, number systems having any number of states per digit can be devised

Figure II-1 A mechanical register.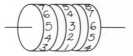

and can be provided with rules for arithmetic and other logical procedures. The binary number system, with just 2 states per digit, while not so compact as others, offers some unique advantages in the field of automation.

First, a field of 2 states only is easily represented mechanistically. This is best illustrated by the establishment of a one-to-one correspondence of the digital state to the state of a switch, a light, or a valve. These devices can be, clearly and unambiguously, in one of two unique states, on or off, and therefore can represent the state of a digit.

Second, there is an almost endless list of attributes that with their negatives, form binary pairs—not true/true; not up/up; not wet/wet; not zero/zero. To emphasize the binary nature of these attributes, the negative states often have their own names. Thus, the list in the sentence above could have been rendered as false/true; down/up; dry/wet, and of special importance for the number system having digits of only 2 states, zero/one. The statement of a sufficient number of attributes or their negatives allows the specification of almost any concept. The familiar game of 20 questions illustrates this versatility.

The binary pair, false/true, also forms the basis for statements of formal logic, and manipulations of binary digits and numbers, defined in a system to represent attributes, can be carried out in accordance with logical rules to reach a coherent result.

The comments above would indicate that the binary number system is a good choice for a versatile language to be used in digitally automated systems. Indeed, it has been almost the exclusive choice.

A binary number or word is usually written as a series of ones and zeros. The decimal number 500, for example, can be written as 111110100. In so far as this binary sequence represents a number, it is a compact way of writing 1 times 2^8 plus 1 times 2^7 plus 1 times 2^6 plus 1 times 2^5 plus 1 times 2^4 plus 0 times 2^3 plus 1 times 2^2 plus 0 times 2^1 plus 0 times 2^0. The same set of binary digits could also be used as a compact ordered statement of nine attributes or their negatives as follows:

True   True   True   True   True   False   True   False   False,
or 111110100

This compact statement has meaning only if each place in the sequence of digits has been assigned in a manner that indicates the state of a specific attribute, just as each place represents the presence or absence of a power of 2 in the sum when the binary word represents a number.

II-3 BINARY ARITHMETIC

Binary numbers can be treated arithmetically in a manner similar to the familiar expression of decimal arithmetic. The rules are simple. Addition, designated by the word *plus* (+ is reserved as a logic symbol), is carried out for each digit in accordance with the rules shown in Table II-1. By way of example, this table can be applied to each digit of the sum of two binary numbers as shown below:

	Digit 4	Digit 3	Digit 2	Digit 1	Digit 0
Augend	0	1	0	1	1
Addend	0	1	0	1	0
Carry in	1	0	1	0	0 ← 0
Carry out	0	1	0	1	0
Sum	1	0	1	0	1

(The numbering of the digits given in this example is in accordance with a usual convention.)

Subtraction is carried out in accordance with rules set up in Table II-2. An example where the minuend is greater than the subtrahend is shown first:

	Digit 3	Digit 2	Digit 1	Digit 0
Minuend	1	1	0	1
Borrow out	(0) 0	1	0	0
Borrow in	00	00	10	00
Augmented digit	01	00	10	01
Subtrahend	1	0	1	0
Difference	0	0	1	1

Table II-1 Binary Addition Table for One Digit in a Sequence

Augend	Addend	Carry in	Sum	Carry out
0	0	0	0	0
0	1	0	1	0
1	0	0	1	0
1	1	0	0	1
0	0	1	1	0
0	1	1	0	1
1	0	1	0	1
1	1	1	1	1

Table II-2 Binary Subtraction Table for One Digit in a Sequence

Minuend	Subtrahend	Borrow in	Difference	Borrow out
0	0	0	0	0
0	1	0	1	1
1	0	0	1	0
1	1	0	0	0
0	0	1	1	1
0	1	1	0	1
1	0	1	0	0
1	1	1	1	1

With the subtrahend greater than the minuend, the requirement to borrow does not stop at the left-hand digit, as shown following:

	Digit 5	Digit 4	Digit 3	Digit 2	Digit 1	Digit 0
Minuend	0	0	1	0	1	0
Borrow out (1)	1	1	1	0	1	0
Borrow in	10	10	10	10	00	10
Augmented digit	01	01	10	10	00	10
Subtrahend	0	0	1	1	0	1
Difference	1	1	1	1	0	1

Obviously the sequence of ones to the left in the last difference will continue indefinitely, and the line labeled *difference* must be interpreted.

The interpretation leads naturally to a formalism by which negative numbers in the binary system are often designated. The formalism, to be unambiguous, requires that a number, positive or negative, be represented by a specified number of digits. Many systems using the binary expression, are designed to manage binary numbers (or words) of 8 binary digits. When the digits are used to represent signed numbers, the digit in the highest place is used exclusively to distinguish the sign of the number. In the 8-digit specification, the two subtractions above may be rewritten as

$$
\begin{array}{r}
00001101 \\
\text{minus} \quad 00001010 \\
\hline
00000011
\end{array} \quad \text{equals positive 3}
$$

$$
\begin{array}{r}
00001010 \\
\text{minus} \quad 00001101 \\
\hline
11111101
\end{array} \quad \text{equals negative 3}
$$

The benefit of this notation may not be obvious without further interpretation. The interpretation requires the introduction of the concept of *complement* as follows:

The n states of a digit used for numeration may be arranged in ascending order of the numerical value they represent. In the decimal system this arrangement is

$$0, 1, 2, 3, 4 : 5, 6, 7, 8, 9$$

In this arrangement of states of the decimal digit the complement of a state n is that state that is symmetrically located with reference to the center (:). In the decimal system the complement of the state n, called the nine's complement $\bar{n}$, can be found in the algorithm $\bar{n} = 9$ minus $\bar{n}$. Thus, $\bar{2} = 7$, $\bar{4} = 5$, and $\bar{8} = 1$.

With decimals of a specified number of digits, using the notion of the nine's complement and a carry in to amend the result, subtraction may be obtained by using the rules of addition. The sign of the result is designated by the state of the highest place, which is reserved in all operands for designating sign. The parallel computations illustrate the nine's complement formalism for decimal subtraction:

Minuend	0536	Augend	0536	
Subtrahend	0123	Addend	9876	$= (\overline{0123})$
		Carry in	1	
Difference	$\overline{0413}$	Result	$(1)\overline{0413}$	

Minuend	0536	Augend	0536	
Subtrahend	0635	Addend	9364	$= (\overline{0635})$
		Carry in	1	
Difference	(minus) $\overline{\;99}$	Result	$(0)9901$	

Final interpretation of these results is as follows: The final carry 1 in the first example result is discarded (it lies outside the defined field of places in the number specification). The result is (plus) 0413, which is identical to the difference found with conventional subtraction. In the second example, the result 9901 is equal to the nine's complement of 0099 plus 1. The seeming complexity and confusion of this formalism applied to decimal subtraction is resolved by adopting the notation for negative decimal numbers as follows:

$$\text{minus} \quad 0\, D_2 D_1 D_0 = 9\, \overline{D_2}\overline{D_1}\overline{D_0} \quad \text{plus} \quad 1$$

With this convention, the examples above may be rewritten.

Augend	0536	original minuend
Addend	9877	$= \overline{0123}$ plus 1, complement of original subtrahend plus 1
Result	$(1)\overline{0413}$	$=$ difference between minuend and subtrahend

Augend   0536   original minuend
Addend   9365 = $\overline{0635}$ plus 1, complement of original subtrahend plus 1
Result   (0)9901 = $\overline{0099}$ plus 1 = minus 99, difference between minuend and sub-
                             trahend

Although this formalism, when applied to decimal subtraction appears to be a bit cumbersome, it is very convenient in the case of binary subtraction since the expression of the binary complement is formed simply by substituting 1's for 0's and vice versa. Thus, from the earlier examples one sees that

$$\text{complement } (00001010) = 11110101$$
$$\text{complement } (00001101) = 11110010$$

and by using the definition for the notation of negative numbers developed in the decimal case one gets

$$\text{negative } (00001010) = 11110101 \text{ plus } 1$$
$$= 11110110$$
$$\text{negative } (00001101) = 11110010 \text{ plus } 1$$
$$= 11110011$$

With these expressions, the subtractions may be written by using the rules of addition, adding the negative of the subtrahend to the minuend.

Augend   00001101   original minuend
Addend   11110110   negative of subtrahend
Result   (1)00000011   difference, discard surplus carry = positive 3

Augend   00001010   original minuend
Addend   11110011   negative of subtrahend
Result   (0)11111101   difference = negative 3

The apparent complication of the formalism arises from the unavoidable inclusion of the state representing the value zero in the digits used to represent numbers. Utilization of this formalism allows a particularly simple mechanization of the arithmetic operation of subtraction.

Multiplication and division are extensions of addition and subtraction, and they are carried out for binary numbers in a manner totally analogous to their expression in the decimal number system. The only complication lies in the number of digits necessary to define the product or dividend. Whereas, in the example above, numbers were specified always to have 8 digits with the digit in the highest place indicating the sign, the product of two n–digit signed number can extend to $2n$ digits including the sign bit. Moreover, if either or both of the factors in the product are negative, they must be written in the

$2n$–digit specification to give the correct result. (Surplus carrys in the product beyond the $2n$th are discarded as before.)

With these comments in mind some examples of multiplication may be written.

(a) Multiplicand   00001010
    Multiplier   00001101

```
              00001010    1st partial product
              00000000    2nd partial product
              00001010    3rd partial product
              00001010    4th partial product
      0000000010000010    product, 16 digits, positive
```

(b) Multiplicand   1111111111110110 = minus (00001010), extended left to 16 digits
    Multiplier   00001101   positive multiplier

```
      1111111111110110
      0000000000000000
     1111111111110110
    1111111111110110
    xxxx1111111101111110    product, 16 digits;
                            discard 4 surplus carries
```

Inspection shows that the 16-digit product in example (b) is indeed the negative of the product in example (a) (as it should be). A third example with both factors negative and in the 2's complement notation can be written (tediously):

(c) Multiplicand   1111111111110110 = minus (00001010)
    Multiplier   1111111111110011 = minus (00001101)

```
                    1111111111110110
                   1111111111110110
                  0000000000000000
                 0000000000000000
                1111111111110110
               1111111111110110
              1111111111110110
             1111111111110110
            1111111111110110
           1111111111110110
          1111111111110110
         1111111111110110
        1111111111110110
       1111111111110110
      1111111111110110
     1111111111110110

    xxxxxxxxxxxxxxxx0000000100000010    product, 16 digits;
                                        discard 16 surplus carries
```

This is, of course, the same result as the 16 digit product in example (a), as expected. Even these cumbersome multiplications of negative numbers adapt themselves well to mechanized systems using binary representation.

Division is carried out by successive subtractions of the divisor digits from the dividend, beginning from the left-hand places in the dividend. The dividend, as was the product above, may be specified with 16 digits and the divisor with 8. This specification will lead to a quotient with at least 8 digits. Other specifications may be used depending on the nature of the problem addressed. Each subtraction of the dividend digits will produce a remainder that is either negative or nonnegative. If the remainder is positive or zero, the corresponding partial quotient digit is 1, the divisor is moved one place to the right, and further subtraction is made. If the remainder is negative after subtraction, the corresponding quotient digit is 0, and the subtraction is reversed before the divisor is moved to the right. Division is complete when the divisor can no longer be subtracted from the remaining part of the dividend to give a positive result. One example of division of two positive numbers will be given:

Dividend	0000010100000000	16 digits
Divisor	00001101	8 digits

Procedure:

Partial quotient	0	
Augend	000001010000000	dividend
Addend	11110011	negative of divisor, placed left
Result	111110000000000	result is negative; reverse the subtraction, displace addend to the right. Quotient digit is (0)

Proceed:

Partial quotient	00	
Augend	0000010100000000	dividend
Addend	111110011	negative of divisor, placed left
Result	11111110100000000	result is negative; reverse the subtraction, displace addend to the right. Quotient new digit is (0)

Proceed:

Partial quotient	001	
Augend	0000010100000000	
Addend	1111110011	
Result	(1)0000000111000000	Remainder remainder is positive; quotient digit is 1

Proceed:

Partial quotient	0011
Augend	0000000111000000
Addend	11111110011
Result	(1)0000000000100000

Remainder   remainder is positive; quotient digit is 1

Proceed:

Partial quotient	00110
Augend	0000000000100000
Addend	111111110011
Result	1111111111010000

result is negative; reverse the subtraction, displace the addend to the right; quotient digit is 0

Proceed:

Partial quotient	001100
Augend	0000000000100000
Addend	1111111110011
Result	1111111110111000

result is negative; reverse the subtraction, . . . ; quotient digit is 0

Proceed:

Partial quotient	0011000
Augend	0000000000100000
Addend	11111111110011
Result	1111111111101100

result is negative; . . . ; quotient digit is 0

Proceed:

Partial quotient	00110001
Augend	0000000000100000
Addend	111111111110011
Result	(1)0000000000000110

Remainder   remainder is positive; quotient digit is 1

Since the final remainder is smaller than the divisor, no further subtraction can be made, and the final quotient is 01100010 with a remainder of 110.

II-4 A PROJECT

A checker set may be used to carry out the steps of binary arithmetic. Colors of the squares on the checker board are of no meaning. The two colors of the checkers themselves can be used to represent the two binary states that binary digits can occupy.

The project is to devise the rules for the four simple games of addition, subtraction, multiplication, and division, and then to play the games. It may be prudent to limit the number of digits specified since there are only 12 markers of each color. A translation table relating binary numbers to their more familiar decimal counterparts may be helpful to monitor the results found in the games.

EXERCISES

1. Using the Arabic symbols, devise a number system having 8 states for its digits including 0. Translate the decimal numbers from 0 to 32 into this (octal) number system, and write a multiplication table for octal numbers.

2. Translate the following decimal numbers into binary notation: 4, 12, 15, 24, 47, 127.

3. The following arithmetic problems are stated using decimal numbers. Perform the arithmetic using binary notation; translate the results into decimal notation and check the results: (1) 12 plus 24; (2) 127 minus 47; (3) 12 times 4; (4) 47 divided by 4.

III

Elementary Digital Logic

An automated system, relying for its information and control on digital expression, often requires operations other than arithmetic to perform its functions. Chapter I described the operation of an automated system that followed a specifically defined plan with a progression of events or steps. If the information and control flow is digital in expression, each event or step in the operation can be associated with one or more digital *statements*. These statements can imply information, instructions for the manipulation of information, results of information manipulation, commands to mechanisms, and so forth. Linking digital statements in a coherent system implies a coherent logic of operation whose rules form the basis for the system design.

Although many mechanisms can be and have been used to implement the management of digital statements, the most common, by far, are based on electric and electronic technology. Subsequent discussions in this book will be limited primarily to the use of electrical and electronic mechanization of systems.

III-1 ELECTRICAL IMPLEMENTATION OF SIMPLE LOGICAL STATEMENTS; BUFFERS AND GATES

The simplest mechanism for electrical implementation is the electrical switch. Electric current may be conveyed from a source to a destination by means of a conductor, and the current may be controlled (interrupted) by means of a switch. Figure III-1 shows the simplest control circuit, consisting of a source (battery), a switch, and a destination (or load). When the switch is open, no current will flow in the load; when the switch is closed, current will flow in the load. The presence or absence of this current can be sensed with a device such as the voltmeter shown in the figure.

Even this very simple mechanism can be used to represent simple logical statements. It can be used, for example, as a 1-digit register. Information is introduced into the register by placing the switch in either the open or the closed position. A convention is adopted to define the selected state as a binary 0 or 1 depending on whether the switch is open or closed, respectively. This convention is commonly used, and the description of devices and operations by this convention are said to be defined in *positive* logic. The state of the register can, of course, be sensed or "read" by the voltmeter.

An alternate use of the mechanism can be defined by using the arrow marked *actuation* (Fig. III-1). In this use, the mechanism lies between two points, labeled actuation (often called *input*) and *output* in Fig. III-1. The actuation itself can be the result of another mechanism. For each state of actuation, there is a logical consequent state of output. If the actuation is present—a state that may be symbolized by a binary 1—the output also occupies the binary state 1. If the actuation is absent—a state that can be represented by a binary 0—the output

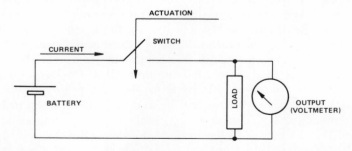

Figure III-1 A simple logic circuit using a switch for actuation and a meter for output indication.

also occupies the state 0. These implications may be summarized in the statements where the overbar on the letter implies the comple-

Actuation	Output
$\dfrac{A}{\overline{A}}$	$\dfrac{B}{\overline{B}}$

mentary state. It is also convenient to write a truth table to describe the operation of a mechanism of this sort, using the binary comple- ments 1, and $\overline{1} = 0$. Thus, the statements above may be represented as

Input	Output
1	1
0	0

A mechanism whose input (I) and output (O) conform to the state- ment of this truth table is equivalent to the battery and switch arrange- ment shown in Fig. III-1. The logical consequences of its use are not dependent on its detailed structure, and, without loss of clarity, it may be given a very simple symbol (see Fig. III-2a). Mechanisms or de- vices of this sort are called buffers—a title often accompanied by a prefixal word or statement describing the function were completely.

The arrow representing actuation in Fig. III-1 was placed in a direc- tion to close the switch when actuation was present [input = 1]. In a similar device the arrow could have been placed in the opposite direc- tion, so that actuation opened the switch and the absence of actuation left the switch closed. The operation of such a device would be sum- marized in the following truth table:

Input	Output
0	1
1	0

This device is also a buffer. It is called an inverting buffer or inverter, while the first device described is more completely called a nonin- verting buffer. The symbol for the inverting buffer is shown in Fig. III-2b.

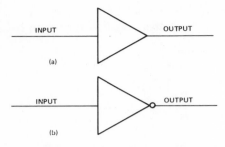

Figure III-2 Symbols representing buffers: (a) noninverting; (b) inverting.

More complex circuits that are able to implement more complicated logical functions can be constructed. Figure III-3a shows a circuit employing two switches arranged so that actuation of one or the other will provide a current in the load. The logical statements appropriate to this circuit are

$$\overline{A} \text{ and } \overline{B} \text{ implies } C$$
$$A \text{ and } \overline{B} \text{ implies } C$$
$$\overline{A} \text{ and } B \text{ implies } C$$
$$A \text{ and } B \text{ implies } \overline{C}$$

which are equivalent to the statement

A or B implies C   (positive logic)

A truth table can be constructed for this circuit as follows:

Inputs		Output
A	B	C
0	0	0
0	1	1
1	0	1
1	1	1

Any device whose inputs and output conform to the statements of this truth table is logically equivalent to the circuit shown and is symbolized as shown in Fig. III-3b. Such a device is called a two-input **or** gate. The origin of the term *gate* lies in the manner of control of the output of the device so titled. A signal present at one input of a two-input gate may influence the output of the gate depending on the state of the other input.

With the arrows on the switches reversed, as in the case of the in-

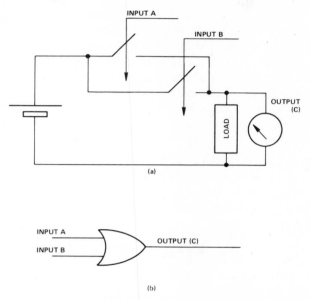

(a)

(b)

Figure III-3 A logic circuit representing the or function: (a) represented by switches for input actuation; (b) symbolic representation.

verting buffer above, the logical statements describing the operation of the circuit are altered as follows:

$$A \text{ and } \overline{B} \text{ implies } C$$
$$\overline{A} \text{ and } B \text{ implies } C$$
$$\overline{A} \text{ and } \overline{B} \text{ implies } C$$
$$A \text{ and } B \text{ implies } \overline{C}$$

There is an equivalent statement that can be made, namely,

$$\overline{A} \text{ or } \overline{B} \text{ implies } C$$

The conventional nomenclature for the gate whose operation is expressed in these logical statements is based on noncomplemented inputs. By this convention, the fourth statement above, $A \text{ and } B = \overline{C}$, prescribes the name inverting **and** gate. The symbol for this gate is shown in Fig. III-4a.

The nomenclature convention should be more completely described at this point. The examples given so far imply that a logical state $\overline{1} = 0$ (or false) is associated with zero (or low) electrical voltage, while a logical state $1 = \overline{0}$ (or true) is associated with a nonzero (or high) electrical voltage. As long as this association conforms to the designer's logical definition, the nomenclature of the circuits and their symbolic alternates is correct. However, when the designer elects to define the zero-voltage (low) state as *true*, the nomenclature for the same devices is changed to conform with the convention elected, namely, the logical statement with uncomplemented inputs prescribes the name of the gate.

Thus, if the zero-voltage state is defined as true, and a nonzero voltage actuates the opening of switches, the circuit named an inverting **and** gate is now described by the logical statements

$$\underline{A}[=(0)] \text{ and } \overline{B}[=(1)] \text{ implies } \overline{C}[=1]$$
$$\underline{A}[=(1)] \text{ and } \underline{B}[=(0)] \text{ implies } \overline{C}[=1]$$
$$\overline{A}[=(1)] \text{ and } \overline{B}[=(1)] \text{ implies } \underline{C}[=0]$$
$$A[=(0)] \text{ and } B[=(0)] \text{ implies } \overline{C}[=1]$$

which is equivalent to

$$A[=(0)] \text{ or } B[=(0)] \text{ implies } \overline{C}$$

giving the device the name *negative* inverting **or** gate. The word negative specifies the designer's choice of low for true to designate the logical state for the binary digits in his system. The symbol for this gate is shown in Fig. III-3b. It is electrically identical to the (positive) inverting **and** gate.

Gates are frequently specified in their positive sense, that is, with the specification that zero voltage (low) is associated with the logical false and the digital state 0. Moreover, truth tables are usually rendered in the positive sense so that 0 implies a zero voltage.

The introduction of a seeming complication into the convention of nomenclature has a use primarily in tracing the logic of a complicated assembly of gates. In a few cases, the design of the gate itself may also be such that the description in negative logic is the more appropriate. Designers do not always adhere completely to the strict conventions in rendering a logic design. If the electrical identity of the devices is

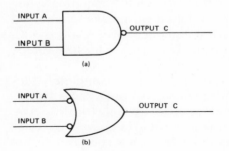

Figure III-4 (a) Symbol for an inverting and gate (positive logic); (b) symbol for an inverting or gate, (negative logic). These can be physically the same device.

kept in mind, the resulting confusion can be resolved. The truth table, stated in terms of positive logic where zero implies zero voltage, is always unambiguous.

The truth table for the devices in Fig. III-4, stated with this implication, is the following:

Input		Output
A	B	C
0	0	1
0	1	1
1	0	1
1	1	0

Its counterpart, stated in terms of negative logic, could also be rendered as

Input		Output
A	B	C
T	T	F
T	F	F
F	T	F
F	F	T

where, to avoid ambiguity, the letters T (true) and F (false) have been substituted for the digital states 0 and 1, respectively.

Symbols ($\cdot$) and (+) have been adopted to connote **and** and **or**, respectively, with the equal sign being used to join a logical input statement with the corresponding output statement. For the devices described so far a convenient shorthand notation results:

$$A = B \qquad \text{noninverting buffer}$$
$$A = \overline{B} \qquad \text{inverting buffer}$$
$$A + B = C \qquad \text{noninverting \textbf{or} gate}$$
$$A \cdot B = \overline{C} \qquad \text{inverting \textbf{and} gate}$$

For an unambiguous description when using this symbology, the type of logic (positive or negative) must still be specified. The statements above refer to positive logic. In changing to a negative logic description, the first two will be unaltered, while the third and fourth become

$$A \cdot B = \overline{C} \qquad \text{noninverting } \textbf{and} \text{ gate, negative logic}$$
$$A + B = \overline{C} \qquad \text{inverting } \textbf{or} \text{ gate, negative logic}$$

In general, the absence of a specification of the type of logic implies positive logic.

III-2 COMBINING GATES FOR MORE COMPLEX FUNCTIONS

Gates may be used in combination to accomplish almost any desired logical end. Figure III-5 shows one way in which a combination of gates may be used to detect a specific logical condition of 8 ordered binary digits, A, B, C, D, E, F, G, H. The specific condition to be detected in $(ABCD\overline{E}F\overline{G}H)$, (positive logic). With the arrangement shown, this sequence will produce a true (1) output. All other combinations will result in a false (0) output. The circuit shown will act as a decoder for the code $(ABCD\overline{E}F\overline{G}H)$. However, it is not compact, in part because it employs only two types of gate.

In order to provide more versatility, additional two-input gates have been developed. Figure III-6 shows the commonly available two-input gates along with their truth tables (positive logic). Using a selection of these gates, the decoder of Fig. III-5 can be simplified as shown in Fig. III-7. Obviously a number of other design choices could lead to the same result.

To facilitate further the construction of more elaborate logical circuits, gates having more than two inputs have been developed. Figure III-8 depicts a variety of gates, along with their logical statements

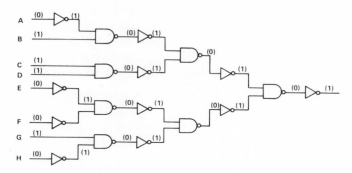

Figure III-5 Combination of buffers and gates to decode a specific combination of 8 inputs.

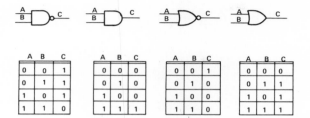

Figure III-6 The simple 2-input gates with their truth tables.

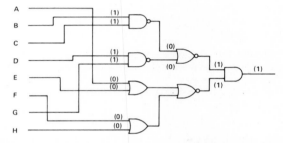

Figure III-7 A simpler decoding than Fig. III-5 using a greater variety of gates.

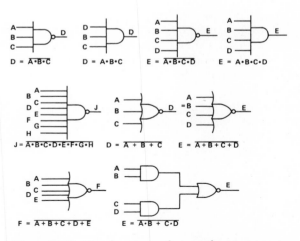

Figure III-8 Simple gates with more than two inputs.

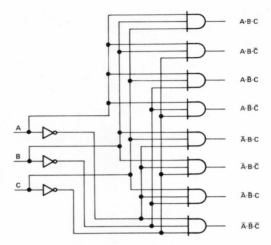

Figure III-9 Medium scale integration to provide complete decoding of a 3-bit input in a single package. (Decoders are often provided with inverting outputs).

(positive logic), that are available to the logic designer. The selection does not show all the devices classed as gates. The last example in the figure is more complex than its fellows but is usually classified as a gate, as are several others like it. It has the impressive name *two-wide two-input* **and or** *invert gate*.

The incorporation of additional inputs considerably broadens the options of the logic designer and allows a simplified design of circuits to perform more complex functions. One of these is shown in Fig. III-9. This circuit decodes separately each of the eight possible combinations of 3 binary digits. There are eight separate outputs to express the decoding. In an automated system, each of the eight outputs could be used to command a different event, the event commanded being chosen by the control word presented at the input (ABC) to the circuit.

A further example of the application of digital logic is shown in Fig. III-10. This circuit performs the function of binary addition, con-

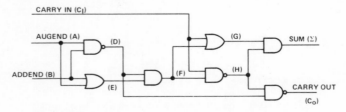

Figure III-10 A 1-bit adder with carry-in and carry-out.

forming to the rules indicated in Chapter II. The circuit can be analyzed by writing a truth table with inputs A, B, and C_I, where A is an augend, B is an addend, and C_I is a carry input. The truth table, listing all the possible inputs is as follows:

Inputs			Intermediate points					Outputs	
A	B	C_I	D	E	F	G	H	Σ	C_O
0	0	0	1	0	0	0	1	0	0
0	0	1	1	0	0	1	1	1	0
0	1	0	1	1	1	1	1	1	0
0	1	1	1	1	1	1	0	0	1
1	0	0	1	1	1	1	1	1	0
1	0	1	1	1	1	1	0	0	1
1	1	0	0	1	0	0	1	0	1
1	1	1	0	1	0	1	1	1	1

where Σ is the digit of the sum and C_O is the *carry out* to the next higher place. Since all four arithmetic operations can be reduced to addition, this useful circuit can serve to implement binary arithmetic in automated systems.

III-3 INFORMATION AND LOGIC

To this point, the chapter has described the operation of gates as it applies to the binary states of inputs and consequent outputs. The utility of these devices results from the assignment of meaning to the states of the gates and the interrelation of inputs and outputs. Each state at each terminal, input or output, can represent one element of information. The shorthand name for one element of information is the *bit*.

An automated system operates through a progression of events, as described in the first chapter. This progression of events in a digital automated system is mediated by an accompanying progression of bits through the system's programming and control component. These bits represent information (including input information from outside the system), program instructions to direct the operation of the system, intermediate results of information manipulation, and output information, including commands. This guiding accompaniment may be visualized as a highly organized march of bits through the system.

The organization and mechanization of this march of data through the system are formulated by the designer, utilizing the logical devices at his disposal, such as the gates already described. The mechanisms represented by gates lend themselves particularly well to this format of dissection of statements. Their logical operation is completely specific, and, in their microcircuit form, they comprise a versatile set having the desirable properties of reliability, very low cost, high speed, low power consumption, standardization, and convenience for assembly into systems. With microcircuit gates, logic design is quite easy, and, with careful attention, successful logic designs can be rendered by amateurs. The distinction of elegant design using a minimum number of gates and efficient management of bits representing the data flow is the hallmark of the superior logic designer. This elegance comes with experience and can be facilitated with certain analytical tools; however, designs that are not optimized can still be completely successful. The circuit of Fig. III-5 is every bit as effective as (though slightly slower than) the circuit of Fig. III-7.

To make the task of the designer even simpler, integrated circuits having many internally connected gates are currently manufactured. Medium- and large-scale integration of circuits is now very highly developed, with devices being offered that incorporate the equivalent of hundreds and even thousands of gates. Acceptance of products incorporating these devices has become quite routine. However, it is still remarkable to note, by way of an example of the application of large-scale integration, that the astonishing capability of the ubiquitous hand calculator resides in a wafer of silicon smaller than the little finger nail.

III-4 TRANSISTORS AS LOGIC CIRCUIT ELEMENTS

A number of projects (see, for example, Section III-5 below) can be undertaken to illustrate the operation of gates and the circuits using them. Equipment requirements are modest, and costs are small. The projects in this chapter will use the transistor–transistor logic (TTL) family of devices, these being the electronic components most widely used in digital logic systems. Although this book is not intended as a source for solid-state electronics, a brief discussion of the structure of these devices is appropriate.

The transistor is the fundamental element in solid-state electronics. It relies for its operation on the electrical properties of crystalline semiconductor materials. The most frequently used material is very pure silicon into which certain impurities have been introduced in carefully controlled and very small amounts.

Metals, in general, are very good conductors of electricity. They rely for their conduction on electrons, which are a universal constituent of matter. In general, electrons are firmly bound to atomic nuclei in matter. However, in metals some of the electrons are more or less free to move about in the bulk of the metal under the influence of electric fields. The number of these conduction electrons is large, comparable to the number of metal atoms. Thus, a foot of copper wire of 0.020-in. diameter has about 3×10^{20} free electrons.

By contrast, semiconductors, including silicon, may have at least a million times fewer charge carriers. Moreover, at the junction of semiconductors with different properties or at the junction of semiconductors and metals, the charge carriers migrate, in the absence of external electric fields, in such a way as to form barriers to the conduction of electric current. These barriers can form even between regions within the same semiconductor crystal, where the controlled impurities differ between the regions. In properly designed structures of semiconductor crystals, having regions containing different impurities in properly controlled quantity and nature, the impressment of external electrical fields permits the electrical carriers within the crystal to overcome the barriers and thereby allows currents to flow.

One such special structure is called the transistor. Figure III-11 shows the incorporation of a transistor into a circuit similar to that of Fig. III-1. The figure shows electrical contacts made to three regions E, B, and C of a silicon crystal. At these contacts no barriers exist. However, owing to the impurity distribution introduced in the regions of the crystal, barriers to electrical conduction, indicated by

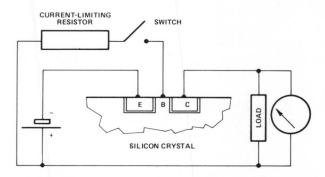

Figure III-11 A highly schematic diagram of a transistor shown in a simple switching circuit.

the double boundary lines, are formed as long as the switch remains open.

When the switch is closed, the external electrical potential impressed on the device acts to depress the barriers, and current can be conducted by the charge carriers between the contacts applied to regions E and C. (A small current also flows to the central contact at region B, limited by the current-limiting resistor.) Since the electrical potentials favorable to depressing the barriers to electrical conduction between E and C can be maintained by much smaller currents flowing at the contact to region B, the device exhibits electrical gain, which is to say that a small current at B can control a very much larger current between E and C. In the use shown in Fig. III-11, the property of gain is used to provide a simple electrically operated switch.

Transistors designed along the lines of the description above are used in microcircuit gates, as well as individually in circuits. The structures are small even in devices able to conduct fairly large currents. In microcircuits, the transistors occupy spaces measured in thousandths of an inch. The regions are formed and the electrical contacts for interconnections are made by a microphotolithography process, with careful deposition and removal of materials in conformity with the microphotographic patterns. The levels of technology involved in the processing are demanding in the extreme, requiring costly equipment and highly skilled operators. However, the lithographic method permits production in very large quantity, allowing for very low unit prices.

Figure III-12 shows symbols for two types of transistors, namely, the NPN and the PNP. Arrows in the symbols show the normal direction of the (positive) current conduction, and the terminals of the transistor are designated as emitter, base, and collector. (See regions E, B, and C in Fig. III-11.) Figure III-13 shows *alternative* internal circuits of two typical TTL two-input gates, with arrows indicating the presence of current conduction in the internal current pathways. The diagrams show device inputs connected each to the emitter of a separate

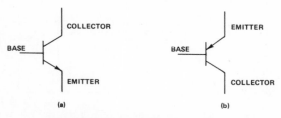

Figure III-12 Symbols for transistors.

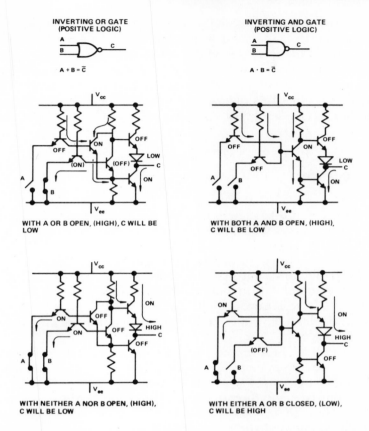

INVERTING OR GATE
(POSITIVE LOGIC)

$A + B = \bar{C}$

WITH A OR B OPEN, (HIGH), C WILL BE LOW

WITH NEITHER A NOR B OPEN, (HIGH), C WILL BE LOW

INVERTING AND GATE
(POSITIVE LOGIC)

$A \cdot B = \bar{C}$

WITH BOTH A AND B OPEN, (HIGH), C WILL BE LOW

WITH EITHER A OR B CLOSED, (LOW), C WILL BE HIGH

Figure III-13 Alternative diagrams for TTL logic devices. Actual TTL devices feature transistors with multiple emitters.

transistor for purposes of visualization. In actual construction of TTL devices, where more than one input is present, multiple emitters are generally attached to the same base region of a single input transistor. The base of this transistor remains saturated for either the high or the low state of the input. This mode of operation provides high operating speed in the input section. Output speed is enhanced by the provision of active devices (transistors) for both pull up and pull down in the output stage.

Current is provided by an external power supply to the terminals marked V_{cc} and V_{ee}. The terminal marked V_{cc} is connected to the positive terminal of the power supply. The negative terminal at V_{ee} is frequently called ground. One device, not previously mentioned, appears in the diagram. This is the diode symbolized by —▷|—. As its symbol suggests, it is a device that permits conduction of (positive) current only in the direction of the arrow.

Although it is interesting to see the internal diagram of a gate or other integrated circuit device detailed to the transistor level, it is seldom necessary that this diagram be used for logic design. The function of the device is almost completely described by the use of its symbol.

III-5 PROJECTS

The projects in this section require integrated logic circuits and a few supplies such as wires, sockets, and switches. In addition, to help in visualization, a number of small lamps, specifically light-emitting diodes (LEDs), are used. Integrated logic circuits, LEDs, and other specialized electronic parts can be obtained from electronic part suppliers. Other supplies and tools can be found in hardware stores. The principal tools required are a small soldering iron and a pair of wire-cutting pliers. Power is supplied to the circuits by a common 6-V lantern battery.

The electronics industry provides a variety of mounting boards for electronic circuits, including specially designed "breadboard" arrangements of various types. The literal "breadboard" approach is not inappropriate, and the projects can be carried out using a number of boards of about $1 \times 4 \times 12$ in. A good starter set for projects includes the following list.

(a)   5 pine boards $1 \times 4 \times 12$ in.
(b)   1 box copper tacks, No. 5
(c)   1 light-duty soldering iron, small tip
(d)   1 wire cutters, light-duty
(e)   1 small pointed-nose pliers
(f)   1 spool rosin-core electronic-grade solder
(g)   1 spool No. 22 bare, tinned, solid copper wire
(h)   1 roll No. 22 insulated copper wire
(i)   3 each 7400 TTL integrated circuit
(j)   3 each 7402 TTL integrated circuit
(k)   2 each 7410 TTL integrated circuit
(l)   2 each 7404 TTL integrated circuit
(m)   5 each 14 pin integrated circuit sockets; sockets with "wirewrap" terminals are convenient

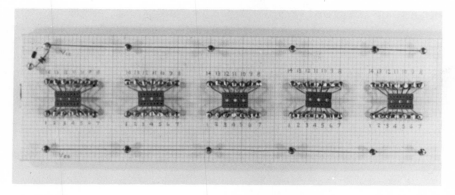

Figure III-14 Photograph of a crude "breadboard" for development of simple integrated circuit logic combinations.

(n) 5 single-pole, single-throw switches
(o) 10 light emitting diodes
(p) 10 each 100 Ω $\frac{1}{4}$-W carbon resistors
(q) 1 each 1N4005 diode
(r) 1 each 6-V lantern battery
(s) 10 each 200 Ω $\frac{1}{4}$-W carbon resistor

Figure III-14 shows a typical arrangement for circuit breadboard. The wire attachment points are the copper tacks that are driven part of the way into the board. Wires are soldered to the tacks, either on top or wrapped around. A slight charring of the base when the soldering takes place is of no consequence, provided the tack is still firm.

Commercial "breadboards" constructed of insulating plastic with guarded contacts properly spaced and able to accept the contact pins of integrated circuits, wires, and small discrete components can be purchased at moderate cost. These boards have their contacts interconnected in a regular pattern and require no soldering. They are very convenient for rapid assembly of experimental circuits.

The diode (1N4005), connected between the V_{cc} line and the battery, serves to protect the circuit against inadvertent reversal of the battery connection, and, in addition, reduces the 6-V supply by about 0.7 V, thereby reducing the electrical stress on the integrated circuits.

Project A.   To Demonstrate the Operation of Inverting Buffers

This project requires a breadboard, laid out as shown in Fig. III-14, with at least one 14-pin socket installed. Pin numbers may be drawn directly on the board (Fig. III-14). The arrangement of the numbers identifies the pins of the 14-pin integrated circuits in the dual-in-line package when the device is viewed from the top.

The type 7404 integrated-circuit package contains six inverting buffers. The diagram identifying the connections is shown in Fig. III-15a. A 7404 may be inserted in a socket on the board, and the connections are shown schematically in Fig. III-15b and diagramatically

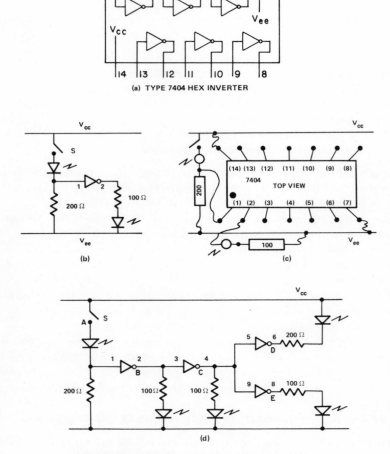

(a) TYPE 7404 HEX INVERTER

(b)

(c)

(d)

Figure III-15 Illustration for projects A and B.

in Fig. III-15c and may be made using the bare leads of the compo-nents without trimming. (They may be used again and again.) Care should be exercised to prevent wires from touching one another, although a momentary short circuit should not damage the integrated circuit. The sense of the LEDs may not be obvious from inspection. If no light appears in LED_1 upon closure of the switch S with power ap-plied to the circuit, its leads should be reversed. Light should then appear. LED_2 may then be connected in the same sense, since there is an identifying difference between the two leads.

The completed circuit should function now to show the operation of the inverting buffer. With the switch S open, the input is kept low and the output is high as indicated by the extinction of LED_1 and the lighting of LED_2. When the switch is closed, LED_1 is lighted and LED_2 is correspondingly extinguished. From this operation, a truth table may be constructed showing the operation.

It should be noted that an amateur's license has been taken in the circuit of this project to emphasize the illustration. Strictly speaking, the output of the TTL device is designed to *sink* a current and not to source one. However, to show the logic and *not* the specification, the pull up transistor of the TTL device output will source a sufficient cur-rent to light the LED, and it is used in this nonapproved way to show the logic more directly.

Project B. Interconnecting Inverting Buffers

Figure III-15d is a schematic circuit for the interconnection of sev-eral inverting buffers. An output may be connected to as many as 10 inputs; thus the output of G_2 can drive the inputs of G_3 and G_4. (In general, outputs of devices should not be connected to outputs of other devices, since they may try to establish opposite states and dam-age can result.) With connections made as shown in the schematic dia-gram, the circuit may be operated. If any lamps do not operate, the connection sense of the LEDs may be wrong. This can be corrected, and with the circuit operating, a truth table can be constructed for points A, B, C, D, and E of the circuit. The truth table should conform to the logical expression

$$A = \overline{B} = C = \overline{D} = \overline{E}$$

Project C. Inverting *And* Gates

Figure III-16a shows the gate connections for the 7400 integrated-circuit package, which contains four inverting **and** gates.

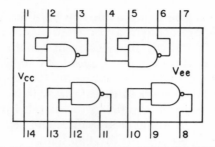

(a) TYPE /400 QUAD 2-INPUT INVERTING **AND** GATE

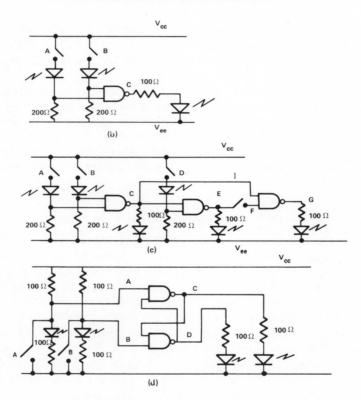

Figure III-16 Illustration for project C.

Figure III-16b shows schematically a circuit that demonstrates the operation of the inverting **and** gate. This circuit may be connected on a board with at least one socket, and the operation of the inverting **and** gate can be demonstrated. From the results, the truth table for the inverting **and** gate can be constructed.

A more complex circuit is shown schematically in Fig. III-16c. Additional gates may be added to the circuit of Fig. III-16b, already constructed, and a truth table can be derived from the results found in operating the switches.

One additional project using inverting **and** gates will demonstrate the very useful circuit of Fig. III-16d. This is a bistable circuit that can occupy either of two states that are set and reset by momentary closures of switches A and B, respectively. The truth table for this circuit may be written in four parts as follows:

A	B	C	D	A	B	C	D	A	B	C	D	A	B	C	D
1	⊔	0	1	1	1	0	1	⊔	1	1	0	1	1	1	0

There is also the anomalous case

A	B	C	D
0	0	1	1

which results when both switches are closed and which leads to an undetermined result if both switches are released at once.

Circuits resembling Fig. III-16d are used very frequently for temporary storage of information, logic, branching control, and other functions, where a momentary input can prescribe a definite state of the output that will remain when the input is removed. These bistable circuits are called, aptly, flip-flops or latches.

Project D. Inverting *Or* Gates

Figure III-17a shows the gate connections for the 7402 integrated-circuit package, which contains four inverting **or** gates. Figure III-17b shows schematically a circuit to demonstrate the operation of the inverting **or** gate. With this circuit connected on the board, the operation may be demonstrated, and a truth table can be constructed for the inverting **or** gate.

In Fig. III-17c a more complex schematic circuit is shown. This circuit can be constructed by adding to the circuit used to demonstrate the operation of the inverting **or** gate. The circuit may be operated, and the results may be used to construct a truth table for the complete circuit.

A flip-flop may also be constructed using inverting **or** gates as shown schematically in Fig. III-17d. In this useful circuit, a momentary contact of either switch can cause a transition to a corresponding state. As was the case for the inverting **and** gate flip-flop, the truth table is written in four parts:

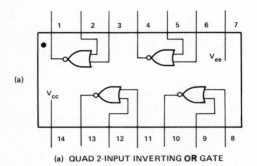

(a) QUAD 2-INPUT INVERTING **OR** GATE

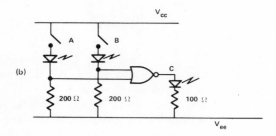

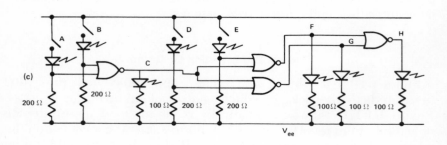

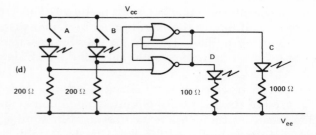

Figure III-17 Illustration for project D.

A	B	C	D	A	B	C	D	A	B	C	D	A	B	C	D
⎍	0	1	0	0	0	1	0	0	⎍	0	1	0	0	0	1

Again, there is an anomalous case

A	B	C	D
1	1	0	0

which results when both switches are closed and leads to an undetermined result if both switches are released simultaneously. The operation of this useful circuit can be demonstrated when it has been constructed. The demonstration will show how the circuit can be used to "remember" a state resulting from a momentary input condition.

EXERCISES

1. Using two-input gates, design a circuit to decode the binary word A, $\overline{B}$, $\overline{C}$, D, E, $\overline{F}$, G, $\overline{H}$ (positive logic).

2. Using any of the gates shown in Fig. III-8, design a circuit to decode the state A, B, C, $\overline{D}$, E, $\overline{F}$, G, H.

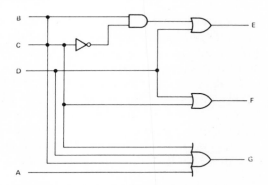

Figure III-18   Illustration for Exercise 4.

3. Design a circuit to decode either of the two states A B C D E $\overline{F}$ $\overline{G}$ $\overline{H}$ or $\overline{A}$ B C D E F $\overline{G}$ H.

4. Write a truth table for the circuit shown in Fig. III-18 when only one of the inputs at a time is high.

5. Write the complete truth table for all of the possible inputs for the circuit shown in Fig. III-18.

IV

Introduction to More Complex Circuits

Chapter III was concerned with the elementary logical units (gates) used in digital automation. Gates, operating on digital data, can be arranged to accomplish a variety of logical functions. Subdivision of a logical requirement to the level of statements that can be expressed by individual gates is always possible, but experience has shown that specific larger blocks of logic frequently appear. The widespread use of these blocks of logic, which can be made up using individual gates, has induced manufacturers to offer integrated circuits in which the blocks of logic, each comprising a number of gates, are preassembled, thereby saving the designer the labor of designing them each time the need arises.

The blocks are actually assembled, primarily by the photo-lithographic process mentioned in Chapter III. The necessary gates, and the interconnections they require to perform the more complex functions, are formed on a single small slice of crystalline silicon. Although the investment required to develop each circuit is high, the lithographic process used in the manufacturing leads to low unit costs when quantities are large. The terms medium-scale integration (MSI) and large-scale integration (LSI) have been attached to these devices depending on the complexity of the blocks in question. The classifications MSI and LSI include circuits to perform functions suggested in the following list:

Arithmetic operations
Register, including shift
   registers
Latches
Memories

Code Converters
Data selectors and
   multiplexers
Counters

No strict lines divide the classification of LSI from MSI, and some circuits of modest complexity are included in the classification of small-scale integration (SSI), which includes all of the integrated circuits that contain only accessible gates. This chapter will deal with a selection of the most frequently used circuits in all three categories, without special emphasis on their classification. In general, examples will be drawn from the TTL family. However, most of the devices have counterparts in other families of technology.

IV-1 FLIP-FLOPS AND LATCHES

Flip-flops generally are classified as small-scale integration devices, and latches bridge the line between small-scale and medium-scale integration. The primary characteristic of these devices is their ability to retain information, which can be introduced into them in a variety of ways. The simplest forms of flip-flops were mentioned in Chapter III. A device containing four flip-flops, made up of inverting **and** gates with the nomenclature $\overline{R}$–$\overline{S}$ (standing for $\overline{reset}$–$\overline{set}$), flip-flop, or latch is available (74279 in the TTL family). A diagram for this device is shown in Fig. IV-1. For each flip-flop, a four-part truth table could be written as shown in Chapter III. However, for economy of writing and for clarity, a function table that includes the concept of the event of transition is generally written. In this table, the input conditions are

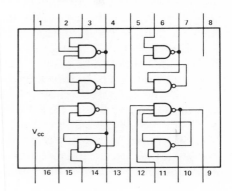

Figure IV-1 Quadruple $\overline{R}$–$\overline{S}$ flip-flop in a single package, type 74279.

indicated in such a way as to show the cause of a transition, if any, and the consequent final state of the output. For the simple inverting **and** gate flip-flop (see Fig. III-15d), the transitional parts of the function table could be rendered as follows:

A	B	C	D
⊔	1	1	$\overline{0}$
1	1	Q	$\overline{Q}$
1	⊔	0	1

where Q and $\overline{Q}$ refer to the retained (complementary) output states, and the symbols in columns A and B imply that the transition to the indicated output state required only a short (negative) input pulse.

More versatile (and more complicated) flip-flops and latches are available. In these devices, the output transition to a state defined by the input occurs as a result of the appropriate excitation of a separate terminal, usually called the clock terminal. In addition, there may be direct *set* and *reset* terminals that allow control of the output independently of the input and clock. The symbol for flip-flops and latches is usually a rectangle to which lines representing the various terminals are attached. Figure IV-2a is an example of this symbol.

One of the lines (the input) attached to the rectangular symbol in the figure is labeled "*D*." This labeling identifies the device as a member of one of the two major classes of bistable flip-flops, namely, the type D flip-flop. In this class, a single input D determines the state to which the output Q will go when the clock line is appropriately excited. In the particular device shown in the figure (found in the type 7474 digital integrated circuit), the transition to the designated output state occurs on the rising edge of a signal applied to the clock line. It is not a high state of the clock line that engenders this transition. If the clock were high, it would have to be brought low momentarily to provide for the required rising edge.

This operation can be made clearer by reference to a timing diagram shown in Fig. IV-2b. In this diagram, the time evolution of logic levels (voltage low or high) is shown for the input D, the clock C, and the outputs Q and $\overline{Q}$. From this timing diagram, the causal relationship between the input and clock, and the output, can be understood.

In addition to the terminals D, the C clock, and the outputs Q and $\overline{Q}$, there are the two terminals labeled P and R. (These labels are shorthand designations for the functions preset and reset or clear.) They are

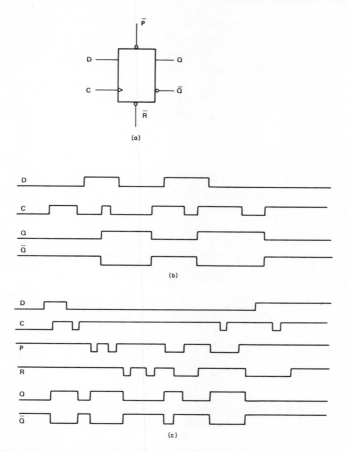

Figure IV-2 (a) Type D flip-flop; (b) timing diagram, input and clock; (c) timing diagram including PRESET and RESET.

direct operating terminals that influence the output immediately without reference to the input and clock lines. Furthermore, they take precedence in determining the state of the output. Their effect is shown in the more complete diagram in Fig. IV-2c. It can be seen from the diagram that, so long as both P and R are in the high state, the operation of the device is as was described. This condition applies to the first two transitions of Q and $\bar{Q}$ shown in the diagram. Following these, the line P, being brought low causes a transition to Q high and $\bar{Q}$ low. This state is maintained when P returns high. Reexcitation of P to the low state has no further effect on the output. A monentary excitation of R to the low state causes a transition to Q low and $\bar{Q}$ high.

This state is also maintained and unaffected by a second excitation of R to the low condition. When both P and R are brought low, it is seen that both Q and $\overline{Q}$ are set high. The output state, when P and R are returned to high, is determined by which rises first. Finally, it should be noted that when either P or R is low, the output state is not influenced by operations at D and C. The versatility of function in the type D flip-flop allows a considerable latitude in its use for the convenience of the designer.

A schematic diagram of the type D flip-flop, or latch, is shown in Fig. IV-3. Detailed analysis of this diagram is an interesting exercise that will be left to the reader. (See Exercise 2.) In addition, a function table can be constructed to describe the operation of the device (see Table IV-1).

Table IV-1   Function Table for ($\frac{1}{2}$) 7474 Type D Flip-Flop

Inputs				Outputs	
D	P	R	Clock	Q	$\overline{Q}$
X	H	L	X	L	H
H	H	H	↑	H	L
H	H	H	L	Q_0	$\overline{Q}_0$
L	H	H	↑	L	H
X	H	L	X	L	H
X	L	H	X	H	L
X	L	L	X	H^a	H^a

^{a} This state is not maintained after the withdrawal of either P or R or both. The final state depends on which is withdrawn first.

In this table, the symbols L and H are used to avoid the ambiguity of the logical 0's and 1's, whose meaning depends on the definition of system logic used to be determined as positive or negative. The symbol X indicates a "don't care" condition at an input whose state or transition does not affect the outputs, given the other conditions present. The arrow symbol ↑ indicates that the transition to the final output state occurs at that instant and as a result only of the positive transition at the clock terminal. The details of one method to provide this feature are the subject of Exercise 1. The specific means for providing it in the 7474 type D flip-flop can be inferred from the gate diagram shown in Fig. IV-3.

A second class of bistable flip-flops in common use comprises type JK flip-flops. They are distinguished from type D flip-flops by the fact that at least two inputs J and K are provided, along with a clock termi-

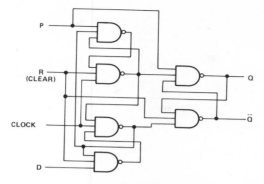

Figure IV-3 Schematic diagram of the type D flip-flop, (1/2) type 7474.

nal. In some JK flip-flops, direct-operating terminals that are analogous to P (preset) and R (reset or clear) in the case of the type D flip-flop, are provided. Other titles are used to describe the direct-operating terminals; S (set) used sometimes for the presetting terminal, and R (reset) used interchangeably with CLR (clear). These titles describe the functions equally well, and no ambiguity need result from their interchangeable use.

JK flip-flops are available with positive or negative edge, or state clocking, and, in some cases, with more than two inputs J and K. In the latter instance, when multiple inputs are present, the several J inputs are internally connected to an **and** gate or a combination of gates. Likewise several K inputs operate through another gate or gates. The gate arrangement for J's and K's is usually included even in the symbolic diagram of the device.

Figure IV-4 shows symbolic diagrams of several JK flip-flops. The input gating of each JK flip-flop shown is obvious from the diagram. The operation of the JK flip-flop can best be described by a function table (see Table IV-2).

Table IV-2 Function Table for ($\frac{1}{2}$) 7473 Type JK Flip-Flop

Inputs				Outputs	
J	K	R	Clock	Q	$\overline{Q}$
X	X	L	X	L	H
L	L	H	$\sqcap$	Q_0	$\overline{Q}_0$
H	L	H	$\sqcap$	H	L
L	H	H	$\sqcap$	L	H
H	H	H	$\sqcap$	$\overline{Q}_0$	Q_0

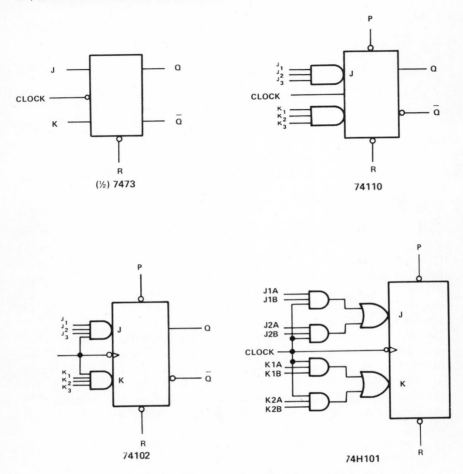

Figure IV-4 Symbolic diagrams of several type JK flip-flops.

In this type of JK flip-flop (7473), as the symbols in the clock column indicate, the transition to the final output state depends on the double transition (up then down) of the clock terminal. The more detailed features of this transition require further description.

Some JK flip-flops, such as the 7473, are described with the term *master–slave*. In these JK flip-flops; there actually exist two bistable circuits: the master, which is attached to the input, and the slave, which is attached to the output. Information existing at the inputs JK is entered first on the master flip-flop and then transferred to the slave flip-flop in a sequence controlled by the clock. This sequence of events for the type 7473 JK flip-flop is shown in the timing diagram of Fig. IV-5a, which shows time horizontally on expanded scale. As the diagram indicates, the master flip-flop has its state changed at point B. Data at JK must be valid for a short interval prior to and including B. During the interval A–D the slave is disconnected from the master and "remembers" its prior state. The final events of the transition cycle occur during the time that the clock level is falling. First, the master is disconnected from the input, (and remembers its state) at time C; second, this state is transferred to the slave and hence to the outputs at time D. The circuit is totally insensitive to the inputs when the clock is low.

Other JK flip-flops are constructed so that output transitions occur at a rising or falling edge of the signal applied to the clock terminal. These devices are not provided with a master and slave as such, rather, the internal circuits are arranged so that information present at the inputs is transferred to the output flip-flop at an intermediate level of the clock, occurring during the clock transition. Thereafter, the JK terminals are disconnected from the circuit to avoid ambiguity in the result if they change. When the clock is returned to its original state, the JK inputs are reconnected to the circuit; however, they do not then influence the output because the trailing clock transition is first communicated to the transfer circuit, disabling any further transfer of information to the output. A timing diagram for the operation of a positive-edge triggering clock is shown in Fig. IV-5b. Both positive- and negative-edge-triggered JK flip-flops are available. Function tables can be written for these two types of edge-triggered JK flip-flops (see Tables IV-3 and IV-4).

Insight to the operation of JK flip-flops is further clarified by an analysis of the gate diagrams of their circuits. Two such diagrams are shown in Figs. IV-6a and IV-6b. The first of these is a type JK master-slave flip-flop (7473); the second is a type JK negative-edge-triggered flip-flop (74H108). Detailed analysis of these circuits is left to the reader (see Exercises 3 and 4).

A third type of flip-flop is found in common use, namely, the monostable "one-shot" flip-flop. In this device, the normal static state is stable. Output Q is low, and output $\overline{Q}$ is high. When the device is appropriately triggered, a single pulse of Q high and $\overline{Q}$ low occurs, the length of the pulse being determined by external discrete components attached to appropriate terminals.

Figure IV-7 shows a symbolic diagram of a monostable flip-flop along with a timing diagram of its operation. From the latter it can be

A. ISOLATE SLAVE FROM MASTER
B. ENTER INFORMATION FROM J, K INTO MASTER
C. DISABLE J, K INPUTS
D. TRANSFER INFORMATION FROM MASTER TO SLAVE (Q, $\overline{Q}$)

(a)

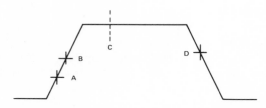

A. ACCEPT JK INPUTS
B. DISCONNECT JK INPUTS
C. TRANSFER CYCLE COMPLETE, JK CAN CHANGE
D. RECONNECT JK INPUTS

(b)

Figure IV-5 (a) State-triggered JK clock transition scheme; (b) edge-triggered JK clock transition scheme.

Table IV-3 Function Table for Type 7470 JK Positive Edge Triggered Flip-Flop

Inputs					Outputs	
J^a	K^a	P	R	Clock	Q	$\overline{Q}$
X	X	H	L	X	L	H
L	L	H	H	↑	Q_0	$\overline{Q}_0$
H	L	H	H	↑	H	L
L	H	H	H	↑	L	H
H	H	H	H	↑	toggle	
X	X	H	H	L	Q_0	$\overline{Q}_0$
X	X	L	H	X	H	L
X	X	L	L	X	L^b	L^b

[a] **J** is the logical consequence of all the J inputs and **K** is the logical consequence of all the K inputs.

[b] This state is not maintained after the withdrawal of either P or R. The final state depends on which is withdrawn first.

Table IV-4 Function Table for ($\frac{1}{2}$) 74H108 Type JK Negative Edge Triggered Flip-Flop

Inputs					Outputs	
J	K	P	R	Clock	Q	$\overline{Q}$
X	X	H	L	X	L	H
L	L	H	H	$\downarrow$	Q_o	$\overline{Q}_o$
H	L	H	H	$\downarrow$	H	L
L	H	H	H	$\downarrow$	L	H
H	H	H	H	$\downarrow$	$\overline{Q}_0$	Q_0
X	X	H	H	H	Q_0	$\overline{Q}_0$
X	X	L	H	X	H	L
X	X	L	L	X	H^a	H^a

^{a} This state is not maintained after withdrawal of either P or R or both. The final state depends on which is withdrawn first.

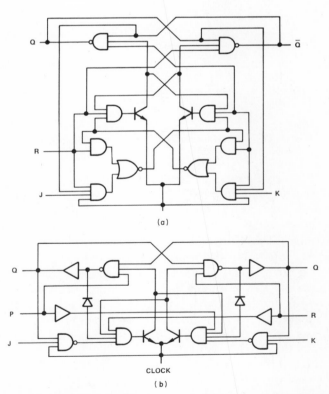

(a)

(b)

Figure IV-6 (a) ($\frac{1}{2}$) 7473-type JK master–slave flip-flop; (b) ($\frac{1}{2}$) 74108-type JK negative-edge triggered flip-flop.

$$T \geq 0.32\ RC\ (1 + \frac{100}{R})$$

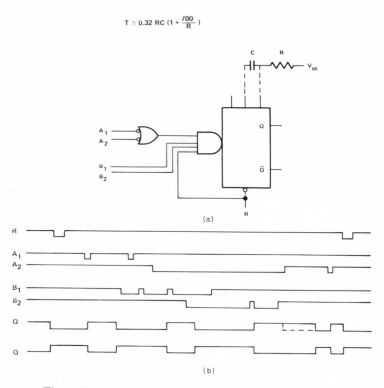

(a)

(b)

Figure IV-7 (a) Monostable flip-flop; (b) timing diagram.

seen that it is a rising edge at the clock input (accessed through gates) that initiates an output pulse. A variety of combinations of input signals can be used to cause an output pulse. Some of these combinations are shown in the timing diagram. All of the possible input combinations can be inferred from the input-gate arrangement shown in the symbolic diagram. In addition to the clock inputs, some monostable flip-flops are furnished with a direct reset or clear terminal. This terminal will return the output to its normal state if it is actuated during the time when an output pulse is present. It also acts to inhibit the initiation of an output pulse by the inputs. In the device shown, the reset terminal can also be used as an additional input by virtue of its internal connection to the input gate.

The timing of the monostable flip-flop is mediated by an externally attached capacitor and an internal or an external resistor. In action, the trigger pulse causes a rapid discharge of the capacitor, accompanied by a transition to the output state having Q high and $\overline{Q}$ low. The capacitor is then recharged by a current inflowing through the internal or external resistor. An internal circuit senses the recharging, and at a certain critical point this sensor initiates a reset operation returning the flip-flop to its normal state with Q low and $\overline{Q}$ high. In some monostable devices, including the one illustrated, actuation of a triggering combination prior to the end of an already initiated output pulse will cause the pulse to be extended by its normal time, beginning with the last triggering event. Convenient charts and formulas are furnished by the manufacturers to determine the normal pulse time length. Gross dependence of this time is simply proportional to the product of the resistance and the capacitance multiplied by a suitable constant:

$$\text{pulse length} = T \cong \tfrac{1}{3}RC \ \mu\text{sec}$$

where R is expressed in ohms, and C is expressed in microfarads.

The function table (Table IV-5) for the monostable flip-flop appearing in Fig. IV-7 is helpful when the device is used in the design of a system. With this diversity of function, the system designer has a considerable latitude to manipulate the input terminals of the device to give output pulses that may be required.

Data latches are devices often titled separately from flip-flops. However, they are simply devices containing flip-flops designed specifi-

Table IV-5   Function Table for 74122 Monostable Flip-Flop

Inputs					Outputs	
A_1	A_2	B_1	B_2	R	Q	$\overline{Q}$
X	X	X	X	L	L	H
X	H	H	X	X	L	H
X	X	L	X	X	L	H
X	X	X	L	X	L	H
L	H	H	H	X	L	H
L	X	↑	H	H	⊓	⊔
L	X	H	↑	H	⊓	⊔
H	L	H	H	H	L	H
X	L	↑	H	H	⊓	⊔
X	L	H	↑	H	⊓	⊔
H	↓	H	H	H	⊓	⊔
↓	↓	H	H	H	⊓	⊔
↓	H	H	H	H	⊓	⊔
L	X	H	H	↑	⊓	⊔
X	L	H	H	↑	⊓	⊔

cally for the storage of data. Single devices with as many as 16 flip-flops are offered for the convenience of the designer. In most of these devices, common clock terminals are provided to transfer data from the inputs to several internal flip-flops simultaneously. Figure IV-8 shows the symbolic diagrams of a few popular data latches. The selection of data latches available to the designer includes edged-clocked and state-clocked devices, devices with direct reset or clear terminals, and devices with enabling terminals for both clocking and output.

In addition to the integrated circuits specified, offered as data latches, there are several devices having more elaborate capabilities,

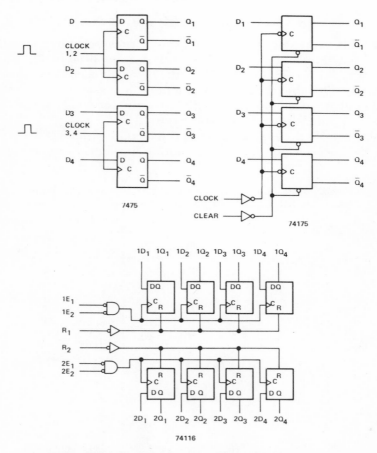

Figure IV-8 Symbolic diagrams of several data latches.

which can also be used as data-storage latches. The ubiquitous flip-flops found in these devices are often accessible in such a way that they can be used to store data as well as to manipulate them. Some of these devices are described below.

The appearance of flip-flops as storage elements in so many of the MSI and LSI devices is indicative of the manner in which data are most frequently used in systems. The most common systems operate with the steps of acquiring data, often before they are required, transferring data from one part of the system to another, manipulating data from a variety of sources, and presenting data to one or more output terminals. All of these operations, in general, require the means for temporary or quasi-permanent storage of data. (Another form of data storage, namely memory, will be discussed in Section IV-3.)

IV-2 REGISTERS AND COUNTERS

Although latches simply act to retain data, registers, which are also devices able to store data, frequently have additional capability. An important member of this class of devices is the shift register. In the shift register, data that are stored in individual flip-flops or cells in an ordered sequence can be moved from cell to cell to left or to right on appropriate command.

Shift registers are functionally typified by the example shown in Fig. IV-9a. In this hypothetical shift register, four JK master-slave flip-flops are connected as shown. There are initial data B_0, B_1, B_2, B_3 in the flip-flops. An upward transition of the clock terminal operates to transfer the input data to the master of the first JK flip-flop, the output of the slave of the first to the master of the second, the output of the slave of the second to the master of the third, etc. (During this time, of course, B_0, B_1, B_2, B_3 are undisturbed; see Section IV-1.) When the clock terminal is returned downward, the data entered in the masters are transferred to their respective slaves and then to the outputs. An abbreviated function table showing this operation follows:

Clock period T						Clock period $T + 1$			
Input	Q_0	Q_1	Q_2	Q_3	Clock	Q_0	Q_1	Q_2	Q_3
I	B_0	B_1	B_2	B_3	⊓	I	B_0	B_1	B_2

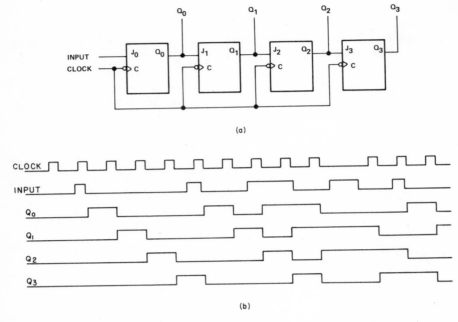

(a)

(b)

Figure IV-9 (a) Schematic diagram of a shift register; (b) shift register timing diagram.

From this table, it is clear that the content of the last cell B_3 disappears from the device, and the new datum, I, enters. All bits B are shifted one space to the right with each clock pulse.

A timing diagram, including an input data stream is shown for the elementary shift register of Fig. IV-9a in Fig. IV-9b. This diagram indicates the progression of data bits through the device under command of the clock terminal. It may be noted in the figure that the regular diagonal pattern of the transitions of Q is altered in an interesting way by the omission of a clock pulse about midway in the progression.

Shift registers may be provided with a variety of additional terminals including individual preset lines (internally gated), a rest terminal, and terminals to mediate shifting either right or left. Some representative shift registers are symbolically shown in Figs. IV-10 and IV-11. Shift registers are frequently used to convert a serial string of data bits into parallel blocks of n bits, where n is the number of cells in the register. Complementary to this, parallel entries can be shifted into serial format. Furthermore, when the data in the ordered cells

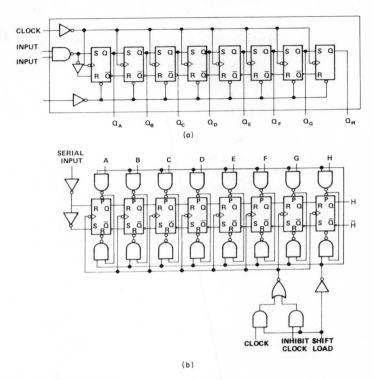

Figure IV-10 (a) Type 74164 8-bit shift register with parallel output terminals; (b) type 74165 8-bit shift register with parallel input capability.

represent binary numbers, a left shift corresponds to multiplication by 2, while a right shift gives division by 2.

Flip-flops may also be interconnected to constitute larger blocks that operate as counters. These counters are necessarily binary in operation. However, using internal connections, the output coding and the overflow condition may be altered to suit a desired coding convention. [The binary coded decimal (BCD) convention will be discussed in an subsequent example.]

An elementary 2-bit binary counter, counting 00, 01, 10, 11 is shown in Fig. IV-12, using two type D flip-flops. The same figure shows a timing diagram illustrating the operation for positive logic definition. In this counter, the reset or clear terminal preempts control of the outputs and inhibits counting when it is held low. Even a momentary actuation will reset the counter outputs to zero.

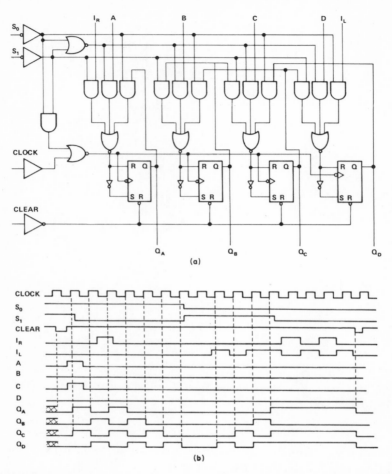

Figure IV-11 Schematic and timing diagrams of a 4-bit universal shift-right/shift-left register, TTL type 74194.

Figure IV-13 shows the symbolic diagrams of four popular 4-bit TTL counters. The first (7493) is a straight binary counter having a divide-by-2 section and a divide-by-8 section. When the output of the divide-by-2 section is connected to the input of the divide-by-8 section, the counter will overflow at the count of 16. Output transitions occur at the falling edge of inputs in the 7493, and transitions ripple through the counter; thus in the transition from count 7 to count 8, (or from 16 to 0), all four bits change in rapid sequence beginning with bit 0. This is shown in an exaggerated way in the timing diagram, Fig.

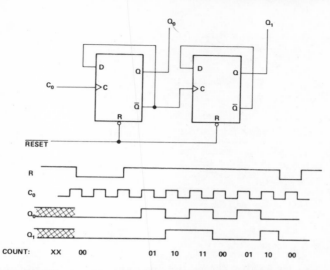

Figure IV-12 An elementary 2-bit counter using type D flip-flops.

IV-14 (top). Since the entire sequence is complete in less than 70 nsec (70×10^{-9} sec), the ripple does not generally cause ambiguity. However, for very fast systems, or for systems with counters that are cascaded to a large number of bits, this must be taken into account where

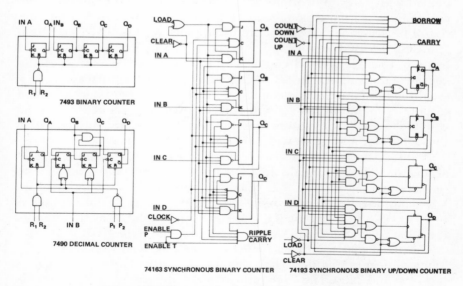

Figure IV-13 Symbolic diagram of 4-bit counters.

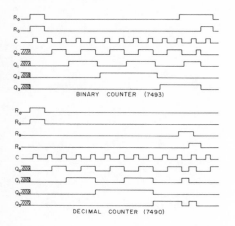

BINARY COUNTER (7493)

DECIMAL COUNTER (7490)

Figure IV-14 Counter timing diagrams, shown (top) exaggeration of ripple delay showing false counting codes and (bottom) binary coded decimal sequence.

the various outputs are viewed simultaneously for purposes of decoding. The difficulty arises because the accumulating delays give rise to ambiguous counting codes during the ripple transitions that will be misinterpreted in the decoder.

The 7490 binary-coded-decimal counter, also illustrated in Fig. IV-13, is a ripple counter and also has two sections as did the 7493. In the 7490, one section is a divide-by-2 and the other is internally connected with gates to overflow at a count of 5. When the output of the divide-by-2 section is connected to the input of the divide-by-5 section, a binary-coded decimal output sequence results. The timing diagram for the BCD-connected 7490 is shown in Fig. IV-14b. At the count of 10, all four flip-flops are reset to 0 by the action of internal decoding of the output state 1010. Table IV-6 shows the binary sequence resulting from the cascade connection of three 7490 counters arranged for BCD operation, along with the decimal representation of the count. The BCD convention does not admit the binary numbers 1010 through 1111, and these will not appear in the table.

The 7493 and the 7490 counters are provided with identical reset arrangements operating through two input inverting **and** gates. Operation is such that when either or both inputs to the reset and gate are low, counting proceeds; when both inputs are high, the counter is reset to 0000 (positive logic), and counting is inhibited. In addition, the 7490 is provided with a gated preset to the state 1001.

The third and fourth examples of counters whose symbolic diagrams appear in Fig. IV-13 have greater capability and versatility than the 7493 and 7490. The 74161 illustrated is described as a presettable synchronous 4-bit counter with asynchronous clear and carry look

Table IV-6 Binary-Coded-Decimal Count for Three
Decimal Digits

Decimal count	Hundreds $Q_DQ_CQ_BQ_A$				Tens $Q_DQ_CQ_BQ_A$				Units $Q_DQ_CQ_BQ_A$			
0	0	0	0	0	0	0	0	0	0	0	0	0
1	0	0	0	0	0	0	0	0	0	0	0	1
2	0	0	0	0	0	0	0	0	0	0	1	0
3	0	0	0	0	0	0	0	0	0	0	1	1
4	0	0	0	0	0	0	0	0	0	1	0	0
5	0	0	0	0	0	0	0	0	0	1	0	1
6	0	0	0	0	0	0	0	0	0	1	1	0
7	0	0	0	0	0	0	0	0	0	1	1	1
8	0	0	0	0	0	0	0	0	1	0	0	0
9	0	0	0	0	0	0	0	0	1	0	0	1
10	0	0	0	0	0	0	0	1	0	0	0	0
11	0	0	0	0	0	0	0	1	0	0	0	1
25	0	0	0	0	0	0	1	0	0	1	0	1
57	0	0	0	0	0	1	0	1	0	1	1	1
101	0	0	0	1	0	0	0	0	0	0	0	1
758	0	1	1	1	0	1	0	1	1	0	0	0
999	1	0	0	1	1	0	0	1	1	0	0	1

ahead. It is provided with enable inputs for both counting and carry functions. Counting occurs with the rising edge of the clock terminal signal. The carry rises on the count of 15 and falls when the count overflows (16 = 0). Preset data are entered, via J and K terminals of the internal flip-flops, under clock control, when the load terminal is held low. When the load terminal is high, the input lines are disconnected. With suitably gated carry outputs connected to successive enable inputs, a synchronous counter of $4n$-bit span can be constructed using n 74161s. In this arrangement, the possible ambiguity due to cumulative delays found in ripple counters such as the 7493 will not be present.

The 74193, also shown in Fig. IV-13, resembles the 74161 inasmuch as it is synchronous. It has the important additional feature of control to count up or down, and both carry and borrow terminals are provided to cascade n devices so as to furnish a $4n$-bit synchronous up–down counter.

Binary-coded-decimal counterparts of the synchronous counters described above are available. In addition, variation of control, enabling, reset, and preset functions are to be found in additional complex counters available to the designer.

IV-3 MEMORIES

As the name implies, memories are devices constructed to retain data either temporarily or permanently. In a limited sense, flip-flops and latches can be thought of and used as small-scale memories of limited utility. Quite apart from the fact that they can store a severely limited number of bits per device, they lack two important features that characterize a general-purpose memory device. These relate to the use of common input and output lines for data flow. Clearly, in any system requiring extensive data storage, it would be inconvenient to provide a separate line or wire for every bit stored. Nevertheless, the information stored must be available on call.

To avoid such an unmanageably large number of lines and connections, data paths in automated systems are limited to the transfer of a relatively small number of bits, often only 4, 8, or 16. The total complement of data is divided into groups of fixed length called *bytes,* which conform conveniently to the number of lines available. (A data word may consist of one or more bytes.) Ordering and selection of the bytes or words of data to be presented to the data paths from storage implies that a unique identity be attached to each byte stored. The cataloging of data that provides this unique identity is almost entirely a cataloging by the location or *address* of the byte in storage. Thus, in most systems there is a two-part expression for data, each part having equal importance. The data bytes themselves are expressed as ordered sequences of bits, usually of fixed length. The identity of the individual bytes is maintained in their respective cataloged addresses.

The useful analogy to this concept is the telephone directory. The telephone numbers represent data words that can be located in an orderly way by consulting the alphabetical listing of telephone subscribers. The subscriber's name corresponds to a catalog location or address in the directory where the data may be found. Without the association of each telephone number with an identity, the collection of telephone numbers themselves would be of little use.

A memory device, then, conceptually, is a collection of cells (which could be flip-flops), each of which is capable of storing 1 bit of information. To be useful, these data bits must be accessible. Bearing in mind an implied requirement of common lines for data transfer, the device must have the means for selectively switching individual data cells to the common lines under some form of logical control. Input to this switching logic consists of the address identifying the location within the device where the required data are located.

This conceptual form is illustrated in Fig. IV-15, which shows a memory device comprised of 16 storage locations, each of which contains 1 bit of information. The memory is organized, in this case, as 16 "words" of 1 bit. To locate one of 16 storage cells requires an address word of 4 bits. This address constitutes the input. The address decoded within the memory activates one (and only one) of the 16 switch-control lines identified by the address word, and thereby connects the corresponding memory cell to the output of the device via the gated logic shown.

The figure also shows the logic that is provided to connect the external "write" terminal to actuate one (and only one) of the flip-flop clock terminals, while all of their "J" terminals are connected to the data input terminal of the memory. By this means, with address bits present on the address inputs and data present at the data input terminal, a data bit can be impressed on the selected memory cell when an appropriate signal is impressed on the write terminal.

Having both output and data entry features, the device illustrated in Fig. IV-15 is a read or write memory of 16 words by 1 bit. The term *random-access memory* (RAM) is commonly used for such a device, and usage associates this term with the write capability in addition to accessibility of the data via the address lines. (Memories whose data cannot be altered during system operation are correspondingly called

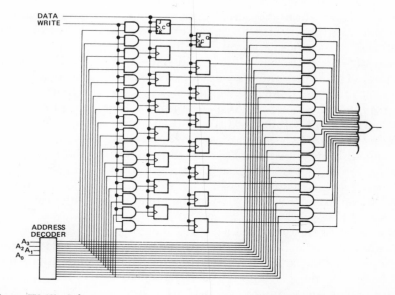

Figure IV-15 Schematic representation of a 16-word by 1-bit read–write memory.

read-only memories (ROM) and are described below.) By virtue of their particular construction, read–write memories, or to use the commonly accepted term RAM's, such as the one in Fig. IV-15, require that the data stored be first entered via data input lines and located by the address lines. Moreover, when power is removed the data are lost. These features of operation characterize most solid-state memories whose content can be altered during the operation of a system.

The alternative form of solid-state memory, having content that can be accessed but not altered is called a read-only memory (ROM). In these memories, the data are entered at the time of manufacture or by special procedures that are not normally part of a system operation. Data stored in ROM's are nonvolatile; that is, they are not lost when power is removed. In keeping with the requirement that data be transferred over common lines, data in ROM's are also located by an address structure and connected 1 byte at a time to a set of output lines. Figure IV-16 shows a representative read-only memory of 4 words by 4 bits along with a table listing its content. In the figure, redundant lines to the output gates are drawn to indicate that the basic structure of the ROM is susceptible to the entry of any data table simply by altering the particular pattern of permanent links joining the address decoder lines and the **or** gate inputs.

The actual construction of RAM's and ROM's resembles the examples drawn in Figs. IV-15 and IV-16 only in a functional way. The internal organization and actual circuits used, often proprietary, are designed for compactness, reliability, low power consumption, economy, and convenience in use. There is a very wide range of choice of both RAM and ROM solid-state devices available to the designer. This choice includes devices having relatively small storage and very high speed, and slower devices in which as many as 16,000 bits may be stored. Very high speed in this reference means that output data are valid within 10 to 100 nsec after the address is presented. In "slower devices," delays of a few hundred nanoseconds to 1 or 2 μsec occur between introduction of address and appearance of valid data on the output lines. Space does not permit any comprehensive listing of memories now available. In later chapters when reference is made to a particular memory, its special features will be briefly mentioned.

One final feature that characterizes most memory devices will be described. Mention has been made of the use of common data paths in systems. If a data path is to be used by more than just one single memory device, some means must be provided to disconnect it entirely from the data lines in the path. In most TTL devices, the outputs occupy a definite state—either high or low—and, in general, only one output should be connected to a line. Multiple connections could be made through **or** gates. However, this adds complexity to a system. To simplify design, memories (and certain other devices including gates) are devised so that their outputs can be connected to common lines. Fig. IV-17 shows the methods by which output connections to common lines are usually handled. In the first method, shown to define the functional requirement, an external **or** gate is simply interposed between several devices and a common line.

In the second method shown, the output of each device is furnished with an "open-collector" transistor. Each device is capable, through its output transistor, of pulling the common line to a low state when it is enabled. The outputs can thus be **or** connected without the hazard of potentially destructive conflict. Ambiguity can be avoided by making sure that only one selected device be enabled at any one time. Open-collector devices necessarily operate on lines that are passively high and actively low, although this limitation need not inhibit the design of systems defined in terms of positive logic.

A_0	A_1	D_3	D_2	D_1	D_0
0	0	0	0	1	1
0	1	1	0	1	0
1	0	0	1	1	0
1	1	1	0	1	1

TRUTH TABLE

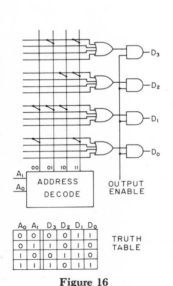

Figure 16

Figure 17

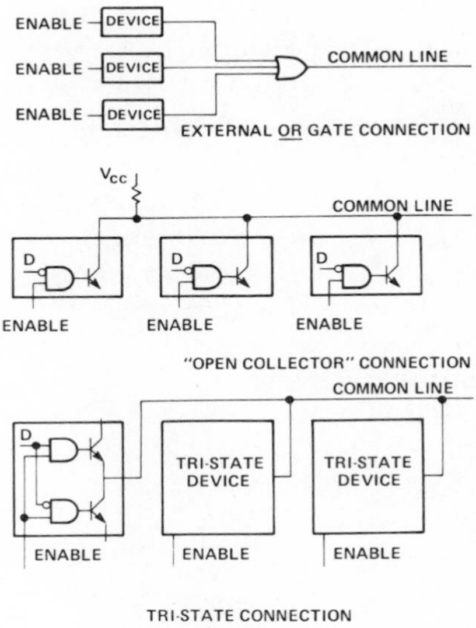

Figure IV-16 Read-only memory of four words by 4 bits. The link pattern can be altered at time of manufacture to alter the memory content.

Figure IV-17 Representative memory output structures suitable for wired or connection.

A third method is also shown in which outputs of the devices provide both high and low states actively. This originally proprietary output structure design, called a *tri-state* output is now offered in a considerable selection of devices whose application may make it desirable to connect several outputs to a common line. In the tristate output two transistors are present, one to pull the output low and the other to pull it high. In addition, the structure is provided with a circuit logically equivalent to the two internal gates shown in each device, which allows complete deactivation of the output (effectively disconnecting both transistors), thereby allowing connection of another device, without conflict, to the common line. In the case of tristate devices with outputs connected to a common line, one and only one device should be enabled at any one time, not only to avoid ambiguity, as with the open-collector devices, but also to avoid the stress of conflicting active states.

Memory devices are available with the equivalent of either open-collector or tristate outputs. This allows the connection of many memories to the same set of data lines without interference. When memories are **or** connected in this manner an expanded system address structure is used to select individual memory devices as required. Figure IV-18 shows how four 16 word by 4-bit memories may be arranged to form a 64 word by 4-bit memory system requiring a 6-bit address. The memory enable line controlling the decoder for address

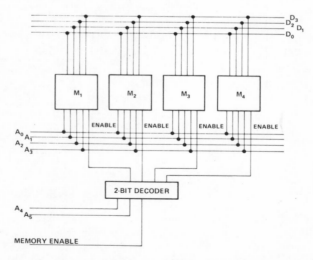

Figure IV-18 Memory select scheme to expand four 16-word by 4-bit memories into a 64-word by 4-bit memory.

bits A4 and A5 can be used to disconnect the memory entirely from the data path by deactivating all four of the individual memory-enable lines. This feature of the circuits allows the data path to be used for functions other than the transfer of memory words.

IV-4 MISCELLANEOUS DEVICES

A great number of special purpose medium-scale integrated-circuit devices have been developed for the convenience of the designer. The scope of this chapter permits the mention of a few having wide application:

a. The *exclusive* or gate (for example, 7486), shown in Fig. IV-19 with its logical equivalent, is a frequently used logic building block. The logical symbol for the *exclusive* or function is $\oplus$. It may be recalled that the 1-bit adder (Fig. III-10) uses a logical sequence corresponding to the **exclusive or** function, and the logical equivalent of the **exclusive or** gate is to be found in that figure.

b. Data selectors, or multiplexers, are used, as the names imply, to connect one of several input lines to a common output. A frequently used 8-line to 1-line multiplexer (74151) is shown in Fig. IV-20a along with its function table. The specific line selected from the eight inputs to have its data state transferred to the output is determined by the binary address impressed on the three data-select inputs. In addition, the enable line must be held low for the transfer to be effected. Multiple-line multiplexers are also available. The 74157 duplexer is one of a family of devices that allows simultaneous switching of 4 output lines to either of two 4-line sources. The logic design of the 74157

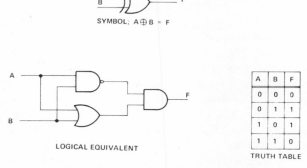

SYMBOL; A $\oplus$ B = F

LOGICAL EQUIVALENT

A	B	F
0	0	0
0	1	1
1	0	1
1	1	0

TRUTH TABLE

Figure IV-19   The exclusive or gate.

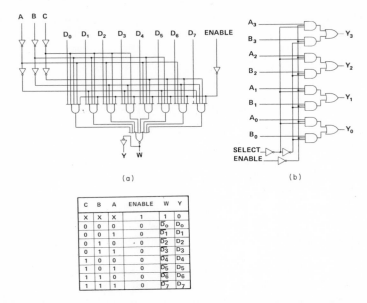

C	B	A	ENABLE	W	Y
X	X	X	1	1	0
0	0	0	0	$\bar{D}_0$	D_0
0	0	1	0	$\bar{D}_1$	D_1
0	1	0	. 0	$\bar{D}_2$	D_2
0	1	1	0	$\bar{D}_3$	D_3
1	0	0	0	$\bar{D}_4$	D_4
1	0	1	0	$\bar{D}_5$	D_5
1	1	0	0	$\bar{D}_6$	D_6
1	1	1	0	$\bar{D}_7$	D_7

Figure IV-20 (a) 1 of 8 data selector (74151); (b) 4-bit data duplexer (74157).

is shown in Fig. IV-20b. Duplexers find frequent application in systems, and the 4-bit width available in the 74157 series is a convenience where multiple-bit bytes are handled.

c. Demultiplexers, sometimes called decoders, perform a function that is complementary to multiplexing, namely, to connect one input line to a selected output line. By way of example, the 3-line to 8-line demultiplexer (74138) is shown in Fig. IV-21 along with its function table. One of the so-called gate or enabling lines can be used in the role of a single noninverting or inverting data line, while the three "address" lines direct the input state to a selected output. The nature of the device makes this application most appropriate to negative logic treatment. The same device may be used as a 3-bit address decoder with a gated enable feature.

d. Decoder is also a term used for devices having purposes other than address decoding. For example, binary-coded-decimal information may be transferred to a display device consisting of a matrix of 7 segments, each 4-bit code word causing the actuation of the appropriate segments to form the corresponding alpha-numeric pictorial of the

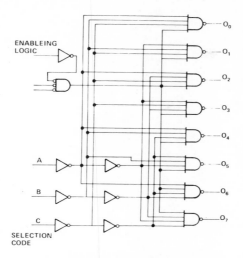

Figure IV-21 3-line to 8-line decoder/demultiplxer which can be used as a 1-line to 8-line demultiplexer or a 3-bit address decoder, type 74138.

decimal digit is represents. Figure IV-22 shows, symbolically, the 7447 BCD to 7-segment decoder, along with its function table and an illustration of the pictorials of the decimal digits.

e. Encoders perform a function that is complementary to the function of decoders. They identify, the state of a number of input lines, usually by binary code at the output lines. An example of an encoder is found in the 74148, a logic diagram that appears in Fig. IV-23, along with its function table. It can be adduced from the logic diagram, and is indicated in the function table, that the output code indicates the line of highest order of the 8 inputs having a low (true) state regardless of the states of lines having lower order. This feature establishes a priority in the ordering of inputs such that the 3-bit output identifies the *highest* priority input present. It also precludes ambiguity in the output when more than one input line is low (true).

Since both encoders and decoders represent devices in which input states are transformed in a unique way to output states, their function can frequently be accomplished with memories. In this case, the memory acts as a code book wherein the input states are impressed on the address lines to the memory, eliciting for each input combination an appropriate output. Memories, particularly read-only memories, are sometimes put to this use for example, in matrix character generation.

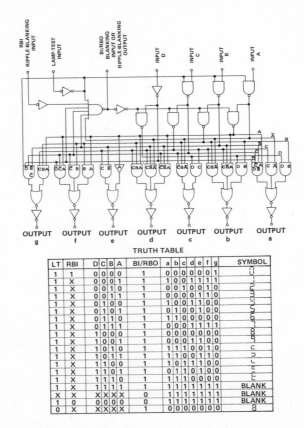

TRUTH TABLE

LT	RBI	D	C	B	A	BI/RBO	a	b	c	d	e	f	g	SYMBOL
1	1	0	0	0	0	1	0	0	0	0	0	0	1	
1	X	0	0	0	1	1	1	0	0	1	1	1	1	
1	X	0	0	1	0	1	0	0	1	0	0	1	0	
1	X	0	0	1	1	1	0	0	0	0	1	1	0	
1	X	0	1	0	0	1	1	0	0	1	1	0	0	
1	X	0	1	0	1	1	0	1	0	0	1	0	0	
1	X	0	1	1	0	1	1	1	0	0	0	0	0	
1	X	0	1	1	1	1	0	0	0	1	1	1	1	
1	X	1	0	0	0	1	0	0	0	0	0	0	0	
1	X	1	0	0	1	1	0	0	0	1	1	0	0	
1	X	1	0	1	0	1	1	1	1	0	0	1	0	c
1	X	1	0	1	1	1	1	1	0	0	1	1	0	⊐
1	X	1	1	0	0	1	1	0	1	1	1	0	0	L
1	X	1	1	0	1	1	0	1	1	0	1	0	0	c
1	X	1	1	1	0	1	1	1	1	0	0	0	0	t
1	X	1	1	1	1	1	1	1	1	1	1	1	1	BLANK
X	X	X	X	X	X	0	1	1	1	1	1	1	1	BLANK
1	0	0	0	0	0	0	1	1	1	1	1	1	1	BLANK
0	X	X	X	X	X	1	0	0	0	0	0	0	0	8

Figure IV-22 4-line to 7-segment decoder, type 7447.

f. Adders are devices designed for the purpose of arithmetic addition of binary numbers. In Chapter II, the rules of binary addition were presented, and Fig. III-10 shows the logical implementation of a 1-bit adder using gates. The 7483, shown in Fig. IV-24, is a device that performs binary addition on two 4-bit binary numbers. It is provided with both input and output carry terminals. Using these terminals, addition of numbers with more than 4 bits can be accomodated by cascading two or more of the devices. As was described in Chapter II, binary adders can also perform digital subtraction using the 2's complement convention, and, by extension, the arithmetic operations of multiplication and division can be accomplished as sequences of additions or subtractions.

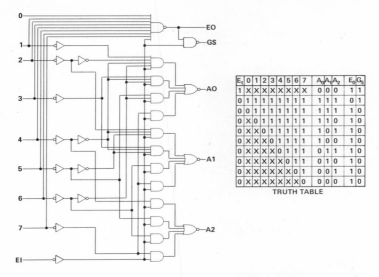

E_I	0	1	2	3	4	5	6	7	A_0	A_1	A_2	E_O	G_S
1	X	X	X	X	X	X	X	X	0	0	0	1	1
0	1	1	1	1	1	1	1	1	1	1	1	0	1
0	0	1	1	1	1	1	1	1	1	1	1	1	0
0	X	0	1	1	1	1	1	1	1	1	0	1	0
0	X	X	0	1	1	1	1	1	1	0	1	1	0
0	X	X	X	0	1	1	1	1	1	0	0	1	0
0	X	X	X	X	0	1	1	1	0	1	1	1	0
0	X	X	X	X	X	0	1	1	0	1	0	1	0
0	X	X	X	X	X	X	0	1	0	0	1	1	0
0	X	X	X	X	X	X	X	0	0	0	0	1	0

TRUTH TABLE

Figure IV-23 8-input priority encoder, type 74148.

g. Digital magnitude comparators function as though they subtract two binary numbers but only show that the difference is greater than, equal to, or less than zero. The 7485 4-bit digital comparator is shown symbolically in Fig. IV-25, along with its function table. The device is furnished with cascading inputs and outputs. Interconnection of two or more 7485's via these cascading terminals allows digital magnitude

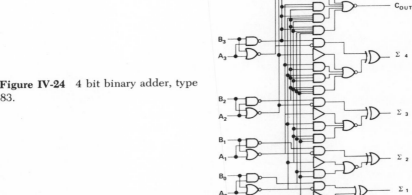

Figure IV-24 4 bit binary adder, type 7483.

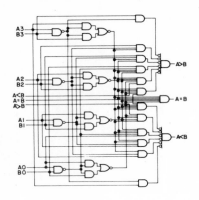

INPUTS A, B				CASCADING INPUTS			OUTPUTS		
							A > B	A < B	A = B
$A_3 > B_3$	X	X	X	X	X	X	H	L	L
$A_3 < B_3$	X	X	X	X	X	X	L	H	L
$A_3 = B_3$	$A_2 > B_2$	X	X	X	X	X	H	L	L
$A_3 = B_3$	$A_2 < B_2$	X	X	X	X	X	L	H	L
$A_3 = B_3$	$A_2 = B_2$	$A_1 > B_1$	X	X	X	X	H	L	L
•	$A_2 = B_2$	$A_1 < B_1$	X	X	X	X	L	H	L
•	$A_2 = B_2$	$A_1 = B_1$	$A_0 > B_0$	X	X	X	H	L	L
•	•	$A_1 = B_1$	$A_0 < B_0$	X	X	X.	L	H	L
•	•	$A_1 = B_1$	$A_0 = B_0$	H	L	L	H	L	L
•	•	•	$A_0 = B_0$	L	H	L	L	H	L
•	•	•	$A_0 = B_0$	L	L	H	L	L	L

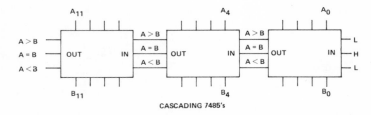

CASCADING 7485's

Figure IV-25   4-bit digital magnitude comparator, type 7485.

comparison of binary numbers of more than 4 bits. The figure includes a diagram that shows how three magnitude comparators may be used to compare two binary numbers each of which has 12 bits.

A number of other specialized devices find less frequent use than the ones so far mentioned. Space does not permit a complete listing. The reader is invited to consult any of the various digital-integrated-circuit data books to see the considerable variety of devices now offered for the added convenience of the system designer.

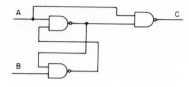

Figure IV-26 Circuit for analysis, Exercise 1.

EXERCISES

1. Analyze the response of the circuit shown in Fig. IV-26, by first drawing up a static function table, then by showing the outputs resulting from the possible input combinations. Next determine the result of transitions at each input. Why is the static table inadequate to describe the operation of the circuit?

2. Analyze the circuit of the type D flip-flop shown in Fig. IV-3. Well-organized tables showing the states and transitions of intermediate points in the circuit are helpful in the analysis.

3. Analyze the operation of the type 7473 master-slave flip-flop whose circuit appears in Fig. IV-6a. Identify the means by which the master is disconnected from the JK input terminals and the means by which its state is impressed on the slave during the clock cycle.

4. Analyze the operation of the type 74108 edge-triggered flip-flop shown schematically in Fig. IV-6b. Identify the transitional event that transfers the information derived from JK to the storage element. Show that the storage element is isolated from the inputs at all times except for the interval occupied by the downward transition of the clock terminal.

5. (a) Using four type D flip-flops, design a 4-bit shift register to shift data serially to the right.

(b) Add the logical control to allow selection of either right or left shifting of data.

V

The Arithmetic Logic Unit

One of the more complex MSI devices is the arithmetic logic unit (ALU). The generic TLL ALU is the 74181 having the equivalent of 75 gates on a single monolithic silicon wafer smaller than a pencil eraser. It is a fast device. The longest time required to establish an output condition is less than 70 nsec. (Even faster versions are available.) It operates on two input operands, of 4 bits each, to deliver an output also basically of 4 bits. In addition, there are terminals for input and output carry functions. The operation joining the two operands to formulate the output is selected by the states of 5 selection or operation-code (op-code) inputs from a repertoire list of 32 operations.

It is this selective capability that gives the device its unique character. Whereas in devices previously encountered, the logical consequence at the output was a fixed function of the input states, the ALU can be instructed to carry out any operation in its repertoire. The choice is designed to cover virtually all of the functions required in the management of data.

The symbolic and logic diagrams of the 74181 ALU are shown in Fig. V-1. Its operation, mediated by the 5 selection or op-code inputs is described in Table V-1. The table is defined in terms of positive logic where 0 = low and 1 = high. The reader is reminded that the symbols $+$, $\cdot$, and $\oplus$ are logical symbols that were previously defined.

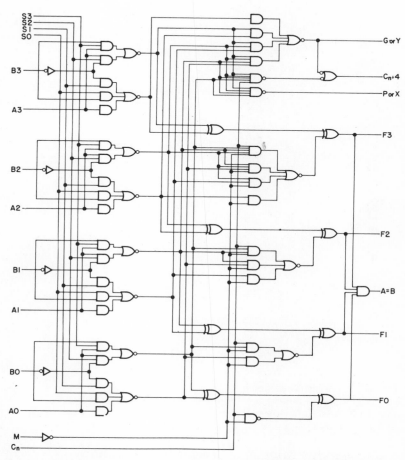

Figure V-1 The arithmetic logic unit showing symbolic and logic diagrams.

Table V-1 Function Table for the 74181 ALU Stated in Positive Logic[a]

Selection code or op-code					Out-put F	Carry-out
M	S_3	S_2	S_2	S_0		
0	0	0	0	0	A plus $\bar{C}_I$	*
0	0	0	0	1	(A + B) plus $\bar{C}_I$	*
0	0	0	1	0	(A + $\bar{B}$) plus $\bar{C}_I$	*
0	0	0	1	1	(minus 1) plus $\bar{C}_I$	*
0	0	1	0	0	A plus (A · $\bar{B}$) plus $\bar{C}_I$	*
0	0	1	0	1	(A + B) plus (A · $\bar{B}$) plus $\bar{C}_I$	*
0	0	1	1	0	A minus B minus $\bar{C}_I$	*
0	0	1	1	1	(A · $\bar{B}$) minus $\bar{C}_I$	*
0	1	0	0	0	A plus (A · B) plus $\bar{C}_I$	*
0	1	0	0	1	A plus B plus $\bar{C}_I$	*
0	1	0	1	0	(A + $\bar{B}$) plus (A · B) plus $\bar{C}_I$	*
0	1	0	1	1	(A · B) minus $\bar{C}_I$	*
0	1	1	0	0	A plus A plus $\bar{C}_I$	*
0	1	1	0	1	(A + B) plus A plus $\bar{C}_I$	*
0	1	1	1	0	(A + $\bar{B}$) plus A plus $\bar{C}_I$	*
0	1	1	1	1	A minus $\bar{C}_I$	*
1	0	0	0	0	$\bar{A}$	‡
1	0	0	0	1	$\bar{A}$ + B	‡
1	0	0	1	0	$\overline{A \cdot B}$	‡
1	0	0	1	1	0	‡
1	0	1	0	0	$\overline{A \cdot B}$	‡
1	0	1	0	1	$\bar{B}$	‡
1	0	1	1	0	A $\oplus$ B	‡
1	0	1	1	1	A · $\bar{B}$	‡
1	1	0	0	0	$\bar{A}$ + B	‡
1	1	0	0	1	$\overline{A \oplus B}$	‡
1	1	0	1	0	B	‡
1	1	0	1	1	A · B	‡
1	1	1	0	0	1	‡
1	1	1	0	1	A + $\bar{B}$	‡
1	1	1	1	0	A + B	‡
1	1	1	1	1	A	‡

[a] 0 = low, 1 = high. The operands are A, B, and carry *in*. The ALU will generate a carry *out* for the arithmetic operations as indicated by the asterisk *. Carry *out* is irrelevent for non arithmetic operations indicated by the double dagger ‡. Both carry in and carry out are inverted.

(See Chapter III.) Arithmetic designations are indicated by written words rather than symbols.

Since the ALU can perform a variety of operations on data, it can be placed in the data path of a system in such a way as to *process* the flowing data according to the requirements of the system. Of course, this sweeping statement is subject to a very fundamental circumscription regarding the required organization of data and the control of its flow. Nevertheless, the power implicit in the use of the ALU to process data is profound and is central to the success of digital automated systems. Whereas the logic designer using gates and more complex fixed-logic elements could devise circuits to accomplish almost any single logical function, he can use the ALU to design circuits whose logical function can be varied at will via the op-codes introduced to it.

The ALU carries out one logical operation at a time on one or two operands to provide an instructed result. In a nontrivial system, the description of data processing is comprised of an ordered series of such instructed operations on an ordered series of operands, each operation being one step of an orderly schedule of events in accordance with a prescribed plan or program. It is natural to account for the individual steps by assigning them numbers serially in order of their occurrence.

Each numbered step implies the marshalling of specific required data. These required data, themselves associated with the enumeration of the respective steps, include the data that make up the operands and the op-code word that, when applied to the ALU, prescribes the operation. The data could simply be stored in a memory location identified (addressed) by the step number. However, since operations may be associated at one time or another with more than one operand, it is more common to associate an op-code with a step number and to provide, in the same association, a code that describes the source in which the operands may be found rather than a code for the operands themselves. The op-code and the source code together provide the necessary information to formulate the complete input to the ALU for one step.

The step itself is incomplete until two additional requirements are met. First, and obviously, the result of the ALU operation is useless unless some disposition is prescribed for the output data. A destination code, specifically describing the disposition of the result, can be included in the information associated with the step number.

A less obvious, but crucial requirement to automate the system is provision of a signal to link the serial operating steps in a timely way. With the suggestion that the steps be serially numbered, the linking process can be provided by simply advancing a counter by one unit to call the next step in the program of events. The linking operation is separate from operand and op-code data. It has a smaller field of choice than the op-code and source and destination codes, although it may afford some descriptive information regarding succeeding steps other than simply the advance of the step counter. One primary function of the linking process is to provide a timing sequence for the events taking place during a step. Finite intervals are required for the unambiguous transfer of data to the ALU, for the operation of the ALU on the data, and for the disposition of valid results. The progression of these events is generally cyclical and is mediated by means of a clock that marks the very small intervals of time associated with each step making up the cycle.

It is convenient to think of the timing and linking component of the system as a semiautonomous control element designed to govern the operation of the system but not its function. Function is then determined by the data and the series of op-codes that are called and executed. The concept is schematically illustrated in Fig. V-2. As the charting of the events shows, the clock of the control unit calls up the events in the operation cycle. Each cycle begins with the generation of a step number and the corresponding address. The address calls the required instruction information including data source code, op-code, and destination code from a memory. Successive events within the cycle are called by the clock ticks until the cycle is complete. It should be noted that the connection of data and op-code to the ALU must be maintained until the cycle is complete. This is symbolized by the bars appearing in Fig. V-2, each of which is carried to the end of the cycle.

Figure V-3 is a simplified schematic diagram of the system described above showing the semiautonomous control component at the lower left and the ALU with its data sources and destinations attached. The function of this system is determined by the content of the memory; that is to say, the system steps at the call of the control component, but the specific function of the steps is vested in the program of codes contained in the memory. Thus, the same set of logical components, with the ALU, can be used in a variety of digitally automated systems simply by changing the content of the memory and the connections to the outside world.

What has been described, using the ALU as its distinguishing component, is a *general-purpose* digital automation scheme. This operating system is divided into two necessary parts. One part is comprised of the physical components of the system whose design and interconnection define the way in which the system operates. This most tangible part of the system is called the *hardware*. The other part of the operating system, variously called program of steps, program of data source codes, op-codes and destination codes, or program of in-

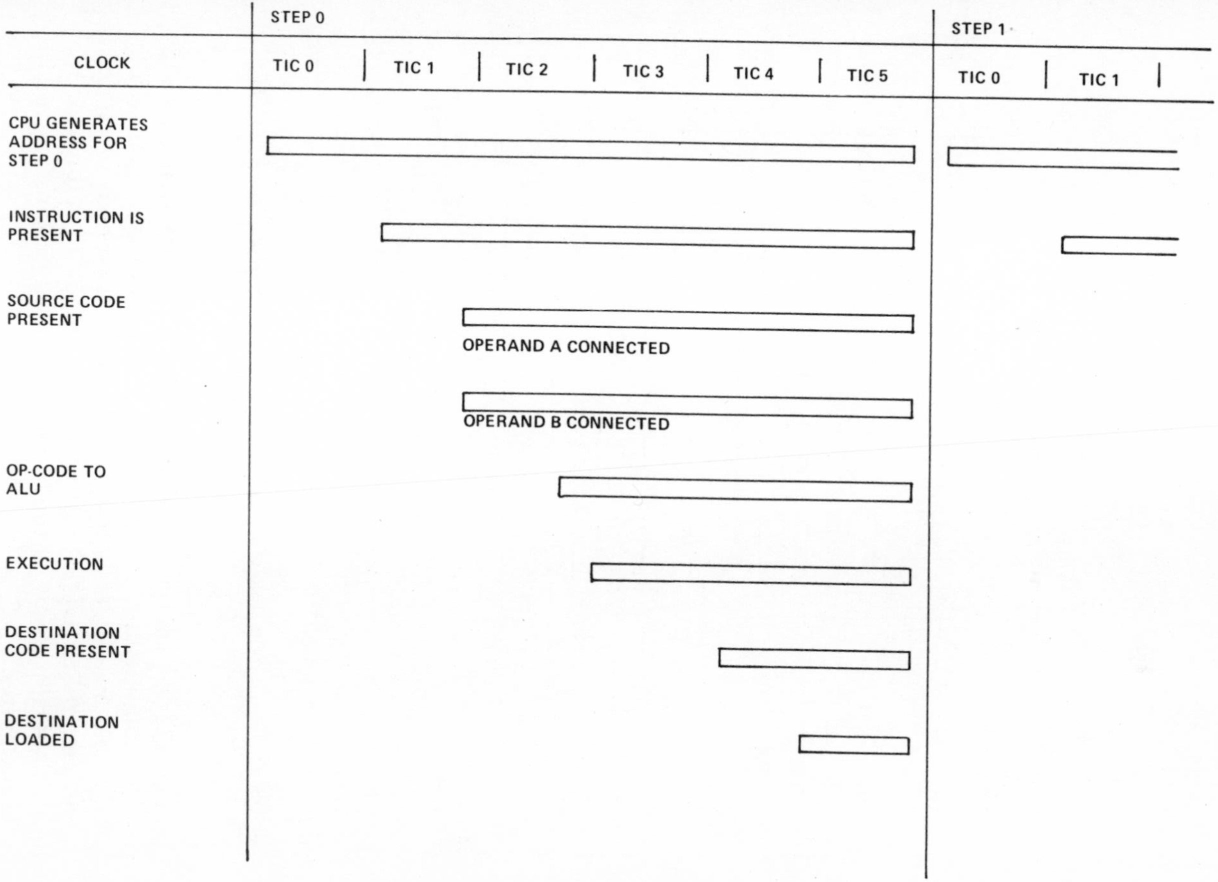

Figure V-2 Schedule of events in an ALU cycle.

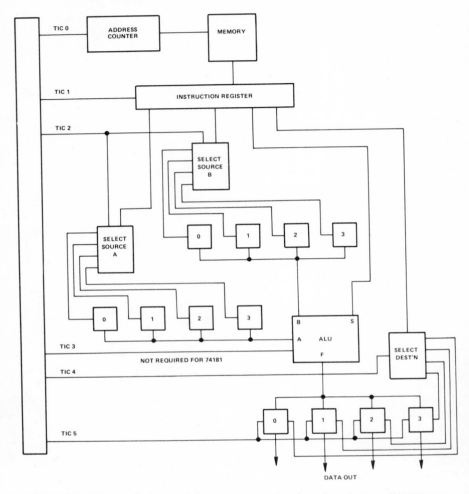

Figure V-3 Schematic diagram of a processor system based on the type 74181 ALU.

structions. A term generally used to compass all of these names is *soft-ware.* The combination of hardware and software, designed specifi-cally to an automation task, can accommodate the needs of that task with virtually unlimited flexibility. It is the capability of the ALU that confers this flexibility by virtue of the fact that it provides a variable logic to the system.

Projects and exercises will be omitted in this chapter since they would be a complicated anticipation of those attached to later chapters. Instead, an example of a simple system using the ALU will be described. The example will be provided with the necessary registers to perform arithmetic addition or subtraction of two 8-bit binary numbers and a memory storing the program and data movement codes.

The example introduces two amplifications on components already mentioned above. First, the semiautonomous control element is provided with a start and stop feature, emphasizing the adverb *semi*, in its title. Second, only one destination register is used, being selected by the destination code. It is provided with a ninth-bit position to accommodate a carry output from the ALU. In addition, the destination register is a shift register, allowing the data to be shifted left or right in response to the state of two additional bits that could be added to the destination code. (This feature is not used for addition or subtraction.) Such a destination register with its additional features is usually called an accumulator.

Finally, since the arithmetic operations sometimes require a carry *in* and sometimes do not, it is expedient to add one additional bit to the op-code, making 6 bits altogether, to designate whether the carry *in* should be set or not set. (Both input and output carry lines of the 74181 are expressed in data complement, and inverters must be used to make their data consistent.)

Figure V-4 shows a schematic diagram of the system divided into a control section and a function section. The control section consists of a clock, a synchronous counter, and a 2-line to 4-line decoder. The counter is inhibited through its terminals P and T whenever the decoder inputs are 11, that is, at counter outputs 0011, 0111, 1011 and 1111. It can be preloaded at any time while it is inhibited, and, of course, if it is preloaded to any number not 0011, 0111, 1011, or 1111, the inhibition is lifted and counting will proceed until the next inhibit condition is encountered.

The function section includes a 4-word by 13-bit read-only memory, input data selectors, latches, the ALU consisting of two 4-bit blocks cascaded to accommodate the 8-bit width required, and a 9-bit accumulator. The number of bits per memory word, 13, is determined by the information requirement to execute a step. One 13-bit word can prescribe all of the events for each of the four arithmetic algorithms offered in the system repertoire, namely, addition without carry, addition with carry, subtraction without borrow, and subtraction with borrow. In addition, the data source codes allow the selection of each operand from one of four separate sources via the source-code bits.

During operation, when there is no external intervention, the con-

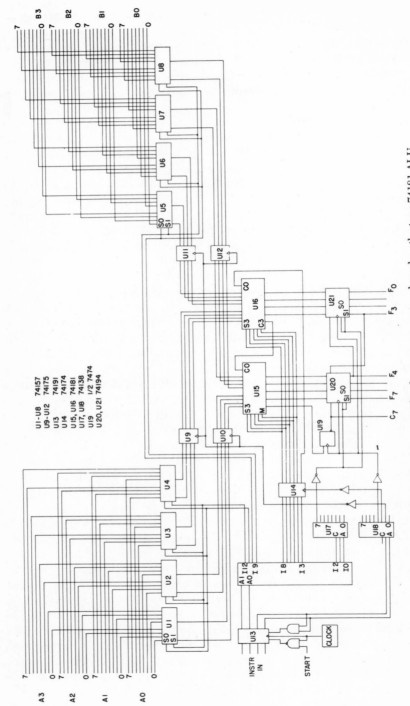

Figure V-4 A more complete example of a processor system based on the type 74181 ALU.

trol system will move quickly to an event whose (counter) number is XX11, at which point it will halt. It is then susceptible to being restarted by an external preload of any number not XX11. In fact, for intelligible results, preload numbers are prescribed to be 0000, 0100, 1000, or 1100, each of which selects one of the four algorithms. When the preload is accomplished, the system will cycle through the algorithm that has been called (four events) and will halt again. The last of the four events that establishes the halt also loads the result of the operation in the accumulator.

The four algorithms in the reportoire, each with its preload call, are described in more detail as follows:

0000: Add without carry the byte found in source A01 to the byte found in source B11 and place the result in the accumulator.

0100: Add with carry the byte found in source A10 to the byte found in source B01 and place the result in the accumulator.

1000: Subtract without borrow the byte found in source B01 from the byte found in source A01 and place the result in the accumulator.

1100: Subtract with borrow the byte found in source B01 from the byte found in source A01 and place the result in the accumulator.

The individual events in each algorithm called are described by the following schedule; the designating counter numbers, sometimes called microstep numbers, indicate the schedule sequence:

XX00: Start the (semiautonomous) controller, address the memory via the bits XX to call the corresponding 13-bit word to the memory output.

XX01: Load the selected operands into the operand latches.

XX10: Load the ALU op-code into the op-code latch.

XX11: Load the result into the accumulator; halt the (semiautonomous) controller.

To promote these operations, the counter output is decoded. This activates the decoder output lines in sequence (via gates to provide the clock edges required) to clock the selected input latches and the accumulator loading, each in its turn. Actual data source and destination selection is determined by the appropriate bits in the 13-bit word as soon as it is present via the respective selection lines to the multiplexer and, in this case, to the accumulator.

The actual construction of the four 13-bit code words can be formulated using the function table for the 74181 and the algorithm list noted above. The code words are divided into fields as shown in Table V-2 and are listed with the preload codes used to call them. The preload word, entered from the outside, serves as an *external instruction*

Table V-2 Function Table for the 74181 Data System

Algorithm	External instruction (preload to counter)	Oper- and A field I_{12} I_{11}	Oper- and B field I_{10} I_9	Operation code field I_8 I_7 I_6 I_5 I_4	Carry- in[a] I_3	Destina- tion field[b] I_2 I_1 I_0
Add without carry: A 01 PLUS B11	0 0 (0) (0)	0 1	1 1	0 1 0 0 1	1	1 1 1
Add with carry A 10 PLUS B 01	0 1 (0) (0)	1 0	0 1	0 1 0 0 1	0	1 1 1
Subtract without borrow A 01 MINUS B 01	1 0 (0) (0)	0 1	0 1	0 0 1 1 0	1	1 1 1
Subtract with borrow A 01 MINUS B 01	1 1 (0) (0)	0 1	0 1	0 0 1 1 0	0	1 1 1

[a] This bit provides the signal to the carry-in gate. In 2's complement expression, the 74181 requires a true carry-in for subtraction without borrow. The carry bit is required in the inverted sense.

[b] 111 is the destination code selecting the accumulator.

to the system. The 13-bit word appearing at the output of the internal memory represents the decoding of the external instruction, in a manner specific to the hardware, to elicit the result called by the external instruction.

Clearly, the system shown in Fig. V-4 could be adapted to a variety of additional algorithms by adding little more than additional internal memory words and the means to address them with external instructions. Moreover, the hardware arrangement could be modified to accomplish more versatile results.

One popular hardware method that simplifies the connection of data sources and destinations to the ALU deserves mention here. In situations when data obtained from many possible sources and directed to many destinations are to be handled, systems are frequently interconnected with data paths common to many sources and many destinations to reduce the number of interconnecting lines. These common data paths, called *data busses* operate in the manner of telephone party lines, and the various sources and destinations are selectively switched to the common lines under direction of the control section.

Individual sources, being **or** connected to the lines, must then have output control, using either open collector or tristate outputs. Similarly, destinations must be equipped with individual entry-enabling means. With these provisions, the control section and instruction decoding can specify data transfers uniquely as to source and destination.

Microprocessors, which are discussed in the remainder of this book, are equipped with internal data busses, and microprocessor system hardware is substantially simplified when data interconnections external to the microprocessor are structured in buss arrangements.

VI

The Microprocessor

The 1960s brought two developments to the science of automation that led to the birth of the microprocessor. The first of these was the development of lower cost digital minicomputers and minicomputer systems, which brought the cost and convenience of high-speed digital data processing within the means of relatively modest enterprises and generated a potential demand for even more widespread application of digital systems. The cost effectiveness and utility of minicomputer systems are attested by the astonishing growth that these systems have enjoyed over the past decade. The second development was the success of increasingly larger scale integration in microcircuits with economically acceptable yields in production.

An important method of microcircuit construction, the metal–oxide–silicon (MOS) technology, was found to be particularly suited to large-scale integration for two important reasons. First, the structure of individual elements in the integrated circuits is simpler than that of other technologies and thus unit areas could be made smaller with reasonable assurance of high yields. Second, the level of electrical power required to operate MOS devices can be considerably less than that required, for example, in TTL devices. This fact reduces thermal stresses on components and allows compact integration without severe demands on thermal design.

These advantages are not entirely secured without performance penalties. MOS devices are not commonly capable of the very high speeds obtainable with TTL devices. Moreover, the signal-output power levels are generally lower. However, the speed of MOS devices is adequate for most applications, and, in situations when signal-output power level is inadequate to drive auxiliary circuit elements (which are often TTL devices) buffers are available to accommodate the loading requirements. The principal factor in the early dominance of MOS devices in the microprocessor field has been the success with which their large-scale integration can be carried out. This success has led to high yields in production and low unit costs.

As might be expected, very low cost digital processing is currently leading to an explosive expansion of the application of digital systems to a large variety of enterprises. Proponents of digital data processing hold that there is no task that cannot use it to advantage. Certainly there are many fields that can benefit significantly from low-cost digital data processing, and this accounts for the very rapid growth in microprocessor applications. Moreover, the added capability introduced into systems by the incorporation of microprocessors results, in some cases, in profound changes in the concept and structure of those systems.

VI-1 THE GENERIC MICROPROCESSOR

Many different models of microprocessors are currently available. In order to describe fully the details of the microprocessor to a suitable level, the description below will be modeled on a particular 8-bit microprocessor enjoying widespread current use. The device is the type 8080 microprocessor manufactured by the Intel Corporation of Sunnyvale, California. The selection of this device for detailed description should not be taken as a specific endorsement to the exclusion of competing devices of other manufacturers, such as, the popular type 6800 of Motorola, or the similarly accepted types F8 of Fairchild Microsystems, the SC/MP Series of National Semiconductor, the CDP1802 of RCA Solid State Division, the PPS-8 of Rockwell International, the 2650 of Signetics and others. Space does not permit detailed description of all of the devices now available. However, a basic understanding of one device facilitates later familiarization with others. The descriptive data furnished by the various manufacturers, are generally readable and accurate and are recommended to furnish further information. Specific automation requirements may be more favorably implemented by the features of one or another microprocessor design.

Most microprocessor designs have been modeled after the structure of general-purpose digital computers. From the start, this natural development enhanced their acceptance, since their operation is familiar ground to the cadre of computer technologists whose large store of experience in the design of operating systems using general-purpose digital computers lends confidence in the utility of microprocessors. The following discussion will describe a typical microprocessor and the rather minimum surrounding hardware that must be furnished to form a simple microcomputer.

Figure VI-1 is a block diagram of the Intel type 8080 microprocessor. The reader will detect features of this diagram that resemble the system utilizing an ALU that is shown in Fig. V-3 in Chapter V. As in Fig. V-3, there is a control section, an ALU, and registers are present for temporary retention of data. The component labeled instruction decoder serves a function analogous to the small memory in Fig. V-3. As with the ALU-based system, the function of the microprocessor is to accept information including both source data and instruction codes, to operate on the data in accordance with the instruction, and to distribute data to designated destinations. Considering the much greater capability of the microprocessor, its resemblance to the example of Chapter V is only a starting point. There are several additional features that distinguish the microprocessor.

First, all data transfers within the microprocessor take place via an internal data buss. Selective switching of devices to this buss for transmitting and receiving information is mediated and scheduled by the control logic as directed by the decoded instruction. An operating cycle includes a specific schedule of several transfers of information on this internal data buss.

Second, a 16-bit program counter is included in the microprocessor. This counter is modified by the microprocessor control section during each operating cycle. The usual modification is an increment of the program counter by one count. However, under the direction of certain instructions, the program counter may be directed to assume other specified values. There are several registers for data storage within the microprocessor. Most of these function as 8-bit accessible registers whose content can be altered via appropriate instructions. There is also a 16-bit register called the *stack pointer* whose purpose is to identify special-purpose locations in the address field. One use of these is a location for temporary storage of the program-counter contents. The stack pointer retains the memory address of this store.

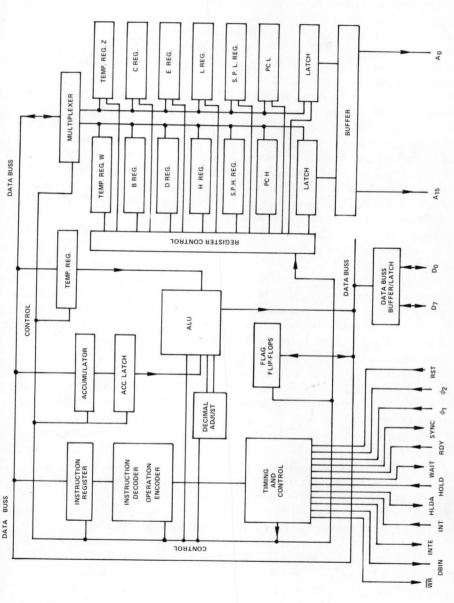

Figure VI-1 Block diagram of the 8080 microprocessor showing overall internal functional structure and external connections.

Third, a set of five flip-flops is provided to store the special conditions resulting from arithmetic and some logical operations, namely, carry, zero result, negative result, parity, and an auxiliary carry for decimal operations. The states of these flip-flops can be tested via certain instructions received by the microprocessor. This useful feature allows testing of input data, of results, and of processing progress against prescribed criteria, allowing the formulation of decisions in the system operation.

Finally, there are several individual special-function control terminals to the microprocessor, including both inputs and outputs relative to the microprocessor boundary. The input control terminals include the *interrupt request*, the *hold request*, the *ready input*, and the *restart*. Output control terminals are the *write strobe*, the *data buss input enable DBIN*, the *interrupt enable status*, the *hold acknowledge*, the *wait*, and the *synchronizing signal* (sync). Utilization of these terminals will be described at appropriate points in the discussion. However, the function of the interrupt and ready inputs deserve special mention.

The interrupt request terminal, when brought true, sets a flip-flop in the microprocessor that, after the current instruction sequence is completed, allows the microprocessor to access an extra instruction which directs the program counter to identify a special memory location for a series of instructions designed to service the needs of the interruption. This feature allows the normal flow of the system operation to be interrupted on demand, to care for an event whose arrival time cannot be precisely anticipated. When the service to this event is completed, the program counter can be returned to the normal sequence to resume system operation.

The *ready* terminal, when held true, permits a continuous flow of microprocessor cycles. If, however, it is brought low, the microprocessor will complete its current cycle and then enter a *wait* state, maintaining the current status of its registers and terminals. The processor signals occupancy of the *wait* state by an output on the *wait* terminal. When the ready line is returned to high, normal operation resumes. This feature allows for a delay of microprocessor operation via external control, to be used, for example, when external data or conditions are not ready for system operation to proceed.

Clearly, the microprocessor, with all its capability, cannot function alone. Although it has features of self-determination and executive function inasfar as it calls for instructions and data and executes prescribed operations, its self-determination, represented in the semiautonomous control section and the internally adjusted program counter,

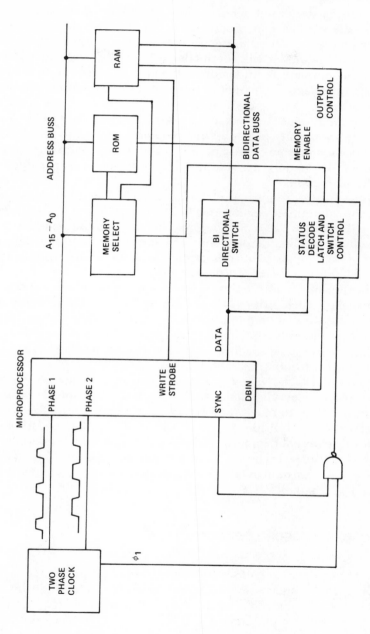

Figure VI-2 Functional diagram indicating the provision of the principal external services required by the 8080 microprocessor.

is incomplete. The microprocessor cannot operate in a purposeful way unless it receives an orderly progression of instructions and data from outside its boundary. When these are present, it can assert its executive role. The nature of this dependence, coupled with assertion, points up the intimate relationship between the hardware and software components and the essential unity of these components in the operating system.

The source of the instructions and some of the data used by the microprocessor are usually provided in a memory external to the microprocessor, although some microprocessors now are even furnished with internal RAM and nonvolatile read-only memory capable of storing short programs. -

In addition to the requirement for an orderly flow of instructions and data, the microprocessor has need of other services. Figure VI-2 is a functional diagram showing some of the devices that can service these needs. (The illustration does not comprise a complete microcomputer. It anticipates the description of a minimum microcomputer, which is the subject of Chapter VII.)

The diagram of Fig. VI-2 shows first a two-phase clock generator which furnishes clock pulses that constitute the heart-beat of the microprocessor system. For technical reasons, the clock pulses must always be present, at least at a minimum rate, to maintain the data in the microprocessor. The spacing and proportionate width of the clock pulses are fairly closely prescribed.

The diagram also shows both read-only and random-access memories. In addition, to service data transfers in both directions at the microprocessor data terminals, there is a bidirectional switch between them and an external bidirectional data buss. The status decode and latch controls external data flow under the direction of the microporcessor. The functions served by these devices must be accommodated in some way in any nontrivial system. Details of this service will be introduced in Chapter VII.

VI-2 MICROPROCESSOR OPERATION

As has been suggested above, the operation of a microprocessor is characterized by a succession of operating cycles, scheduled by the control section and specified by input instructions and data. The repertoire of the 8080 microprocessor includes several types of cycle, designated by the instruction and identified at the microprocessor boundary by timed signals issued at its data terminals.

The most basic cycle obtains an instruction by a reference to memory at the address identified by the program counter; execution of that instruction follows. The microprocessor operations in this execution may be simple and may include no operation at all other than to update the program counter. They may be simple data-transfer operations. They may be operations that perform arithmetic or logical processes on data. Operations may be more complex, for example, the microprocessor may prepare for operations called in succeeding cycles, or may execute events such as conditional modification of the program counter to a nonserial address, depending on the state of condition flip-flops previously set. Every instruction sequence, including linked cycles for more complex executions, begins, at least, with a memory reference cycle to acquire an instruction.

Figure VI-3 shows a timing diagram of a memory reference cycle. The clock pulses delivered to the clock terminals are shown next to the top of the diagram. The next successive line shows the address terminal transitions, collectively indicated. It is followed below by a line

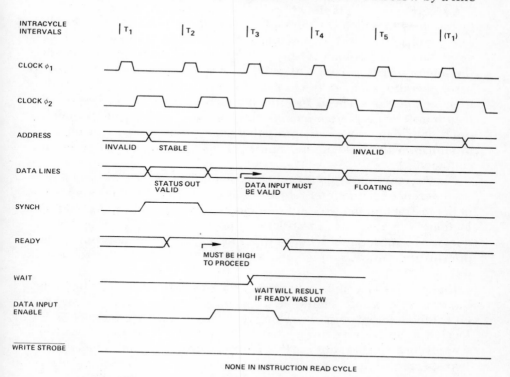

Figure VI-3 Timing diagram of events in a memory reference cycle.

in which the data buss events are shown. The next five lines indicate the states and requirements of the synchronizing pulse; the ready line; a line indicating whether the microprocessor is in a *wait* state; the data input enabling signal, which directs the external data switch to transfer the word present on the external data buss to the microprocessor data terminals; and, finally, when required, an output from the microprocessor write strobe terminal, which can be used to latch valid words in external registers or to write to memory.

As shown in Fig. VI-3, parts of the microprocessor cycle are timed in reference to the clock pulses, being scheduled by the microprocessor control logic. To facilitate the description of the schedule of events occurring in an instruction sequence, it is convenient to mark its timing diagram into sequentially numbered intervals that can be derived from the clock pulses and synchronizing signals. These intracycle intervals are labeled with the capital T and subscripts as shown at the top of the figure. Using these designations, the events in a memory reference cycle can be cast into a cycle-operation table (Table VI-1).

A single cycle is sufficient to complete the execution of many of the instructions to which the microprocessor can respond. These 1-cycle instructions include many of those that involve operation on data words that are temporarily stored in the interal working registers of the microprocessor itself. Other types of instructions and microprocessor operations may require more than one microprocessor cycle for their completion. These include instructions that involve operand data transfer to and from *outside* the microprocessor, such as operations with data stored in external memory, data input and output to and from the system, and nonserial modification of the program counter.

For the multiple-cycle instructions, the first cycle is always a memory reference instruction cycle as described above. The decoded bits of the instruction that are acquired modify the operation of the control logic in such a way as to restructure the microprocessor utilization of one or two subsequent bytes of input data in a manner appropriate to the instruction. Examples of several multiple-cycle instructions follow.

Figure VI-4 is a timing diagram for a 2-cycle instruction directing the transfer of a data word from a specified location in the memory to one of the microprocessor working registers. The 1-byte instruction is located at an address designated by the program counter. The data word is located at an address that has been previously introduced into two specific working registers in the microprocessor. During cycle 1 of the instruction execution, the microprocessor latches the instruc-

Table VI-1 Schedule of Events in a Typical Memory Reference Cycle

Schedule time	Identified	Event	Comment
$T_1\phi_1$	—	—	Address buss may be invalid
$T_1\phi_2$	$\phi_2 \cdot$ Sync	(a) Program counter output to address terminals	Address data certainly valid after ϕ_2 falls
		(b) Identity of cycle type, encoded and output to data terminals	Identity code is certain at $T_2\phi_1$ and is valid until *after* ϕ_1 falls
$T_2\phi_1$	$\phi_1 \cdot$ Sync	Microprocessor samples ready line	If ready line is low at this point, microprocessor will delay entering interval T_3 and enter a *wait* state wherein all conditions except the clocks are static after $T_2\phi_2$.
$T_2\phi_2$	$\phi_2 \cdot$ Data enable	Set up for data transfer on data terminals	This is a signal to prepare data for input to the microprocessor. The data are usually identified by the address lines and the bidirectional switch is directed to transfer data *in*.
$T_3\phi_1$	$\phi_1 \cdot$ Data enable	Microprocessor accepts input data; that may be an instruction.	Input data must be valid at this time. For an instruction cycle, data area latched in the microprocessor instruction register.
$T_3\phi_2$	$\phi_2 \cdot$ Data enable	Instruction execution commences	During this and the next four intervals, the microprocessor executes the necessary internal data transfers and such operations as are required by the instruction under the direction of the control logic and mediated by the output information from the instruction decoded.
$T_4\phi_1$	—	Address terminals may become invalid	
$T_4\phi_2$	—		
$T_5\phi_1$	—	Instruction execution complete	
$T_5\phi_2$	—		
$\rightarrow$			
$(T_1\phi_1)$	—		Of the succeeding cycle

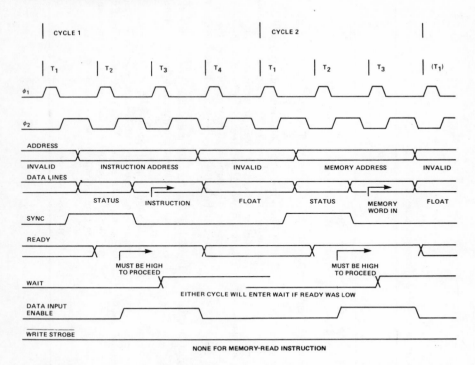

Figure VI-4 Timing diagram of events in an execution involving transfer of data from memory to a designated microprocessor register.

tion in the instruction register at the time $T_3\emptyset_1$. Decoding of this instruction modifies the operation of the control logic to provide for a second cycle.

In the second cycle, the control code directs the microprocessor to disconnect the program counter from the address terminals and to replace it with the 16 bits contained in the two working registers specified to define the high and low bytes of the memory address of the data word to be transferred. This is accomplished at $T_1\emptyset_2$ of the second cycle. At the same time, the data input enable line is again set high, providing for external connection of the external data buss to the data input terminals via the bidirectional switch. Data transfer to the microprocessor takes place at $T_3\emptyset_1$ of the second cycle, with the internal destination determined by destination bits in the original instruction. Execution is complete after this transfer has taken place, and the microprocessor then proceeds to call for the next instruction designated by the incremented program counter.

Data transfer *to* memory is accomplished with a similar 1-byte 2-cycle instruction. Figure VI-5 represents the timing diagram for this transfer instruction. As in the case of transfer from memory, the first cycle of the instruction consists of the acquisition by the microprocessor of the instruction from the address contained in the program counter. As before, the instruction is latched on the instruction register, and decoding of this instruction directs the microprocessor to place the designated memory address on the address terminals during the second cycle, identifying the eventual destination of the data word to be transferred from the microprocessor.

Further decoding of the memory write instruction, acquired during the first cycle provides that the status code appearing on the data terminals from $T_1\emptyset_2$ to $T_2\emptyset_2$ of the second cycle identify this cycle as one in which a data word is to be transferred out of the microprocessor. The source of this data word in the microprocessor is identified in the source code of the instruction. The status bits are decoded externally

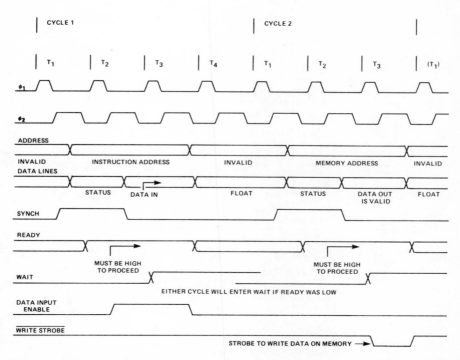

Figure VI-5 Timing diagram for transfer of data from a microprocessor register to memory.

to actuate the external bidirectional switch so as to transfer data *out* of the microprocessor. The source code is used internally to direct the data word from the identified source within the microprocessor to its data terminals at the end of $T_2\emptyset_2$ of the second cycle.

In the transfer of data to memory execution, the microprocessor control section does not actuate the data input enable line during the second cycle. Instead, at $T_3\emptyset_1$, the write line is depressed and held low to the end of the cycle. This signal is impressed on the external memory write enable terminal to write the data word at the memory address designated, completing the execution of the instruction. The microprocessor then proceeds to call for another instruction.

In Fig. VI-6, the timing diagram for a 2-byte, 3-cycle instruction is shown. This instruction is provided to permit data transfer to the microprocessor from a source other than memory and is called an input instruction. In many respects the operation engendered by this instruction resembles that of the data transfer from memory to the microprocessor. However, the address identifying the location of the data to

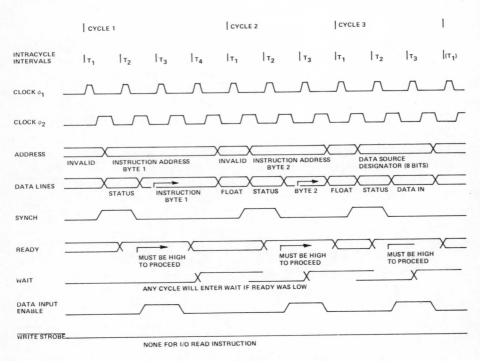

Figure VI-6 Timing diagram for execution of an input instruction.

be transferred is specified in the second byte of the input instruction by a single 8-bit address word that is accepted by the microprocessor during the second cycle and is transferred to the address terminals during the third cycle. This address lies outside the field of memory addresses and must be accessed by switching under control of the status word in the third cycle of instruction execution. The same switching must disable the memory and connect the external data buss to the designated input port. Data present at the input port of the system are accepted by the microprocessor at $T_3\emptyset_1$ of the third cycle, and at the end to T_3, the input instruction execution is complete.

An analogous 2-byte, 3-cycle output instruction, resembling the data transfer from the microprocessor to the memory, is provided. It is also structured for addressing an output port outside the field of memory addresses. Both the input and output addressing schemes represent an artifice—using the status word—to expand the address field. [Special treatment of the regular memory address field, reserving specified blocks to be empty of memory, allows an alternative means of input/output (I/O) access to the microprocessor, using ordinary memory-transfer instructions.]

Figure VI-7 represents the timing diagram of a different type of instruction. This instruction, consisting of 3 bytes and 5 cycles, is designed to facilitate a nonserial change of the program counter, allowing temporary access to a program routine that may be frequently used. The originating program counter address is stored in order to allow unambiguous return to the main program sequence. The temporarily accessed routine is called a subroutine, and the instruction is named a *call* instruction.

In the call instruction the first of the 3 bytes contains the instruction itself. The second and third bytes comprise the low and high 8 bits, respectively, making up the 16-bit address of the subroutine entry point. In the first cycle of execution, the instruction byte is accepted in the microprocessor instruction register. During the second and third cycles, the address bits making up the subroutine address are accepted into temporary storage, to be transferred to the program counter after completion of the fifth cycle of the call instruction.

In the fourth cycle, at $T_1\emptyset_2$, the microprocessor disconnects the program counter (whose content has been incremented in the normal way), from the address terminals and connects to them the content of the stack pointer register, which has been decremented by one. At the same time, the data lines are engaged with a status code indicating that a microprocessor output to memory is impending, in manner identical to the second cycle of the data transfer to memory instruc-

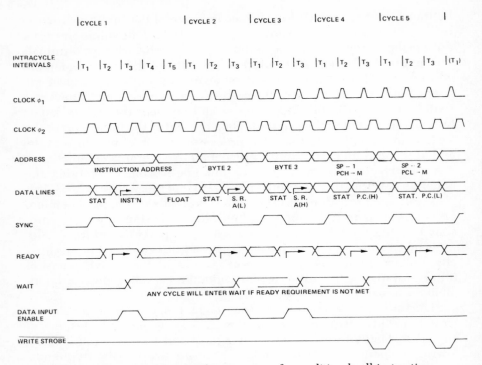

Figure VI-7 Timing diagram for execution of a conditional call instruction.

tion. This status indication must be used externally to actuate the bi-directional data switch to transfer data from the microprocessor to memory. At $T_2\emptyset_2$ of the fourth cycle, the high 8 bits of the program counter are impressed on the data terminals, and at $T_3\emptyset_1$, the $\overline{\text{write}}$ line is depressed. This signal is used, as it was in the memory write instruction, to write the high 8 bits of the program counter at the memory location identified by the content of the stack pointer. After this output is signaled, the stack pointer register is *decremented* again, and the microprocessor enters the fifth cycle.

The fifth cycle resembles the fourth. The decremented stack pointer content is impressed on the address terminals at $T_1\emptyset_2$. At the same time, the status signals on the data lines condition the external bi-directional data switch to transfer data from the microprocessor to the memory. At $T_2\emptyset_2$, the low 8 bits of the program counter are impressed on the data terminals, and the $\overline{\text{write}}$ line is depressed at $T_3\emptyset_1$, resulting in the writing of the low 8 bits of the program counter to the designated memory address. At the completion of the fifth cycle, the program counter is set to the subroutine address, completing the call instruction.

Call instructions can be conditional as well as unconditional, with reference to an operational consequence stored in the condition flip-flops. If the condition designated by the call instruction is not met, the instruction execution described above is broken off after the third cycle, and the microprocessor proceeds to the next serial instruction as though nothing had happened. The microprocessor repertoire includes conditional and unconditional return instructions of 1 byte and 3 cycles, which use the stack pointer to locate the originating program address in memory. The low and high bytes of address are recalled sequentially from memory to reconstruct the former content of the program counter, thereby terminating the subroutine called and returning the program operation to its main sequence.

Conditional and unconditional jump instructions are also provided to modify the content of the program counter. These 3-byte 3-cycle instructions resemble the call instructions but do not save the originating address designated by the program counter and do not alter the content of the stack pointer register.

The interrupt instruction is unique in that it does not reference the memory for its initiation. A single input terminal to the microprocessor, when actuated from the outside, sets a flip-flop in the microprocessor, which interrupts the normal program flow upon completion of all of the cycles in the current instruction sequence. At that point, the interrupt sequence is begun. The 3-cycle sequence whose timing diagram appears in Fig. VI-8 begins at $T_1\theta_2$ with a status word on the data terminals identifying the interrupt status. This identification must be used externally to disconnect the memory from the external data buss, leaving the buss free for the mandatory impression of a special 1-byte interrupt instruction or a 3-byte *unconditional* call instruction. The 1-byte interrupt instruction is equivalent to an unconditional call instruction to a specified address reserved for interrupt servicing. The last two cycles of the interrupt sequence are identical to the fourth and fifth cycles of the call-instruction execution, providing for the saving of the prior content of the program counter in order to allow a return to the interrupted program sequence after the requirements of the interrupt have been met.

Upon completion of the interrupt instruction, the program counter, whose former content is saved in the stack, is set to the interrupt service address specified by the interrupt instruction introduced into the microprocessor, and this address is used by the microprocessor to locate the first instruction in the interrupt service (sub)-routine. Execu-

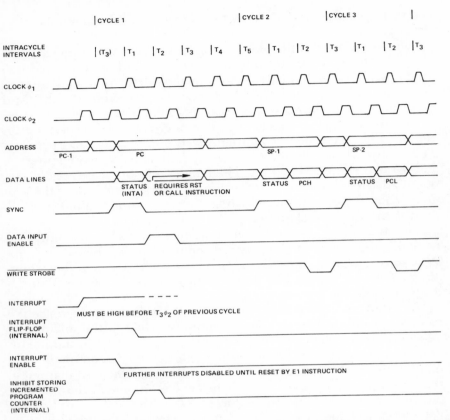

Figure VI-8 Timing of events in an 8080 interrupt sequence leading to the unconditional call to the interrupt servicing address. The prior content of the program counter is saved in a specially identified memory location, (stack), pending a return to the main program.

tion of the interrupt service routine proceeds in a normal manner until it is completed, the termination *usually* being designated with a *return* instruction that restores the program counter to the location in the main sequence at the point where the interrupt occurred.

This chapter describes the operation of the microprocessor in a representative way. Some mention was made regarding external requirements whose representative accommodation was shown in Fig. VI-2. Chapter VII continues the discussion by describing microcomputer systems that take account of the microprocessor architecture and its external requirements.

VII

From Microprocessors to Microcomputers

In this chapter two microprocessor operating systems will be described. The first will be a limited-performance system that uses a small number of gates and latches to provide for minimum external service requirements. The second will be a higher performance system using several special purpose MSI devices to accomodate most of the performance features designed into the microprocessor. The second system is capable of substantial expansion to accomodate additional memory and input/output (I/O) facility. A brief introduction to simple software also will be included.

For the sake of continuity and with no bias against other devices such as those mentioned in Chapter VI, the microprocessor featured in the systems described in this chapter also will be the Intel Type 8080.

VII-1 A SIMPLE LIMITED-PERFORMANCE SYSTEM

The system described in this section is purposely designed in an unsophisticated way to illustrate the most basic requirements for operation. It is furnished with 256 8-bit words each of ROM and RAM, with the facility to add an additional 512 words, in blocks of 256, of RAM or ROM as might be required. (Alternative means for management of the address lines would allow further expansion of the memory field.) In addition to memory, the system is provided with one port each of input and output that, for simplicity, are addressed as memory locations. Expansion of the I/O field can be provided by external decoding of the low address bits if desired.

Control of *interrupt* and *hold* is omitted. However, circuits are included to actuate the *ready* and *reset* terminals to permit single-step operation and restart at address zero.

The manner in which circuits external to the microprocessor are arranged does place constraints on the utilization of the system; in particular, there is no facility for interrupt, and the normal 2-byte I/O instructions will ordinarily be misinterpreted. In addition, the memory field is limited, and this limitation must be observed in programming the system. Figure VII-1 is a schematic diagram of the limited-performance system. The 8080 microprocessor is central to the diagram.

The requirement of clock pulses to the microprocessor is met by the block in the center left area of the figure. The specially marked gate (74132) at the left of this block is a TTL inverting **and** gate, whose input operates as a Schmitt trigger. The Schmitt trigger input circuit features considerable hysteresis, which allows a stable response to a slowly varying input signal at levels that are quite precise. The output transitions are characteristically rapid. The gate is connected at its input with a delay circuit, consisting of a resistor and a capacitor, that operates as a reliable oscillator having adequate stability to clock the microprocessor. (The Schmitt trigger gate can also be used as an ordinary TTL gate when its inputs are normally connected.) The falling edge of the oscillator output clocks the first of three cascaded monostable flip-flops. Two of these generate the two-phase clock pulses required by the microprocessor, and their outputs are connected through level shifting buffers to provide the 11-V clock-pulse levels needed at its clock terminals. Figure VII-2 shows a timing diagram for the clock-pulse generator, indicating the function of the monostable flip-flops in forming the repeating clock-pulse train.

The reset circuit, at the top left in Fig. VII-1, is provided with a simple bistable flip-flop to buffer the action of the manual reset switch shown. This flip-flop guarantees stable transitions on the microprocessor reset line, obviating the possible confusion that would result from the inevitable switch-contact bounces. The reset flip-flop is followed by a type D latch, which is clocked by the leading edge of

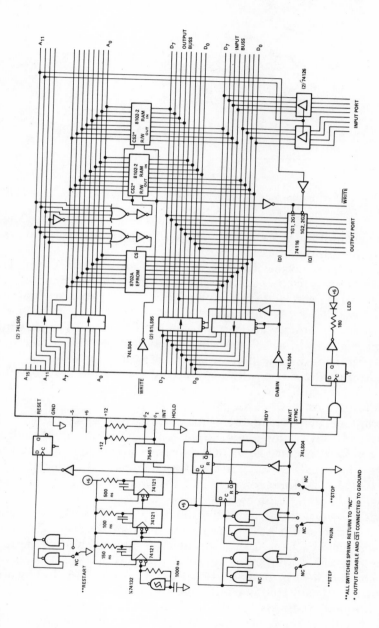

Figure VII-1   Schematic diagram for a limited performance microprocessor system.

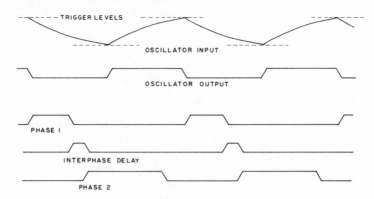

Figure VII-2 Timing diagram of the relaxation oscillator driven clock generator.

phase two ($\emptyset_2$) of the system clock so that the reset signal occurs at a specified time in the clock cycle.

At the lower left in the figure, circuits are provided to accomodate either single-step cycling of the microprocessor or continuous running. Control is exercised via the microprocessor ready line. Momentary contact switches are provided to select a "step" or a "run" operation. These switches are also isolated by flip-flop circuits to preclude problems that would arise from contact bounce. A third momentary contact, requiring no flip-flop isolation, provides for reversion to a *wait* state from the run condition, allowing the subsequent selection of either step or run.

The address terminals of the 8080 are able to sink only 0.75 mA. To avoid problems of overload, these terminals are buffered. The 74LS04 is a 6-bit buffer with low-power inputs and sufficient output to drive the address buss requirements of the low-performance system. Of the 16 address terminals only 12 are used to accomodate the address fields required (A_0–A_{11}). Moreover, of the 12, the high 4 bits A_8–A_{11} are used inefficiently to simplify decoding.

Individual word addresses in the ROM and RAM blocks are identified by the address bits A_0–A_7, giving a field of 256 for each. The ROM block is selected when A_8–A_{11} are all low; thus, its address field is numbered 0–255. The RAM is selected with A_8 high and A_9–A_{11} low, and its memory field is numbered 256–511. (Address 512–1023 would be accessible by suitable decoding with A_9 high.)

For simplicity, address bits A_{10} and A_{11} are not decoded and thus must be used separately. To give intelligible results only one can be set high at a time. They are used for selection of input and output, respectively. Treatment of the input and output ports as memory fields, of course, restricts the field available for actual memory. However, this arrangement avoids the more elaborate status decoding that would otherwise be required for the specialized input and output instructions in the 8080 instruction set.

Address bit A_{10}, when high, activates the (eight) tristate gates connecting the input port to the input buss. It is also conveyed to the system boundary to provide an input control line, signaling to the outside that an input transaction is taking place. Similarly, address bit A_{11} serves to select and enable a strobe to an 8-bit latch that serves as an output port. The input of the latch is connected to the system output buss. Activation of A_{11} serves also to signal to the outside world that an *output* transaction is taking place. The buffered *write* line effects the *actual* transfer of data to the latch. Both A_{11} and write are carried to the system boundary. (The write line is also actuated, of course, for normal memory write instructions.)

As mentioned above, the simplified use of the address structure, including the treatment for I/O function does place constraints on the software. These constraints are not difficult to manage. They involve, simply, the proscription of certain instructions and proper use of the address field. Figure VII-3 shows the system address field, identifying the utilization of addresses 0-4095.

Two external data busses are provided for the low-performance system: one, named the input buss, conveys information *to* the data terminals of the microprocessor; the other, called the output buss, accepts data *from* the data terminals. A bidirectional buffer and switch is furnished, using two DM81LS95's.* The operation of this switch is

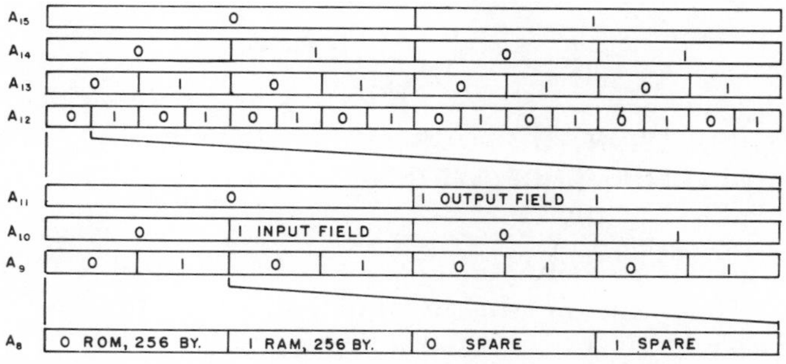

Figure VII-3 Address field utilization in the limited performance system.

* Manufactured by the National Semiconductor Corporation.

normally to connect the data terminals of the microprocessor to the output buss, allowing access to the memory input (RAM) and the output port latches. (It should be noted that the data on this buss are relevant only at *write* time. Unused or invalid data may be present at other times.)

At the time when the microprocessor issues the DBIN signal,* the bidirectional switch is actuated to disconnect the output buss from the microprocessor data terminals and to connect the input buss to them. The input buss receives data from the memory or from the input buffer depending on the address generated by the microprocessor. These data are valid at DBIN time and are accepted by the microprocessor via the bidirectional switch.

One additional peripheral function is incorporated in the service arrangements. At $T_2\emptyset_1$, the data terminals of the microprocessors are engaged with valid status information. In particular, bit D_3, if high, indicates that the microprocessor is in a *halt* state. Since valid status time is uniquely identified by the coincidence of SYNC and $\emptyset_1$, the *halt* status can be captured by latching D_3 on a type D flip-flop with SYNC $\cdot \emptyset_1$ as a strobe. The output of the type D flip-flop is used (with a buffer) to actuate a light emitting diode (LED) signaling the *halt* state. Its indication is a useful clue as to when the system exhibits unexpected and otherwise puzzling behavior.

Although the limited-performance system is implemented with very simple service circuits, it is a fully independent system and, within the limitations of its memory, can demonstrate a considerable range of performance in control and data processing with only modest proscriptions on the use of microprocessor instructions. It is, of course, unable to operate without a program entered in the memory. Section VII-2 provides an introduction to hand programming by using a simple example.

VII-2 INTRODUCTION TO PROGRAMMING, USING THE LOW-PERFORMANCE SYSTEM

The subject of programming and software is extensive and complex, not to say monolithic. Bearing in mind that, for complex problems, formalized treatments are a virtual necessity to the generation of effective software in a reasonable time, it is appropriate for the nonprofessional programmer to make a back-door entry into the subject. For

---

* See Section VI-1, timing diagrams.

simple problems, "machine language" programming with a minimum use of formalized programming aids is possible and sometimes expedient. Thus, the programmer can proceed without the panoply of formal languages and computerized formulation of object code. Indeed, from the standpoint of understanding the conjunctive operation of hardware and software, there is a palpable advantage to undertake programming of simple problems in machine language.

The low-performance system described in Section VII-1 operates under a program of instructions stored in the ROM or introduced into the RAM. The programmer "writes" a program from a lexicon of instructions to which the microprocessor will respond. The monologue (and sometimes dialogue) that is generated by the program words is conceived and encoded by the programmer to accomplish his desired result. Only the simplest of sequences are easily written directly in instruction codes. For even slightly elaborate routines, some forms of programming aids simplify the process of writing a program.

One of the more useful aids to programming is the flow chart. This chart is, in effect, an outline of the program to be constructed. Figure VII-4 is an example of a very simple flow chart for a program. In this

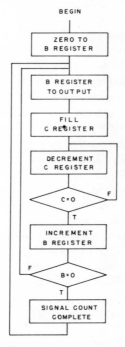

Figure VII-4 Flow chart for a program to generate an incremental binary number.

figure, the rectangular boxes represent forward events, and the diamond-shaped boxes indicate condition tests leading to program branching. The flow of events is indicated by lines joining the labeled boxes. The starting and terminating points are of particular importance in the organization of the flow chart. These boxes must always be present to indicate the boundaries placed on the operation of the program. The termination point of a program or a program fragment should be accompanied by a statement of what is to come next, for example, a termination could be made with a halt, a return to the starting point, or another linking statement.

The program, whose outline is presented in the flow chart of Fig. VII-4, has the purpose of generating an incremented binary number and delivering this number to the output port. In order to slow the rate at which numbers are delivered to the output, the program includes a software-generated delay or timing loop. The termination block of the program is reached after the count of numbers reaches 255 (decimal), which is the largest number that can be represented by 8 bits. The termination statement directs a return to a point that recycles the routine, creating, in this case, an endless loop.

The instructions for this routine are to be stored in a ROM at a sequence of address beginning with a start address. Part of the programmers task is to organize the address field to accommodate conveniently the programs needed. In this example, the program can be assigned to start from address zero. With this address, in the low-performance system, the assignment provides that the program can be accessed by means of a restart sequence. Programmable ROMs (PROMs) and erasable programmable ROMs (EPROMs) are offered by a number of vendors. Introduction of program into these devices involves the use of special equipment. Sellers will usually furnish a programming service of PROMs and EPROMs gratis or at a nominal charge, to the buyers listing.

Having located the program's starting point, the programmer's next task is to generate the coded instructions to be installed serially into memory by following the sequence of events shown in the flow chart. If he is very familiar with the instruction codes, the programmer can produce the sequence of instructions in microprocessor code directly from the flow chart. However, it is generally helpful to generate a list of the instruction sequence that includes additional information to aid the process. The list shown in Fig. VII-5, which presents the program outlined by the flow chart, includes columns for address and instruction codes. In addition, it has a column for the mnemonic name of each instruction and a column for clarifying remarks. The intellectual

REF	ADDRESS			INSTRUCTION				CALL	COMMENT
	BINARY	OCTAL	HEX	BINARY	OCTAL	HEX	MNEMONIC		
NUMB	00000000 00000000	000 000	00 00	00000110	006	06	MVI B		ZERO TO B REGISTER
NMB2	00000000 00000001	000 001	00 01	00000000	000	00			
	00000000 00000010	000 002	00 02	01111000	170	78	MOV A,B		B REGISTER TO A REGISTER
	00000000 00000011	000 003	00 03	11010011	323	D3	OUT		A REGISTER OUT
	00000000 00000100	000 004	00 04	00000001	001	01			TO PORT 1
	00000000 00000101	000 005	00 05	00001110	016	0E	MVI C		FILL THE C REGISTER
	00000000 00000110	000 006	00 06	11111111	377	FF			FOR TIMING COUNT
NMB1	00000000 00000111	000 007	00 07	00001101	015	0D	DCR C		DECREMEMT COUNTER
	00000000 00001000	000 010	00 08	11000010	302	C2	JNZ		IF COUNT DOWN IS NOT
	00000000 00001001	000 011	00 09	00000111	007	07		NMB1	COMPLETE, GO BACK
	00000000 00001010	000 012	00 0A	00000000	000	00			TO DECREMENT AGAIN
	00000000 00001011	000 013	00 0B	00000100	004	04	INR B		INCREMENT B REGISTER
	00000000 00001100	000 014	00 0C	11000010	302	C2	JNZ		TEST OVERFLOW CONDITION;
	00000000 00001101	000 015	00 0D	00000010	002	02		NMB2	IF NOT COMPLETE,
	00000000 00001110	000 016	00 0E	00000000	000	00			CYCLE PROGRAM AGAIN
	00000000 00001111	000 017	00 0F	11010011	323	D3	OUT		ELSE OUTPUT A SIGNAL
	00000000 00010000	000 020	00 10	00000010	002	02			TO PORT 2
	00000000 00010001	000 021	00 11	11000011	303	C3	JMP		AND DO THE LOOP OVER
	00000000 00010010	000 022	00 12	00000000	000	00		NUMB	
	00000000 00010011	000 023	00 13	00000000	000	00			

Figure VII-5 Coded program for incrementing a binary number.

process of generating the program is actually contained in these two columns, and they are often written first. The translation of the named instructions into machine code is, then, simply a process of looking them up.

The microprocessor responds, of course, to instructions encoded in binary bits, and, in the listing shown, both the addresses and the instructions are written in binary form. This writing is tedious, so shorthand representations are also shown in the listing to be used as alternatives. The most commonly used shorthand notations are the *octal* and *hexidecimal,* both directly derivable from binary notation. Both notations are shown in Fig. VII-5.

The octal number scheme admits the decimal digits 0–7 followed by 10 . . . 17, 20 . . . 27, 30 . . . , etc., where 10 (octal) is equivalent to 8 (decimal). The hexidecimal scheme requires 16 digits, 0–9 followed by the upper case letters A, B, C, D, E, F. Table VII-1 shows

Table VII-1 Correspondence of Decimal, Octal, and Hexidecimal Number Schemes

Decimal	Octal	Hexidecimal	Decimal	Octal	Hexidecimal
0	0	0	15	17	F
1	1	1	16	20	10
7	7	7	24	30	18
8	10	8	25	31	19
9	11	9	26	32	1A
10	12	A	27	33	1B
11	13	B	31	37	1F
12	14	C	32	40	20
13	15	D	:	:	:
14	16	E	255	377	FF

how numbers may be represented, by relating the octal and hexidecimal schemes to the decimal sequence.

By using the listing of Fig. VII-5, or by using only the more condensed octal or hexidecimal notation, a reader has sufficient information to follow the process defined by the instruction sequence listed with mnemonic designations and code. Other programs may require additional information to be understandable, particularly when the program is broken into parts distributed nonserially in the memory field, and when subroutines are used.

(A notation has been devised for program listing, called assembly language. It adheres to a rather strict formalism, defined for each microprocessor type, that permits computer generation of its address and object codes. This notation is reminiscent of the simpler listings illustrated in this chapter. The programmer, if he has access to a computer system provided with a program assembler appropriate to the microprocessor in his system, needs only to use instruction mnemonics, embedded in the strict assembly-language formalism, to generate programs. For a more detailed description of assembly language and its procedures, the reader is referred to other publications.* The scope of software methods covered in this book will be limited to machine-language programming with simple informal listings.)

The codes used in the listing of Fig. VII-5 are drawn from the lexicon of instructions for the 8080 microprocessor (see Table starting on p. 183). As the listing indicates, the short program uses a few of these instructions to transfer data from point-to-point to increment registers, and to perform conditional and unconditional program-directed changes of the program counter (JUMPS).

The systematic structure of the codes representing instructions can be, for the most part, deduced from the instruction list. Although it is not necessary to penetrate this structure in order to write programs, recognition of the general form of its systematics is helpful in programming and program checking in machine language. An example of the code structure in the 8080 microprocessor is to be seen in the set of simple register-to-register data-transfer instructions. The bits of these 1-byte instructions are arranged in three fields. The first field, which consists of the first two binary bits, contains the code 01 that, for this set, is the operation code for data transfer. The next three bits designate the destination for the data, and the final three bits, the source.

---

* See, for example, Intel 8080 Assembly Language Programming Manual, INTEL Corporation, 1975.

The 8080 microprocessor has seven accessible working registers, including the accumulator. For the simple data-transfer instructions (and a number of others), these registers are designated by 3-bit codes as shown in Table VII-2.

The remaining 3-bit code, 110, is reserved to identify the "memory," which is treated as a register whose address is identified by the current content of registers H and L.

Table VII-2 8080 Accessible Register Codes

Register name	Locating code
Accumulator	111
B	000
C	001
D	010
E	011
H	100
L	101

With this scheme, for example, the instruction, 01 111 010, calls for the transfer of data from register D to the accumulator, and 01 011 110 calls for transfer from a memory location (identified by the 16-bit address stored in H and L) to register E. (Registers H and L define the address indicating destination or source for data transfers to or from memory. Apart from this function they may be used in the same way as the other working registers.)

In the 8080 microprocessor, all logical operations and all 8-bit arithmetic operations are formulated with one of the operands introduced by the accumulator and with the result of the operation returned to the accumulator. The source of the second operand is identified by register codes as described above.

The instruction set of the microprocessor defines all of the transactions that it can conduct. The program designer must be familiar with the instruction set and the facilities available in the microprocessor system. Operations called out in the program that involve interaction with external hardware devices must, of course, be undertaken in a manner that is compatible with the devices and their connections to the microprocessor system. The flow chart mentioned above is an aid not only for the rephrasing of the problem into series of simple statements that can be placed in one-to-one correspondence with a sequence of instructions, but also to keep track of the external hardware relationship.

VII-3 A HIGHER PERFORMANCE SYSTEM

Manufacturers of microprocessors have been quick to follow their offering of microprocessors with a selection of devices that make their use more convenient. Most have recently introduced MSI devices that perform many of the external control and service tasks required for a microprocessor system, thereby reducing the labor in its implementation and freeing the system designer to concentrate on the ultimate utilization of the system. Again, for the sake of continuity, this chapter will continue with description of a system based on the Intel 8080 microprocessor and some of the specialized devices offered by Intel to interconnect with it. In addition, proprietary devices of other manufacturers will be included when their functions are particularly applicable. This book is not intended to describe all of the devices currently offered or even to indicate the range of engineering choices that can be made to optimize any special system property. In most of the simple systems likely to be developed by nonprofessionals, the microprocessors and auxiliary devices offered by many maufacturers will serve with equal facility.

The higher performance of the system to be described in this section does not specifically depend on the specialized devices that are connected around the microprocessor. The same results could be achieved with nonproprietary high-speed TTL components. However, the specialized devices allow an elegant economy of parts and are sufficiently diverse to satisfy most of the design requirements of the system, including those which extract a maximum performance from the microprocessor. The parts of the higher performance system will be introduced one at a time, beginning with the clock.

Figure VII-6 shows the connection of the microprocessor to the Intel type 8224 clock generator. In addition to providing clock pulses, this device satisfies other timing needs of the system. Its functional diagram is also shown in the figure. It is provided internally with an oscillator section that is capable of being frequency controlled either by a quartz crystal operating in its fundamental mode or by an overtone mode crystal, via the "tank" terminals. (Most systems rely on quartz-crystal resonators for frequency determination.) The high-frequency oscillator signal is connected to a modulo 9 counter whose output is decoded to deliver the two clock phases. With a minimum clock period specified at 480 nsec, oscillator frequency can be as high as 18.7 MHz. The 8224 is furnished internally with high-level clock buffers to deliver the required 11-V clock pulses to the 8080. (To pro-

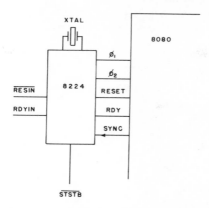

Figure VII-6   Illustrating the use of the Intel-type 8224 clock generator.

vide these pulses it requires a power source of $+12$ V, as well as $+5$ V.)

In addition to the clock pulses, the 8224 will also deliver properly timed signals to the ready and reset terminals when requested at its appropriate inputs. It will be recalled that these signals must be presented to the microprocessor at precisely determined points in the clock cycle. Furthermore, the 8224, by using the SYNC line and internal timing generates a strobe pulse to capture status data when they are stable at the microprocessor data terminals. Finally, a TTL level output of the clock phase two is provided for possible external timing needs. A timing diagram for the 8224 operation is shown in Fig. VII-7.

Since some of the required timing is critical, particularly in a system operating near its maximum speed, it is a considerable help to use the 8224 that, by design, is well matched to the 8080 microprocessor.

In the higher performance system, as was the case in the simple system described in Section VII-1, a buffer is connected to the 8080 address terminals and drives the address buss. It is convenient to use two DM81LS95's, each able to accomodate 8 bits. The buffer input demand is appropriately low, and its tristate output can provide for the address requirements of large blocks of MOS memory. The limiting factor in the buffer output drive capability, with MOS memory, is the capacitance of the memory address inputs and the interconnecting lines. Parallel expansion with more DM81LS95s permits additional extension of memory. High-power drivers such as the 75451 could be attached to the busses to satisfy still greater drive requirements, particularly if high capacitance interconnecting cables are to be used.

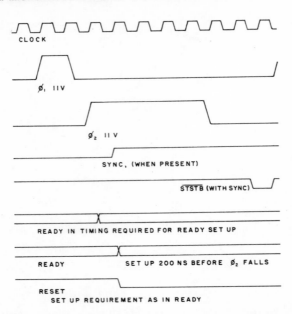

Figure VII-7   Timing diagram for the output of the Intel-type 8224 clock generator.

The tristate output control terminals of the DM81LS95's permit disconnecting the address buss from the microprocessor, which allows the use of this buss for independent access to the memory. Their output control terminals are connected to the hold acknowledge (HLDA) terminal of the 8080 microprocessor for this purpose.

In many systems, the use of multipurpose buss structures has become popular. The 8-bit data terminals of the 8080 are used bidirectionally and for multiple purpose. To carry this feature into the service parts, the higher performance system is provided with an external bidirectional data buss. Management of this external buss is accomplished with the help of another special purpose device—the Intel 8228. This device includes a bidirectional buss driver and switch, a status latch, and the necessary gates and logic to decode the status bits and control five status terminals. The connection of the 8228 to the 8080 is shown in Fig. VII-8, along with a memory select system consisting of three 74LS138's that allow selection of up to 16,384 words. (This system is expandable for memory selection from the entire field of 65,356 words that can be directly addressed using a 16-bit address structure.)

Inputs required by the 8228 include the data terminals of the 8080

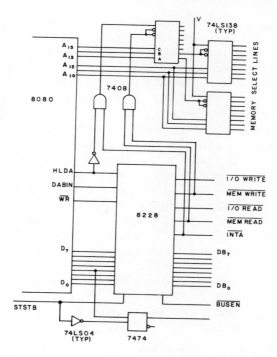

Figure VII-8 Representative utilization of the Intel-type 8228 data buss controller and status latch.

(when they are active), the external data buss, the $\overline{\text{status}}$ strobe from the 8224 mentioned above, and the lines DBIN, $\overline{\text{WRITE}}$, and HLDA from the microprocessor. A separate enable terminal $\overline{\text{BUSEN}}$ is also provided in the 8228 if additional buss control is required. Five outputs of the 8228 declare the status of the microprocessor and are used for control of data flow. The five status conditions operate in the higher performance system as follows:

$\overline{\text{MEMR}}$: This defines a memory read cycle. Memory selection is enabled, and data are transferred to the microprocessor at DBIN time.

$\overline{\text{MEMW}}$: This defines a memory write cycle. Memory selection is enabled, and data are transferred at $T_3\emptyset_2$ (see Chapter VI).

I/O READ: This defines an input cycle from an input address outside the memory address field. The address buss is active and defines the input address from a field counted by 8 bits. Memory selection is disabled, and the input field is enabled. Data transfer occurs at DBIN time.

I/O WRITE: This defines an output cycle to an output address outside the memory address field. The address buss is active and defines the output address from a field counted by 8 bits. Memory selection is disabled, and the output field is enabled. (For most applications, the address buss is set up, in an I/O WRITE cycle, in sufficient time to allow the use of I/O WRITE as a strobe signal to latch the output data into the output device.)

INTA: This signal occurs after the microprocessor accepts and acts on an interrupt request. Although the address terminals still retain their content from the prior instruction sequence, the microprocessor expects a call instruction. If no instruction is placed on the data buss, the 8228 can issue a default 1-byte call instruction to address 56 (decimal) at DBIN time with no additional external hardware. (This call instruction is issued when an appropriate current source is applied to the INTA terminal of the 8228.) Alternatively, a 1- or 3-byte call instruction may be introduced using a gated interrupt instruction port. INTA will be maintained during the call instruction sequence, whether it is called by 1 byte or 3 bytes. Since MEMR and MEMW are inactive (high) during the first cycle of the interrupt sequence, the memory select system is disabled, leaving the data buss free to accept the gated interrupt instruction.

The are two additional status conditions to be accounted for, namely, HLDA and HALT.

HLDA: This status defines the isolation of the microprocessor from the busses in response to a hold request. The disengagement of the external address buss has already been mentioned. The 8228 also responds to HLDA by disconnecting the external data buss from the microprocessor and restoring any of INTA, MEMR, and I/O READ to high. (MEMW and I/O WRITE are high by definition at the time HLDA becomes active.) With these conditions, the memory enable system is disabled and will function only under the external memory enable control line shown in Fig. VII-8. While HLDA is active, the memory is released for direct external access independent of microprocessor operation.

HALT: This status may be entered under program control, for example when the microprocessor is first turned on and may also be entered via an instruction elsewhere in the program. The 8228 has no provision for detecting this status, therefore, a separate type D flip-flop clocked by the status strobe from the 8224 is used to sense the HALT condition. This indication may be useful for external monitoring of microprocessor operation.

The other major components of the higher performance system are the memory and the I/O port systems. The detailed provision of these components is usually based on the detailed requirements placed on the system. The specific structures included in the example of a higher performance system described here are typical. A memory of 4096 words equally divided between ROM and RAM is installed. Three 8-bit ports each of input and output are provided, along with eight 1-bit sense and eight 1-bit control lines. With the use of additional decoding of address bits accompanying the input and output operations, the I/O facility may be expanded to handle additional ports as might be required. (There are many other ways in which the I/O functions can be managed, including the use of very capable specialized MSI devices.*)

The memory elements chosen for the high-performance system are moderately high-speed MOS devices. Competitive sources can be found for both ROM and RAM devices, satisfying the setup timing requirements of the higher performance system. The use of slower devices, which are available at only slightly lower cost, would possibly entail the introduction of a WAIT interval in each instruction cycle, thereby reducing the speed of operation.

Memory speed is specified by manufacturers in various ways. In a high-speed application, the critical timing considerations are best understood by reference to a timing diagram. In Fig. VII-9, the timing diagram of a typical RAM of adequate speed is shown in conjunction with the timing of relevant events in a high-performance 8080 microprocessor system (see also Fig. VI-5).

In the system described in this section, the critical interval in a memory–read event is the delay between the memory select signal (CS), and the time at which data are required. With a clock cycle time of 480 nsec, allowing 140 nsec from the rise of $\emptyset_1$ in T_2 to the actuation of the decoded memory select, this time is 340 nsec. Thus, the memory, when selected, must furnish valid data in less than 340 nsec after memory select.

Similarly in a memory write event, the critical intervals can be identified. All setup times are measured backward from the rising edge of the $\overline{\text{write}}$ signal occurring at the end of T_3. In the system described in this section, in a write cycle, the shortest interval presented to the memory is the time during which data are stable. With a cycle time of 480 nsec, this time is approximately 630 nsec, a figure compatible with the specifications of many MOS RAMs. The address setup time and

* For example, the Intel 8255 programmable peripheral interface.

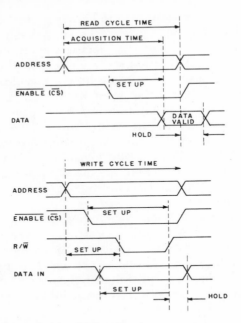

Figure VII-9 Timing diagram for a typical random access memory, (RAM).

the memory select interval are longer than this. No hazard to the memory content is posed by the fact that the interval of valid data is the shortest, provided it is sufficiently long. However, the address to which data are to be written must be set up some time before the write pulse arrives at the memory. In the system under discussion, the address becomes valid approximately 200 nsec before $\overline{\text{WRITE}}$, thereby satisfying this requirement.

All of the critical times discussed in the paragraphs above are consistent with the capability of medium-speed MOS RAMs. A superficial single-number "cycle time" for reading and writing memory is often specified. If this cycle time is less than the microprocessor cycle time, the memory is likely to be satisfactory. However, a more detailed inquiry into the timing of both the system and the memory is necessary in order to be certain of satisfactory performance.

Selection of the type of ROM for a system is generally made on the basis of functional use and economics. For most systems produced in small quantities, electrically programmable ROMs (PROMs) are most suitable. For systems produced in large quantities, mask programmed ROMs are less expensive after amortization of a substantial charge for mask preparation. In systems where changes in stored program are contemplated, erasable electrically programmable ROMs are the best choice, though these are even more expensive than PROMs. These "EPROMs" are furnished with a transparent quartz cover. They can be erased by the application of strong ultraviolet light from a mercury lamp and reprogrammed as often as desired.

The address structure designed into the higher performance system is structured to accomodate blocks of 1024 words (10 address bits). The generic EPROM with 1024 words of 8 bits is the 2708 (now 8708) manufactured by Intel. Similar devices that are pin-compatible are offered by other manufacturers including Signetics (2708). In RAM, the most popular units feature 1024 words by 1 bit, although devices with greater capacity are becoming available. The generic 1024 word by 1-bit static RAM is the 8102-A4 by Intel with a more recent Signetics counterpart (2102). Many other manufacturers offer competitive devices. With the 1024 by 1-bit configuration, a block of 1024 words requires eight devices, addressed and selected in parallel, and the 2048 words of RAM suggested for the system requires 16 packages all together.

Clearly, there is a premium on economy of memory, and, even in high-performance systems, designs of software that reduce the memory requirements are worthwhile.

To implement the I/O functions of the higher performance system, three buffers accomodate three 8-bit input ports and three 8-bit latches comprise three 8-bit output ports. The input buffers have tri-state outputs that can be connected directly to the data buss. The output 8-bit latches are able to retain data impressed during an output sequence. Selection of both input and output buffers is accomplished using a 74138 with enabling logic and selection dependent on address bits and the engagement of either I/O READ or I/O WRITE. Unused select lines are brought to the system boundary for possible I/O expansion.

In addition to the 8-bit input and output ports, the system provides for the reading of eight independent 1-bit sense lines and for writing to eight independent 1-bit control lines. These are selected by address bits and I/O READ or I/O WRITE as appropriate. The former are monitored via DB_1 on the data buss via a 74251 multiplexer with a tri-state output. The latter may be set individually high or low using address bits only.

Figures VII-10a and VII-10b show the complete diagram for the higher performance system including memory and I/O structure. As shown in Fig. VII-10b the memory select terminal for each block of

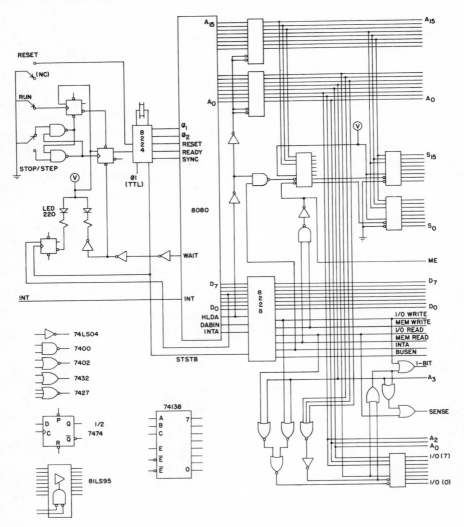

Figure VII-10a High performance microprocessor system, central processor section.

memory is connected to the appropriate output terminal of the memory select system.

ROM is selected by low addresses including address 0–1024, allowing for startup directly in the stored program. ROM outputs are **or** connected to the external data buss, being effectively disconnected when deselected.

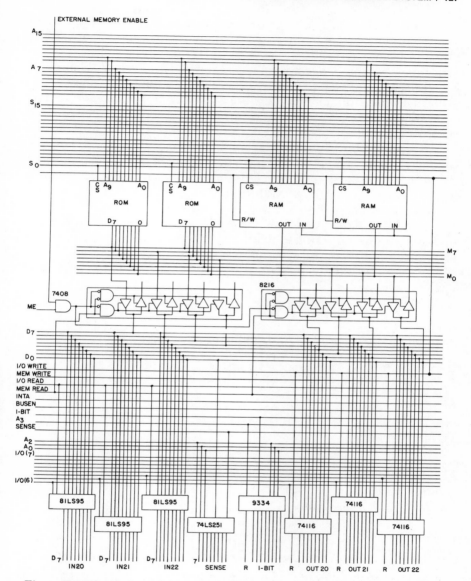

Figure VII-10b High performance microprocessor system, memory and input/output section.

The RAM data lines must be treated differently to allow for devices whose output may not be internally disabled during a write operation. Since a common data buss is being used for read and write, an 8-bit bidirectional switch consisting of two Intel 8216's is used. Control of switching is exercised through a 7408 **and** gate normally allowing internal control with memory enable (ME) from the memory select system. When HLDA is present external control is substituted, the microprocessor being disconnected.

The description of the higher performance system has been presented, in part, as a vehicle to introduce some of the special-purpose devices that make system design simpler and allow systems with fewer components. A basic system, in fact, can be constructed using the 8080, the 8224, and the 8228 plus a small memory and I/O facility. Figure VII-11 shows such a system, which can operate with the full instruction repertoire of the 8080 at maximum speed. At the opposite extreme, more complex systems can be designed using additional MSI devices to add greater capability, particularly with regard to I/O facility.

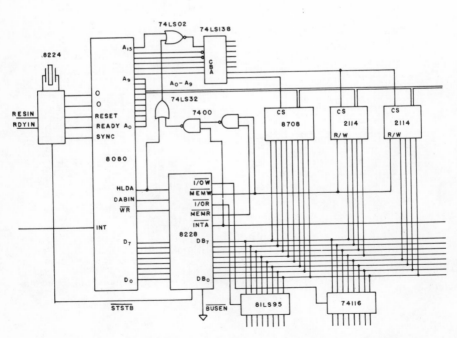

Figure VII-11 A minimum microprocessor system which still gives high performance.

VII-4 ANOTHER PROGRAMMING EXAMPLE INCLUDING I/O AND ARITHMETIC OPERATIONS

The low cost of microprocessors allows microprocessor driven systems to be applied with considerably less than maximum efficiency and full utilization. For example, a programming example is given for an application that requires both arithmetic and I/O facility, as well as management of a flow of events. The program incorporates some grossly inefficient steps, and in this sense it underutilizes the capability of the microprocessor system.

The problem to be solved is for the microprocessor to accept a series of digital data values from a single source at intervals defined by that source, to formulate a digitally filtered value from the input data with a programmed filter time constant, and to deliver the filtered value to one display and the difference between the current datum and the filtered value to a second display.

The statement of the problem defines the minimum requirements the microprocessor system must possess to fulfill the application. The system described in Section VII-3 is more than sufficient to accomodate the problem stated, and the programming can be structured according to its configuration.

With the problem and the microprocessor system defined, one more consideration is necessary prior to the writing of the program, namely, the external hardware, which may be central to the utilization of the system from the user's point of view. It includes devices that actually generate the data to be processed and display the processed results. The microprocessor system simply acts as a processing conduit. The external hardware comprises merely one or a few of many "peripheral" devices that the microprocessor can accomodate when appropriately programmed. For example, the input part of the external hardware is a data source described simply as a black box with a set of digital lines for data transfer. To make the operation more specific, the box could represent a device to measure the temperature of an oven. A system incorporating this function is shown in Fig. VII-12. Eight of ten lines from temperature-measuring equipment deliver a binary number representing the temperature at stated intervals. The ninth is a line that goes true when a new temperature measurement is ready on the eight data lines. It is sensed by a sense line from the microprocessor. The tenth is a line *to* the box by which the microprocessor can reset the "data ready" indication to false after it has acquired the latest temperature data.

The external hardware also includes display devices. In this case,

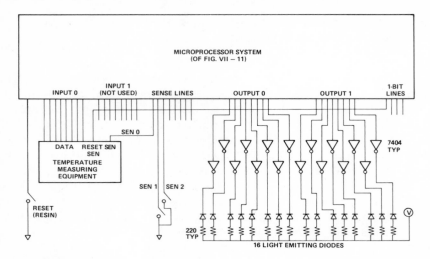

Figure VII-12 Schematic representation of the connection of a microprocessor system to external hardware.

for simplicity, the display devices will be just two sets of eight LEDs, one to record the filtered temperature value and the other to show the difference between the filtered value and the current reading. For the microprocessor, these are simply two data destinations.

The programmer is required to know not only the properties of the microprocessor system and the problem to be solved, but also the nature of the external hardware in order to generate operable software. It is convenient to have a functional diagram of the complete hardware system with the functions defined. For the present problem, such a diagram is shown in Fig. VII-12. Armed with this diagram, the programmer is ready to proceed with a program flow chart.

A workable flow chart for the stated problem is shown, in gross form, in Fig. VII-13. The numbered sections of this flow chart are detailed in Figs. VII-14, VII-15, VII-16, and VII-18.

The first of the six sections is the entry to the program; it also serves as its terminus. This section and an initialization sequence are detailed in the flow chart in Fig. VII-14. The program allows for an operator-selected idle state when the "process" switch is set false. Following the branching point of this state is an important sequence to many programs, namely, the initialization. The program will use the stack pointer, therefore, an area is defined in RAM and reserved as a short memory stack. An address 8 bytes above the top (highest address) of this stack is entered in the stack pointer. The stack pointer

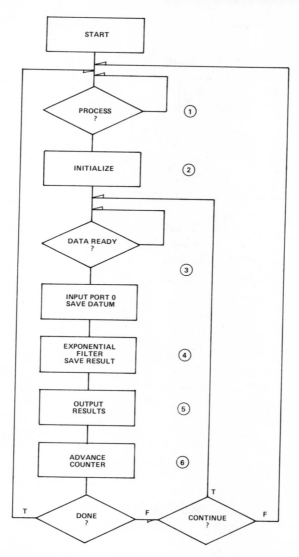

Figure VII-13 Overall flow chart to display current and filtered values of an input.

can then be used, as will be seen later, to clear the stack locations and to place an initial address in registers H and L, which are used as memory pointers.

Section 3 in Fig. VII-13 represents a data-acquisition step. There are many ways to handle data acquisition, depending, among other

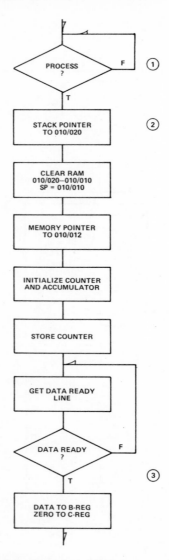

Figure VII-14 Flow chart detail, initialization sequence and data acquisition.

things, on the nature of the data source, the data rates, the validity criteria, and the other requirements placed on the microprocessor. The data-acquisition step in the flow chart shown is very wasteful of microprocessor time, since the microprocessor will sample the "data ready" sense input repeatedly until it is set true by the data source. Data acquired are saved, and a 1-bit output is issued to reset the sense source.

Section 4, the step entitled exponential filter (EXPF), represents the principal data-processing assigned in the problem statement. The requirement is not difficult to implement. It is convenient to enumerate the equal measurement intervals serially and designate the sequence with an index k. A data value D_k can be identified by this index. Further, for each interval, a filtered value F_k will be computed. The algorithm for this computation is

$$\frac{1}{\tau} * [(F_k) \text{ minus } (F_{k-1})] = \frac{1}{T} * [(D_k) - (F_{k-1})]$$

where τ is the interval between measurements, and T is the smoothing time. This algorithm is a digital implementation of the differential equation

$$dF/d\tau = (1/T)(D - F)$$

for an exponential filter with time constant T.

The algorithm above may be rewritten in an equivalent form more convenient to programming

$$[F_k] = [F_{k-1}] \text{ plus } \left[\frac{\tau}{T}\right] * [(D_k) \text{ minus } (F_{k-1})]$$

The arithmetic operations that are required are a subtraction, a multiplication, and an addition, in that order. Addition and subtraction are explicit instructions in the microprocessor instruction set. Multiplication could be set up in the software as an addition of partial products (see Chapter II). However, the microprocessor can perform multiplication by powers of 2 using a data-shift instruction. The system designer has an opportunity to simplify the problem by restricting the values of T such that $T = 2^m\tau$, with m an integer >0. (This condition is not as restrictive as it might seem, since the system designer can vary both m and τ in order to achieve the desired values for the smoothing time T. In this instance, the hardware is modified to simplify the software by modifying the measurement time τ; in other examples it may be more appropriate to adapt the software to accomodate strict hardware requirements. With $T = 2^m\tau$, the algorithm for exponential filtering becomes

$$[F_k] = [F_{k-1}] \text{ plus } 2^{-m} * [(D_k) - (F_{k-1})]$$

Figure VII-15 shows a more detailed flow chart to implement computation of the filtered value of the data according to this algorithm. In order to preserve precision of results, arithmetic operands are extended to 2 bytes. A convention for signed arithmetic performed on extended operands uses the highest bit of the high-order byte for sign.

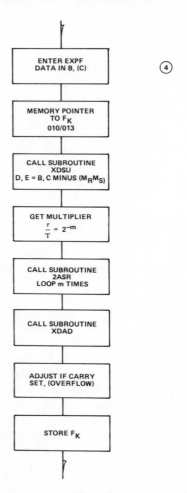

Figure VII-15 Flow chart detail, data processing to render exponentially filtered data.

The lower byte occupies all 8 bits giving a complete operand with 15 bits plus sign. Arithmetic operations carried out with extended operand word lengths are aptly described with the adjective *double precision.**

Since the double-precision arithmetic operations may be carried out

---

* Some conventions omit the high bit of the low-order byte for expressing signed double-precision numbers.

more than once in a program, they are frequently entered into programming as subroutines. This saves the labor of writing the routine for each use and also conserves memory space.

There are three subroutines in section 4 of the program. The use of a subroutine requires the programmer to make the operands conform to a consistent format, since the subroutine, necessarily, always operates in a standardized way. The specific format used is, of course, the choice of the programmer.

The subroutines for double-precision addition and subtraction, XDAD and XDSU, are shown diagramatically in Figs. VII-16 and VII-17. In the format choice, the first operand is located in the B and C registers with the low-order byte in C. The second operand is at two memory locations, M_R and M_S with the low-order byte in M_R. Registers H and L are loaded to point to M_R. Addition is carried out one byte at a time, beginning with the low byte and observing the carry for the second byte addition. In signed addition, the association of carry with overflow and the sign bit may be ambiguous. To resolve the ambiguity, a short routine must be undertaken that sets the carry flip-flop unambiguously for overflow. This routine begins with a test for mixed algebraic signs $(+ -)$ of the operands (no overflow possible). If the signs are unmixed $(+ +$ or $- -)$ the overflow condition is determined by testing the carry and high byte sign bits in accordance with Table VII-3. The two bytes of the results are placed in registers D and E. If overflow is indicated, still further interpretation of the sum may be required.

Double-precision subtraction is accomplished by addition of the 2's complement of the subtrahend to the minuend, using the subroutine XDAD. The overflow test, which is part of XDAD, is valid in forming the result of XDSU. Carry is set by the program for overflow, and further interpretation of the result may be necessary again.

Table VII-3 Resolution of Ambiguities
When Overflow Occurs

Condition flip-flop states		True conditions	
Carry	Sign	Overflow	Sign
0	0	No	Positive
0	1	Yes	Positive
1	0	Yes	Negative
1	1	No	Negative

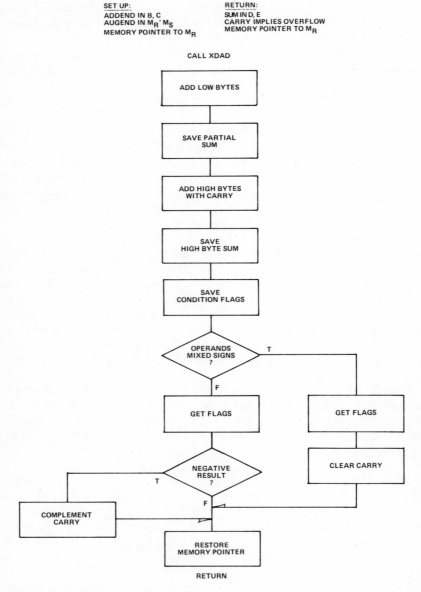

Figure VII-16   Flow chart for XDAD, a subroutine for double precision addition.

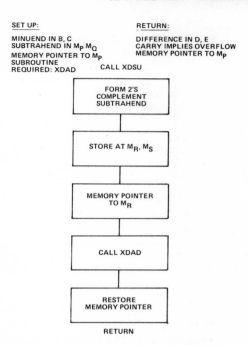

SET UP:

MINUEND IN B, C
SUBTRAHEND IN M_P M_Q
MEMORY POINTER TO M_P
SUBROUTINE
REQUIRED: XDAD

RETURN:

DIFFERENCE IN D, E
CARRY IMPLIES OVERFLOW
MEMORY POINTER TO M_P

CALL XDSU

FORM 2'S
COMPLEMENT
SUBTRAHEND

STORE AT M_R, M_S

MEMORY POINTER
TO M_R

CALL XDAD

RESTORE
MEMORY POINTER

RETURN

Figure VII-17 Flow chart for XDSU, a subroutine for double precision subtraction.

The third arithmetic operation required in the subroutine EXPF is a double-precision arithmetic shift to the right by m places. This routine, XASR assumes an adjusted and signed operand. In the routine EXPF, if the quantity $D_k - F_{k-1}$ is in overflow, the adjustment is made before entry. Figure VII-18 shows the flow chart for the double-precision arithmetic shift right.

The final steps in the flow chart of Fig. VII-13 are quite simple. When the routine EXPF is completed, a new value of F_k has been generated and is carried in the B and C registers. It is stored and becomes F_{k-1} for the next cycle of the program. The byte of F in the B register is transferred to the accumulator and delivered to its display by an appropriate output instruction. Next, the datum D_k is recalled to the accumulator and F_k is subtracted (B register). This result is also sent to *its* display. Finally, the cycle counter is decremented, tested, and, if the count is complete, the program is returned to the initialization point; otherwise, it simply returns to acquire another data point and repeats the cycle.

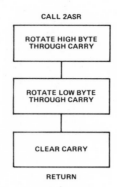

SET UP:	RETURN:
OPERAND IN D, E	SHIFTED RESULT IN D, E
CARRY SET IF NEGATIVE	CARRY CLEARED

Figure VII-18   Flow chart for XASR, a subroutine for right arithmetic shift of two registers.

The program flow charts can be converted to a program listing in a shortened format resembling Fig. VII-5. The programmer has a choice of octal or hexidecimal expression for address and code. The following listing includes both. It also has a column at the left labeled REF (reference) in which the entry points to routines and subroutines are named, each by a 4-character code. A map of the RAM entries appears at the end of the listing. This map, built up during the course of writing the listing, helps to keep track of the addresses required in the memory pointers H, L and the stack pointer.

PROGRAM LISTING: FILT
PURPOSE: TO ACQUIRE DATA PERIODICALLY: TO PER-
    FORM EXPONENTIAL FILTERING: TO OUTPUT FIL-
    TERED DATA, OUTPUT DEVIATION OF CURRENT
    DATUM FROM HISTORICAL VALUE
ENTRY ADDRESS: 000 (TO BE ADJUSTED)
MEMORY REQUIRED: 176 WORDS ROM, 14 WORDS RAM
EXTERNAL HARDWARE: DATA SOURCE
    MANUAL TIME CONSTANT ENTRY SWITCHES
    MANUAL PROCESS CONTROL SWITCH

PROGRAM: FILT

REF	ADDRESS OCTAL	ADDRESS HEX	CODE OCTAL	CODE HEX	MNEMONIC	CALL	COMMENT
FILT	000/000	00 00	333	DB	IN		TEST SWITCH ZERO FOR IDLE LOOP
	1	1	000	00	000		
	2	2	037	1F	RAR		
	3	3	332	DA	JC		
	4	4	000	00		FILT	SWITCH WAS NOT SET, TRY AGAIN
	5	5	000	00			
	6	6	061	31	LXI SP		SET A STACK POINTER
	7	7	020	10			
	10	8	010	08			
	1	9	001	01	LXI B		SET UP TO ZERO 7 SPACES
	2	A	000	00			
	3	B	000	00			
	4	C	305	C5	PUSH B		ZERO EIGHT SPACES
	5	D	305	C5	PUSH B		
	6	E	305	C5	PUSH B		
	7	F	305	C5	PUSH B		
	20	10	341	E1	POP H		ZERO H, L
	1	1	071	39	DAD SP		GET TABLE ADDRESS
	2	2	227	97	SUB A		
	3	3	365	F5	PUSH PSW		INITIALIZE COUNTER, IRRELEVANT CONDITIONS TO 8TH PLACE
DRDY	4	4	333	DB	IN		GET DATA READY LINE
	5	5	001	01	001		
	6	6	037	1F	RAR		AND TEST IT
	7	7	332	DA	JC		
	30	8	024	14		DRDY	NOT READY, TRY AGAIN
	1	9	000	00			
	2	A	333	DB	IN		ELSE GET A DATA POINT
	3	B	022	12	022		
	4	C	167	77	MOV M,A		STORE IT AT 010/012
EXPF	5	D	107	47	MOV B,A		ALSO SET UP MINUEND FOR XDSU
	6	E	016	0E	MVI C		
	7	F	000	00			

REF	ADDRESS OCTAL	ADDRESS HEX	CODE OCTAL	CODE HEX	MNEMONIC	CALL	COMMENT
	000/040	00 20	043	23	INX H		GET ADDRESS OF SUBTRAHEND
	1	1	315	CD	CALL	XDSV	CD = DK MINUS FK
	2	2	230	98			
	3	3	000	00			
	4	4	333	DB	IN		GET "TIME CONSTANT" (ALWAYS READY)
	5	5	021	11	021		
	6	6	107	47	MOV B,A		SAVE IT IN B-REGISTER
	7	7	322	D2	JC	EXF1	NO CARRY MEANS NO OVERFLOW
	50	8	067	37			
	1	9	000	00			
	2	A	362	F2	JNM	EXF2	ELSE ADJUST FOR OVERFLOW,
	3	B	056	2E			HIGH BIT ON MEANS POSITIVE OVERFLOW
	4	C	000	00			
	5	D	077	3F	CMC		CARRY → 0 GIVES NO FILL FROM LEFT
EXF2	6	E	315	CD	CALL	XASR	SHIFT IT
	7	F	255	AD			
	60	30	000	00			
	1	1	365	F5	PUSH PSW		SAVE THE CONDITION (M ONLY; XASR CLEARS CARRY)
	2	2	005	05	DCR B		DECREMENT SHIFT COUNTER
	3	3	312	CA	JZ	EXF5	IF DONE
	4	4	103	43			
	5	5	000	00			
EXF4	6	6	361	F1	POP PSW		ELSE CONTINUE
EXF1	7	7	362	F2	JNM	EXF3	SKIP IF POSITIVE
	70	8	073	3B			
	1	9	000	00			
	2	A	067	37	STC		ELSE SET CARRY TO FILL FROM THE LEFT
EXF3	3	B	365	F5	PUSH PSW		SAVE THE CONDITION (MINUS)
	4	C	315	CD	CALL	XASR	SHIFT AGAIN
	5	D	255	AD			
	6	E	000	00			
	7	F	005	05	DCR B		DECREMENT SHIFT COUNTER

REF	ADDRESS OCTAL	ADDRESS HEX	CODE OCTAL	CODE HEX	MNEMONIC	CALL	COMMENT
	000/100	00 40	302	C2	JNZ	EXF4	NOT DONE, GO BACK FOR MORE
	1	1	066	36			
	2	2	000	00			
EXF5	3	3	361	F1	POP PSW		RESETS STACK POINTER
	4	4	102	42	MOV B,D		SET UP AUGEND FOR XDAD
	5	5	113	4B	MOV C,E		
	6	6	315	CD	CALL	XDAD	COMPUTE NEW FK
	7	7	156	6E			
	10	8	000	00			
	1	9	163	73	MOV M,E		STORE IT
	2	A	043	23	INX H		
	3	B	162	72	MOV M,D		
	4	C	172	7A	MOV A,D		ROUND OFF ADJUSTMENT FK TO 1 BYTE
	5	D	263	B3	ORA E		COMBINE HIGH BIT, HIGH AND LOW BYTES
	6	E	362	F2	JNM	EXF6	HIGH BYTE POSITIVE, LOW BYTE LESS THAN
	7	F	126	56			1/2 HIGH BYTE LOW BIT; NO ADJUSTMENT
	20	50	000	00			ELSE MIXED, HIGH BYTE NEGATIVE, LOW BYTE
	1	1	253	AB	XOR E		LESS THAN HALF OR VV
	2	2	372	FA	JM	EXF6	ALSO NO ADJUSTMENT
	3	3	126	56			
	4	4	000	00			
	5	5	024	14	INR D		OTHERWISE ROUND OFF CORRECTION
	6	6	172	7A	MOV A,D		AND DISPLAY ADJUSTED FK HIGH BYTE
	7	7	323	D3	OUT		
	30	8	021	11	021		
	1	9	053	2B	DCX H		GET ADDRESS FOR DK
	2	A	053	2B	DCX H		
	3	B	176	7E	MOV A,M		GET DK
	4	C	222	92	SUB D		AND SUBTRACT ADJUSTED FK
	5	D	323	D3	OUT ·		DISPLAY THE DEVIATION
	6	E	022	12	022		
	7	F	053	2B	DCX H		ADJUST MEMORY POINTER

REF	ADDRESS OCTAL	ADDRESS HEX	CODE OCTAL	CODE HEX	MNEMONIC	CALL	COMMENT
	000/140	00 60	065	35	DCR M		
	1	1	312	CA	JZ	FILT	256 POINTS TAKEN, START OVER
	2	2	000	00			
	3	3	000	00			
	4	4	333	DB	IN		TEST THE ESCAPE SWITCH
	5	5	002	02	002		
	6	6	037	1F	RAR		SWITCH STATE TO CARRY
	7	7	322	D2	JNC		
	50	8	000	00		FILT	ESCAPE SWITCH SET, GO TO IDLE
	1	9	000	00			
	2	A	043	23	INX H		ADJUST MEMORY POINTER
	3	B	303	C3	JMP		
	4	C	024	14		DRDY	GET ANOTHER DATUM DK
	5	D	000	00			
XDAD	6	E	136	5E	MOV E,M		GET LOW BYTE AUGEND
	7	F	043	23	INX H		ADJUST MEMORY POINTER
	60	70	126	56	MOV D,M		GET HIGH BYTE AUGEND
	1	1	171	79	MOV A,C		ADD LOW BYTES
	2	2	203	83	ADD E		
	3	3	137	5F	MOV E,A		AND SAVE IN E-REGISTER
	4	4	170	78	MOV A,B		ADD HIGH BYTES
	5	5	212	8A	ADC D		
	6	6	127	57	MOV D,A		AND SAVE IN D-REGISTER
	7	7	365	F5	PUSH PSW		SAVE CONDITIONS
	70	8	170	78	MOV A,B		CHECK FOR MIXED SIGNS
	1	9	256	AE	XOR M		
	2	A	362	F2	JNM	SKP1	SIGNS WERE NOT MIXED, OVERFLOW POSSIBLE
	3	B	201	81			
	4	C	000	00			
	5	D	053	2B	DCX H		RE-ESTABLISH LOW BYTE ADDRESS
	6	E	361	F1	POP PSW		
	7	F	267	B7	ORA A		CLEAR CARRY

REF	ADDRESS OCTAL	ADDRESS HEX	CODE OCTAL	CODE HEX	MNEMONIC	CALL	COMMENT
SKP1	000/200	00 80	311	C9	RET		DONE IF NO OVERFLOW
	1	1	301	C1	POP B		GET CONDITIONS, (C-REGISTER)
	2	2	305	C5	PUSH B		SAVE THEM AGAIN
	3	3	171	79	MOV A,C		
	4	4	007	07	RLC		CARRY TO BIT 1, MINUS TO BIT 0
	5	5	346	E6	ANI		MASK FOR CARRY AND MINUS INDICATOR
	6	6	003	03			
	7	7	312	CA	JZ		NEITHER SET
	10	8	225	95		SKP3	SKIP CARRY ADJUSTMENT, NO OVERFLOW
	1	9	000	00			
	2	A	075	3D	DCR A		DECREMENT INDICATOR
	3	B	312	CA	JZ		
	4	C	222	92		SKP2	POSITIVE OVERFLOW, SET CARRY
	5	D	000	00			
	6	E	075	3D	DCR A		DECREMENT INDICATOR
	7	F	312	CA	JZ		
	20	90	225	95		SKP3	NEGATIVE OVERFLOW, CARRY IS SET
	1	1	000	00			
SKP2	2	2	361	F1	POP PSW		ELSE CARRY SET BUT NO OVERFLOW, SAVE SIGN,
	3	3	077	3F	CMC		COMPLEMENT CARRY
	4	4	365	F5	PUSH PSW		
SKP3	5	5	053	2B	DCX H		ADJUST MEMORY POINTER
	6	6	361	F1	POP PSW		RESTORE CONDITIONS
	7	7	311	C9	RET		DONE XDAD
XDSU	30	8	136	5E	MOV E,M		GENERATE THE NEGATIVE OF THE SUBTRAHEND
	1	9	043	23	INX H		GET LOW BYTE AND HIGH BYTE
	2	A	227	97	SUB A		ACCUMULATOR = ZERO
	3	B	127	57	MOV D,A		SAVE A ZERO
	4	C	223	93	SUB E		SUBTRACT LOW BYTE
	5	D	137	5F	MOV E,A		SAVE THE RESULT
	6	E	172	7A	MOV A,D		RESTORE ZERO TO ACCUMULATOR
	7	F	236	9E	SBB M		SUBTRACT THE HIGH BYTE (WITH BORROW)

REF	ADDRESS OCTAL	ADDRESS HEX	CODE OCTAL	CODE HEX	MNEMONIC	CALL	COMMENT
	000/240	00 A0	043	23	INX H		ADJUST MEMORY TO POINTER
	1	1	163	73	MOV M,E		2S COMPLEMENT SUBTRAHEND TO ADDEND ADDRESS,
	2	2	043	23	INX H		LOW BYTE
	3	3	167	77	MOV M,A		AND HIGH BYTE
	4	4	053	2B	DCX H		SET UP MEMORY POINTER FOR XDAD
	5	5	315	CD	CALL		
	6	6	156	6E		XDAD	
	7	7	000	00			
	50	8	365	F5	PUSH PSW		SAVE CONDITIONS
	1	9	053	2B	DCX H		ADJUST MEMORY POINTER
	2	A	053	2B	DCX H		AND AGAIN
	3	B	361	F1	POP PSW		RESTORE CONDITIONS
	4	C	311	C9	RET		DONE XDSU
XASR	5	D	172	7A	MOV A,D		GET HIGH BYTE
	6	E	037	3F	RAR		ROTATE RIGHT; CARRY TO HIGH BIT, LOW BIT TO CARRY
	7	F	127	57	MOV D,A		SAVE RESULT
	60	B0	173	7B	MOV A,E		THE SAME FOR LOW BYTE
	1	1	037	3F	RAR		
	2	2	137	5F	MOV E,A		
	3	3	267	B7	ORA A		CLEARS THE CARRY
	4	4	311	C9	RET		DONE XASR

ENTRY LIST

ENTRY	ADDRESS	
	OCTAL	HEX
XASR	000/255	00 AD
XDSU	000/230	00 98
SKP3	000/225	00 95
SKP2	000/222	00 92
SKP1	000/201	00 81
XDAD	000/156	00 6E
EXF5	000/103	00 43
EXF3	000/073	00 3B
EXF1	000/067	00 37
EXF4	000/066	00 36
EXF2	000/056	00 2E
EXPF	000/035	00 1D
DRDY	000/024	00 14
FILT	000/000	00 00

RAM MAP

ADDRESS		TITLE
OCTAL	HEX	
010/000	08 00	RAM BASE ADDRESS
010/007	08 07	TOP OF STACK
010/011	08 09	COUNTER
010/012	08 0A	STORAGE DK
010/013	08 0B	STORAGE FK LOW BYTE
010/014	08 0C	STORAGE FK HIGH BYTE
010/015	08 0D	XDSU WORKING SPACE
010/016	08 0E	XDSU WORKING SPACE

This completes the listing for the program defined. It would ordinarily be written with either hexidecimal or octal notation only, depending on the preference of the programmer. There is a trend toward the use of hexidecimal for compactness. The instruction mnemonics have been entered in the form that is acceptable to an 8080 assembler, however, the other conventions of assembly formalism have been omitted.

Obviously, there are other ways of writing the program that could give the same result, possibly with more compactness and lucidity.

There are also some "tricks," that an experienced programmer might use, which have been omitted in order to keep the program statements direct. For example, in order to maintain a simple sequence, the instructions PUSH PSW and POP PSW have been used at several points in the program to save the states of carry and the condition flip-flops that otherwise would be lost prior to the tests requiring the condition information. Alternate treatment of the intervening steps might preclude the need for this precaution. Although the result of this maneuver may lack some elegance, it's application is practical unless the program is severely limited as to stack space or time.

The reading of the program is considerably facilitated by consulting the instruction lexicon reproduced at the end of the chapter. The entries include not only the title of the instruction, but also the effect of the instruction on the relevent registers and condition flip-flop states.

Since the format of the listing is *not* intended to conform to any specific assembly procedure, it is arbitrarily structured only to facilitate the reading of the instruction-code sequences. Although it does resemble an assembly language arrangement, it cannot be used for computer-assisted assembly. The instruction codes required in the listing are drawn from the 8080 instruction set.

Mention was made at the beginning of this section that the program described is grossly inefficient. The inefficiency is primarily represented by the fact that the microprocessor, having acquired a data value and having processed that value, is effectively disabled from other occupation until the next data ready condition is signaled. Alternate designs of the program could utilize a considerable part of the waiting time. For example, the polling of the data ready line could be interlaced with other operations, or the data ready signal could engage an interrupt sequence.

Although the program for data filtering described above is moderately long, it is quite comfortably negotiable to hand programming. A well-thought plan rendered in flow charts is very helpful in constructing the program sequences. The flow charts also help in keeping track of the necessary details and avoiding such problems as dead-end logic loops, which effectively stop the operation, and mystifying JUMPS to oblivion.

The programmer normally expects a number (hopefully a small number) of errors or "bugs" in the first execution of a new program. Short programs can frequently be "debugged" by operating the system in a manually stepped mode. Both simple and elaborate debugging programs have been written to facilitate the discovery and correction of errors. Ordinary debugging routines are not easily applied to programs contained in ROM, since entries cannot be changed, although single-step monitoring is possible in most cases. One method for editing a program is to translate it to RAM (with appropriate address reference changes), where it can be corrected one word at a time with a simple edit routine.

Some bugs stay hidden in program testing, only to emerge later under unusual operating circumstances. However, program problems generally yield to methodical analysis.

Almost any data processing routine that can be logically stated can be formulated into flow charts and thus into programs. Moreover, the steps representing data acquisition and the later transfer of data to display or recording devices comprise relatively simple operations. Particular requirements may be facilitated by the inclusion of auxiliary hardware in the system (see Chapter VIII). The more elaborate programs for system control and data processing can be submitted to more powerful programming procedures, including a computer-generated assembly of program statements into an object program. Programming at even higher levels of abstraction using a variety of special "languages" is suitable to complex problems. These levels of programming lie outside of the scope of this book. They require the services of medium- or large-size computer-operating systems with extensive software, and, for the noninitiate, the help of professional programmers. Rather, the purpose here is to stress the solution of simple problems in an economic and advantageous way by users having a professional grasp of the problems and a somewhat amateur stance toward digital automation.

VII-5 A PROJECT

The project of this chapter is to construct a small 8080 microprocessor-operated control and data-processing system. The design of the project is based on the higher performance system described in Section VII-3. Although it is small, the system can be expanded to almost any degree within the capability of the 8080 microprocessor. The system is provided with an operator's panel with control switches and register displays. The project statement includes a ROM listing for a short editing program that permits the entry of operating programs and data into RAM. These programs are then accessible both to review and alteration, and exercise via the operating switches. The input and output ports provide the entry and display facilities for the system.

The complete system is shown in the block diagram, Fig. VII-19a.

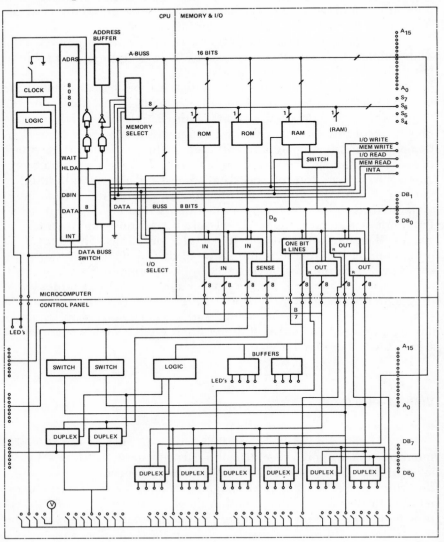

Figure VII-19a Consolidated diagram for a microprocessor system project. The diagram is divided into sections marked CPU (central processing unit), memory and I/O, and control panel.

This diagram is divided into three sections, viz., the CPU section, the memory and I/O section, and the control panel section in Figs. VII-19b, c, d, respectively. Individual components are identified in the latter figures.

With a project of this degree of complexity, construction methods

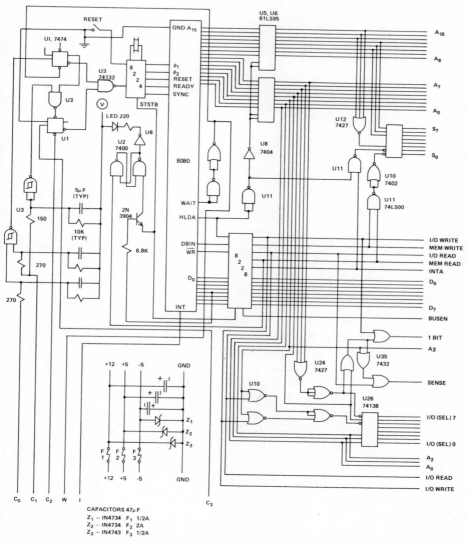

Figure VII-19b Microprocessor system project, detail of CPU section.

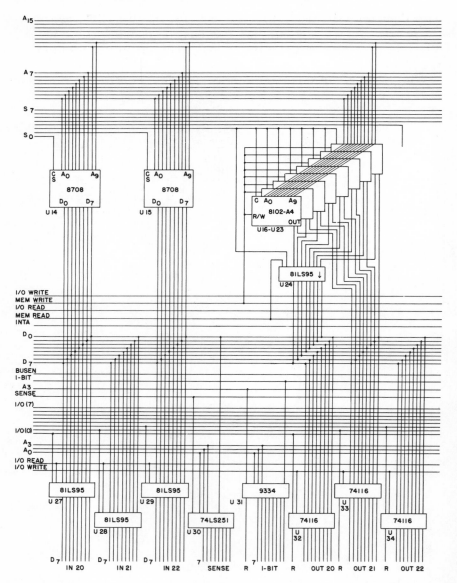

Figure VII-19c Microprocessor system project, detail of memory and I/O section.

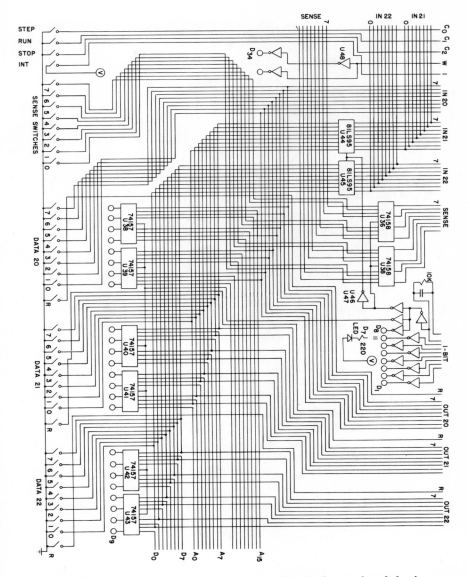

Figure VII-19d Microprocessor system project, detail of control and display section.

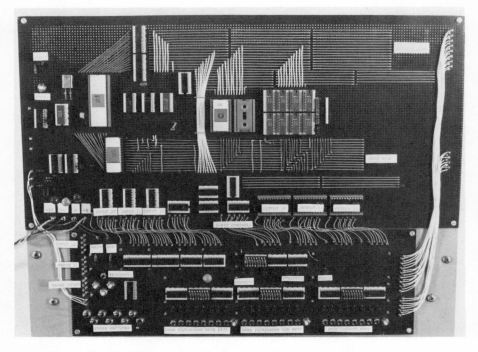

Figure VII-20   Photograph of the completed microprocessor system project.

and organization are important. Figure VII-20, shows a construction carried out on a prepunched glass reenforced epoxy board $\frac{1}{16}$ in. thick, having holes on 0.100-in. centers. This hole pattern matches the pin spacing on integrated circuit sockets, and it helps in laying out the wiring in an orderly way. A materials list for construction is shown in Fig. VII-21. Judicious substitution for many of the small hardware items is appropriate in cases of more convenient availability; however, the electrical components should follow the specification closely.

Wiring should be carried out with care. The author wired the board shown in the photograph using solder pin sockets and insulated wire wherever wire crossovers occur. The major buss structures were laid down with No. 18 bare tinned copper wire anchored to the board at 3-in. intervals. (Since a number of connections are made to these busses, the use of bare wire is quite a convenience to accomodate their attachment). Of course, wires connected to the busses must be insulated. Solder pin sockets are not recommended. Sockets with

0.025 in.^{2} (wire-wrap) pines (0.750 in. long) are easier to use. A wire-wrap tool facilitates speedy work. Otherwise, the pins can be cut to about $\frac{1}{4}$ in. length, and the connecting wires can be soldered.

The orderly arrangement of the buss and control line structures is a considerable help in circuit layout. Unfortunately the pin-out arrangement of the integrated circuits themselves follows no such ordered sequence (for reasons of internal connections). Thus, the connections between the busses and the sockets on the back side of the board become a rather tangled scramble and must be made with insulated wire. Completing these connections and the interwiring of the sockets on the back of the board is tedious. Spacing the work out over a period of time helps to prevent the fatigue that could lead to troublesome wiring errors.

When the circuit board is completely assembled and wired, a wiring check using a circuit test meter (ohmmeter) is advisable. The board should be tested before integrated circuits are installed in the sockets. Particular attention should be directed to the continuity of connections and to pin-to-pin isolation. When the wiring test is complete, the microprocessor board may be loaded with its complement of integrated circuits, excluding the ROM if it is not yet programmed.

The control-panel board is simpler than the microprocessor board. Construction with the same methods used for the latter is quite straightforward. When it is completed and the wiring checked, it can be interconnected with the microprocessor board with lines not exceeding about 2 ft in length.

With this connection, the hardware is complete. Power supply is the next order of need. The system requires a well-regulated and filtered source of +5 V at 1.4 A. In addition, −5 V at 50 mA and +12 V at 100 mA, must be furnished. The system is protected from improper connection of power by the combination of fuses and zener diodes shown in the diagrams. However, care should be exercised with all power connections in order not to endanger expensive components.

The system cannot be operated without a programmed ROM. Vendors will usually furnish programming service for programmable ROM devices either at low cost or for no charge. Any valid program may be entered on a ROM used in the system. Expansion to 2048 words of ROM can be accommodated directly on the board using the two sockets provided.

An exercise program is described and listed below. This program has been designed to furnish the user with RAM alteration and diagnostic facilities and to allow independent operation of programs entered in RAM. (The user should remember that RAM entries are vola-

MATERIAL LIST FOR THE MICROPROCESSOR PROJECT

INTEGRATED CIRCUITS

ITEM	IDENTIFICATION	MANUFACTURER
U_1	7474, TTL IC	Any
U_2	7400, TTL IC	Any
U_3	74132, TTL IC	Any
U_4	8214, STTL IC	Intel
U_5	8080, MOS Microprocessor	Intel
U_6	DM81LS95, LSTTL IC	National Semiconductor
U_7	DM81LS95, LSTTL IC	National Semiconductor
U_8	7404, TTL IC	Any
U_9	8228, STTL IC	Intel
U_{10}	7402, TTL IC	Any
U_{11}	74LS00, LSTTL IC	Any
U_{12}	7427, TTL IC	Any
U_{13}	74138, TTL IC	Any
U_{14}	8708, MOS EPROM	Intel
U_{15}	8708, MOS EPROM	Intel
$U_{16} - U_{23}$	8102–A4, MOS RAM	Intel
U_{24}	81LS95, LSTTL IC	Any
U_{25}	7427, TTL IC	Any
U_{26}	74138, TTL IC	Any
$U_{27}-U_{29}$	81LS95, LSTTL IC	Any
U_{30}	74251, TTL IC	Any
U_{31}	9334, TTL IC	Any
$U_{32} - U_{34}$	74116, TTL IC	Any
U_{35}	7432, TTL IC	Any
U_{36}, U_{37}	74158, TTL IC	Any
$U_{38} - U_{43}$	74157, TTL IC	Any
U_{44}, U_{45}	81LS95, LSTTL IC	National Semiconductor
$U_{46} - U_{48}$	7404, TTL IC	Any

MATERIAL LIST FOR THE MICROPROCESSOR PROJECT

COMPONENTS

ITEM	IDENTIFICATION	MANUFACTURER
Z_1, Z_2	IN4734A Zener Diode	Any
Z_3	IN4743A Zener Diode	Any
$D_1 - D_{35}$	Light Emitting Diodes, HP 5082-4484 or equivalent	
(35 ea)	200 Ω 1/4 Watt Carbon Resistors	
(5 ea)	10 KΩ 1/4 Watt Carbon Resistors	
(1 ea)	6.8 KΩ 1/4 Watt Carbon Resistor	
(2 ea)	270 Ω 1/4 Watt Carbon Resistors	
(1 ea)	150 Ω 1/4 Watt Carbon Resistors	
(40 ea)	SPST Momentary Contact Switches	For example, Grayhill, Inc. No. 39-1
(3 ea)	5 μf 20 V Electrolytic Capacitors	
(3 ea)	47 μf 20 V Electrolytic Capacitors, preferably tantalum	
(10 ea)	1 μf 50 V Ceramic Capacitors; these are not shown on the diagram. They are to be installed at sockets dispersed around the system between power pins and ground.	

Figure VII-21   Materials list for the microprocessor system project.

ITEM	IDENTIFICATION
(2 ea)	Fuses 1/4 Ampere
(1 ea)	Fuse, 3 Ampere, quick acting
(12 ea)	14-pin Dual In-Line Sockets
(21 ea)	16-pin Dual In-Line Sockets
(8 ea)	18-pin Dual In-Line Sockets
(3 ea)	24-pin Dual In-Line Sockets
(3 ea)	28-pin Dual In-Line Sockets
(1 ea)	40-pin Dual In-Line Sockets
(1 ea)	Crystal Resonator ≈ 18 MHz

MATERIAL LIST FOR THE MICROPROCESSOR PROJECT

MISCELLANEOUS REQUIREMENTS

Circuit Board, Vector Manufacturing Corp. No. 169P84-062WE prepunched G-10 fibreglass epoxy
    board is convenient to use, obtain 2

Interconnecting Wire and Solder

Terminals, Vector Manufacturing Corp. offers a selection convenient to use with the board identified
    above

Patience

Figure VII-21 *Continued.*

tile and will disappear when the system's power is removed.) The program has been deliberately structured to give examples of useful routines and maneuvers that can be borrowed for other applications. Although it is generally straightforward and not dazzling, it does exhibit a degree of sophistication, including a single major section INTR able to handle the needs of two separate routines.

With the exercise program entered in ROM an operator can make use of the system to enter programs into RAM, to diagnose their operation, and to run them for useful results, all under control of front-panel switches. To this end, the program is divided into four major sections as follows:

ENTRY AND EXECUTIVE SECTION, (EXRC)
EDIT RAM SECTION, (ALTR)
PROGRAM RUN ROUTINE, (PRAM)
PROGRAM DIAGNOSTIC ROUTINE, (DIAG)

The operator need not analyze the operation of the exercise program itself to utilize it, although it may be instructive to do so. The front-panel procedures are simple, and attention can be focused primarily on additional programs written for entry and operation in the RAM. Such programs as may be permanently useful can be impressed on alternate ROMs to be used without the need of features in the exercise program.

The individual sections of the exercise program are accessible under control of the operator's panel switches. These switches are identified in the figures and function as follows:

The RESTART switch introduces a restart request to the microprocessor forcing its program counter to zero. This location is the entry into the beginning of the executive program EXRC that will clear any operation under way, but will not destroy RAM entries already made. The RESTART is, in a manner of speaking, a final escape from any intractable situation, such as a microprocessor halt or an inadvertant jump to an improper address.

The RUN, STOP, and STEP switches control the ready line of the microprocessor. STOP forces the system into a WAIT state after the completion of the current cycle. From the WAIT state, the microprocessor can be directed to operate one cycle at a time by successive actuations of the STEP switch. When full autonomous operation is required, the RUN switch is pressed once. The program itself may stop the system, to allow reading registers, etc. Successive operation of the RUN switch will then cause the program to progress after the programmed stops.

The eight SENSE switches provide for manual selection of program modes and other procedures. In the exercise program, the executive section relies on SENSE zero, SENSE three, and SENSE four to select the operating routines. Other switches are used within the routines themselves.

The INTERRUPT switch is mainly used for a temporary exit from an operating RAM program, either in the PRAM or DIAG routines. INTERRUPT is under program control and is disabled while the system is operating from the ROM programs.

All of the SENSE switches on the panel are disabled when the program is operated in RAM via PRAM or DIAG. During this time, the sense lines could be carried off the board for RAM program inquiries.

A description of the operation of the program routine follows: EXRC, the executive routine, is entered at turn-on or whenever the restart switch is actuated. In this routine the OPERATE light is off, and the WAIT light will be on. If the sense switches—SENSE zero, SENSE three, and SENSE four—are disengaged, EXRC will simply poll these switches until one has been set, whereupon the program jumps to the selected routine. In the EDIT routine, the OPERATE light remains off. In PRAM or DIAG, it is lighted, and the panel registers and data lights are connected to the address and data busses. These can be monitored in the step mode. If any of the three sense switches were engaged at the time of entry into EXRC, the FAULT light will show until all three are cleared. The operator can reenter EXRC at anytime by suitable operation of switch sequences.

ALTR, the RAM altering routine, is entered from EXRC by actuation of SENSE zero. The panel will then display the RAM base address 010, 000 and the RAM content at this address and enter a WAIT state. If only SENSE zero is engaged, pressing RUN will increment the displayed address by one and then display the content of that address while waiting for the next operator command. While the system is in the WAIT state, the operator may clear the address display and enter a new address by means of the register switches. The next RUN actuation will then set up the new address in the program routines and display the content of the new address. No other action follows a change of address regardless of which switches are set. If SENSE one is also engaged, the address counter is decremented rather than incremented, thereby giving the next lower address with its content when RUN is actuated.

With SENSE zero or SENSE zero and SENSE one engaged, the operator can examine the content of any memory location including ROM. The RAM content is not altered in this condition. However, if SENSE two is also engaged, a new entry may be installed in the RAM address and is indicated by clearing the object byte display and entering the new word thereon. Entry into memory is accomplished with the actuation of RUN. Entries can, of course, only be made in RAM. If a ROM address is present, the new entry is ignored by the hardware. After entry, the address is advanced or decremented in accordance with the state of SENSE one. A manual change to the address display precludes acceptance of a change entry to the object byte display. The program is returned to EXRC on the next RUN cycle by engagement of SENSE six or by a restart command.

Two options are present for PRAM entry. In the first option, commanded by the *prior* setting of sense switch 2, the program displays, in succession, the microprocessor register store beginning with the accumulator and the condition flags. Since no prior entries were made in the program relating to the register store, the content displayed will be random and meaningless. However, the operator may clear each display as it appears and enter any word desired. The register store displayed is identified by the three function lights with the individual registers being shown in D21 and D22 (see Fig. VII-20). This identification is detailed in accordance with Table VII-4. Each display status is called in succession by operation of the RUN switch. New values may be entered by first operating the appropriate display clear switch and its entering data using the individual bit switches. Entry of the values into the program occurs with the actuation of RUN.

If entry data are not required, the RUN switch may be actuated rapidly until function 110 is shown. This display is a call for the entry of a

Table VII-4 Interpretation of Function Light Codes

Function light code	Register display	
	D22	D21
001	Condition states	Accumulator
010	B	C
011	D	E
100	H	L
101	Stack top content high byte	Stack top content low byte
110	Stack pointer high byte	Stack pointer low byte
111	Entry or exit address high byte	Entry or exit address low byte

stack pointer. Any valid stack pointer greater than 010/024 may be used. Actuation of RUN enters the stack pointer and brings up a display of 111 on the function lights. At this point the operator is obliged to enter a valid start address before proceeding. Acceptance of this entry is followed by a shift of the address from D21, D22 to D20, D21 and another pause in WAIT. This sequence allows a final escape to EXRC in case an improper entry had been made. Escape is engaged by setting sense switch 6 *before* operating RUN. Otherwise, RUN will start the program at the entry point designated.

If no register entries were required, sense switch 2 would not be engaged before entry into PRAM from EXRC. (The switch can also be turned off after entry into the PRAM start-up sequence.) In this case, the entry sequence goes directly to status 110 and then proceeds as before to status 111 for start address entry as described above.

When the jump to RAM program takes place, the gated connection between output ports 21 and 22 and input ports 21 and 22 is disengaged under program control, and these ports are completely free for external use. The eight sense lines are also available for external and on-board actuation. Seven of the 1-bit control lines and output port 20 may also be used. However, the latter is still connected to input port 20. For this reason, input port 20 cannot be used externally.

Once set in PRAM, the system will continue to operate as required by the program entered in RAM in either single-step or RUN mode. D22, D21, and D20 display the content of the address and data busses for observation in single-step mode. Escape from operation of the RAM program can be made by the operator by simply actuating restart, or as was specifically designed, into the EXRC program by actuating the interrupt switch. In the latter instance, the program prescribes retention of the program exit address and the microprocessor state, including all registers and conditions, for examination, if desired, in a routine headed by the reference INTR. (A detailed description of the major part of this routine is presented later in this section.)

From the interruption point the RAM program may be reentered without reversion to EXRC, simply by a suitable number of RUN actuations. The entry point back to RAM and the microprocessor state can be accessed and changed, if desired, by the use of SENSE one and SENSE two. Where neither is set, the microprocessor stops only to show the program counter at INTR, and, with RUN actuated twice, picks up the program at the point where it was left off. When SENSE one is set, a series of RUN actuations will cause the display of the accumulator and the states of the condition flip-flops, the register pairs BC, DE, HL, the original stack top content, and the SP. All registers can be changed prior to resumption of operation; if SENSE two is engaged. The program always permits a change in the address of the reentry point. In all of the RUN steps following the engagement of SENSE one or SENSE one and SENSE two, the display source is identified in binary code by the three display function lights with meanings as described in the table above.

During the RUN sequence, the program function lights for both EXRC and ROM operation are turned off. At INTR, the OPERATE light is turned off when INTR is entered. The entire operation can be returned to EXRC, either by a restart switch actuation at any time or by actuation of SENSE six during INTR.

DIAG, the diagnostic routine, is called from EXRC by the engagement of SENSE four. DIAG requires the entry of two addresses, namely, a breakpoint or terminal address for the intended RAM operation and a start address as in PRAM. Entry accompanied by the setting of SENSE two permits the display and alteration of the microprocessor register content as before. After the stack pointer is displayed, DIAG calls for a mandatory entry of the breakpoint address for the diagnostic essay, selected by the operator. This demand is identified as before by the function-light code of 111 and display of 001/001 in D21 and D22. When the trap address is entered and RUN is actuated, the address display is shifted to D20 and D21, while the RAM instruction is shown in D22. The pause at this point allows reexamination of the address and instruction. If the word at trap address is a second or third byte of a multiple-byte instruction or is lodged in a data sequence, the trap will misfire and may lead to problems. The pause at this point in the entry sequence allows for second thoughts. Engagement of SENSE five, followed by RUN, allows for another entry if the first was faulty. Otherwise, RUN sets the trap by installing a

RESTART 7 instruction at the trap address. The next demand is signaled by display of 111 in the function lights and 002/002 in D21 and D22, calling for the selected start address. The procedure from this point in the sequence is identical to that described for PRAM entry above.

The final actuation of RUN causes a jump to the designated RAM start address, as was the case with PRAM, with the same switching of the input and output ports zero and the sense and control lines. In DIAG, however, the RAM program will normally run only to the designated breakpoint whereupon it is automatically directed to INTR by the RESTART 7 instruction and does not require actuation of the interrupt switch. A fault in the RAM program may preclude this automatic termination, in which case the operator can intervene by actuating the interrupt switch, which will normally cause an entry to INTR, or, if failing to get a response, he can actuate the restart switch, which causes a return to EXRC.

INTR itself is a dual-purpose sequence whose primary function is, first, to retain the pertinent microprocessor entries obtained at the interrupt or restart point. If only SENSE three (from PRAM) were engaged, the exit address would be displayed by INTR. Subsequent actuation of RUN (twice) will simply cause a reentry into the RAM program at the point of exit. If just SENSE four (from DIAG) were set, the exit address, which is the trap address plus one, would also be displayed. (In DIAG, the exit is normally under program control of the RESTART 7 instruction inserted in the RAM program at the intended breakpoint.) Subsequent actuation of RUN clears the address display and actuates the function-counter-code lights to show 110 (binary), indicating that the program is waiting for a new stack pointer to be entered as in the normal sequence for setting another diagnostic trap and RAM entry point.

If the prior diagnostic cycle did not cause an exit at the designated breakpoint, but entered INTR, for any reason, with a different address, this address would be shown in the address display, and the fault light would be lighted by INTR. This condition is virtually certain to arise if the operator intervenes in DIAG by actuating the interrupt switch as a preferred escape from a failed diagnostic cycle. INTR always restores the instruction substituted in the RAM program by DIAG, regardless of a faulty condition. However, an escape to EXRC by using the restart switch will not do so.

Upon the display of the exit address, several options are open via switch selection, whether the fault light is present or not, with the next actuation of RUN. First, if SENSE six is engaged, the routine will return to EXRC, and the microprocessor status will be lost. Second, if SENSE one is engaged, INTR will allow a look at the microprocessor status prior to further operation. In this case, the system will display in succession the registers along with the corresponding function codes.

Third, if neither SENSE six nor SENSE one is engaged, INTR will call for either a start address, operating in PRAM, or for terminal address and start address, operating in DIAG, depending on which routine was previously in operation.

In every option, if SENSE six is engaged, return to EXRC will eventually occur, although several actuations of RUN may be required to complete a series of steps before this return takes place. The return is signaled by the display of the FAULT light, whereupon the operator may select another mode.

After INTR has cycled the "look" at the microprocessor as described above, additional options are open to the operator. First, when only SENSE one is engaged upon the actuation of RUN, the call for start address or the call for terminal address and start address is issued as before depending on whether the entering routine is PRAM or DIAG. Second, if SENSE two is also engaged, the parade of the microprocessor status is again presented, but this time it is presented with the option of changing the entries, if desired, including the possibility of changing the top bytes of the original stack. (A new stack pointer entry would make such a change meaningless.) Subsequent to the completion of the change cycle, the address calls for PRAM or DIAG are issued and the operation in RAM can proceed. As before, SENSE six can be used to direct a return to EXCR prior to the execution of the jump to RAM.

The listing for the exercise program appears on the following pages. The routine ALTR could be lifted from this program to provide a short resident editor to accompany other programs. In this application, minor modification, allowing either direct or indirect jumps to operating programs under control of a sense switch, should be included. The modification is left as an exercise for the reader.

PROGRAM LISTING: EXRC
PURPOSE: TO PROVIDE EDITING AND DIAGNOSTIC FACIL
       ITY FOR CONSTRUCTING PROGRAMS IN RAM
ENTRY ADDRESS: 000/000
MEMORY REQUIRED: 547 WORDS ROM 49 WORDS RAM
EXTERNAL HARDWARE: ONLY AS REQUIRED FOR PRO-
   GRAMS CONSTRUCTED

REF	ADDRESS OCTAL	ADDRESS HEX	CODE OCTAL	CODE HEX	MNEMONIC	CALL	COMMENT
EXRC	000/000	0000	061	31	LXI SP		SET STACK POINTER TO RAM BASE PLUS 020 OCTAL
	1	1	020	10			
	2	2	010	08			
	3	3	315	CD	CALL		CLEAR THE FUNCTION LIGHTS AND OUTPUT REGISTERS
	4	4	016	0E		CLRO	CONNECT THE CONTROL PANEL
	5	5	002	02			
EXC1	6	6	323	D3	OUT		SET FAULT LIGHT
	7	7	010	08	010		
	10	8	333	DB	IN		GET SWITCH 0; BIT 0 = 0 MEANS SWITCH WAS ON
	1	9	000	00	000		
	2	A	107	47	MOV B, A		SAVE IT
	3	B	333	DB	IN		
	4	C	003	03	003		
	5	D	240	A0	ANA B		COMBINE SWITCH 3
	6	E	107	47	MOV B, A		
	7	F	333	DB	IN		
	20	10	004	04	004		
	1	1	240	A0	ANA B		COMBINE SWITCH 4
	2	2	107	47	MOV B, A		
	3	3	333	DB	IN		
	4	4	006	06	006		
	5	5	240	A0	ANA B		COMBINE SWITCH 6
	6	6	037	1F	RAR		BIT 0 TO CARRY
	7	7	322	D2	JNC		A SWITCH WAS ON, TRY AGAIN
	30	8	006	06		EXC1	
	1	9	000	00			
	2	A	323	D3	OUT		TURN OFF THE FAULT LIGHT
	3	B	000	00	000		
POLL	4	C	333	DB	IN		GET SWITCH 0 (EDIT)
	5	D	000	00	000		
	6	E	037	1F	RAR		BIT 0 TO CARRY
	7	F	322	D2	JNC		

REF	ADDRESS OCTAL	ADDRESS HEX	CODE OCTAL	CODE HEX	MNEMONIC	CALL	COMMENT
	000/040	00 20	172	74		ALTR	GO TO ALTR IF SWITCH WAS SET
	1	1	001	01			
	2	2	333	DB	IN		GET SWITCH 3 (PRAM)
	3	3	003	03	003		
	4	4	037	1F	RAR		BIT 0 TO CARRY
	5	5	322	D2	JNC		GO TO PRAM IF SWITCH WAS SET
	6	6	134	5C			
	7	7	001	01			
	50	8	333	DB	IN		GET SWITCH 4 (DIAG)
	1	9	004	04	004		
	2	A	037	1F	RAR		BIT 0 TO CARRY
	3	B	322	D2	JNC		GO TO DIAG IF SWITCH WAS ON
	4	C	151	69			
	5	D	001	01			
	6	E	303	C3	JMP	POLL	ELSE NO SWITCH SET; GO TRY AGAIN
	7	F	034	1C			
	60	30	000	00			
	1	1	EMPTY				
	2	2	EMPTY				
	3	3	EMPTY				
	4	4	EMPTY				
	5	5	EMPTY				
	6	6	EMPTY				
	7	7	EMPTY				
INTR	70	8	042	22	SHLD		SAVE H, L REGISTERS 010/052 CONTAINS H
	1	9	051	29			
	2	A	010	08			
	3	B	353	EB	XCHG		EXCHANGE DE, H, L
	4	C	042	22	SHLD		SAVE D, E REGISTERS
	5	D	047	27			
	6	E	010	08			
	7	F	140	60	MOV H, B		

REF	ADDRESS OCTAL	ADDRESS HEX	CODE OCTAL	CODE HEX	MNEMONIC	CALL	COMMENT
	000/100	00 40	151	69	MOV L, C		
	1	1	042	22	SHLD		
	2	2	045	25			
	3	3	010	08			SET UP TO CAPTURE ORIGINAL STACK POINTER
	4	4	041	21	LXI H		
	5	5	002	02			
	6	6	000	00			GOT IT
	7	7	071	39	DAD SP		GET EXIT ADDRESS
	10	8	321	D1	POP D		GET ORIGINAL STACK TO P
	1	9	301	C1	POP B		
	2	A	061	31	LXI SP		INTERRUPT STACK ADDRESS A
	3	B	045	25			
	4	C	010	08			
	5	D	365	F5	PUSH PSW		SAVE ACCUMULATOR AND CONDITION FLAGS
	6	E	325	D5	PUSH D		SAVE EXIT ADDRESS
	7	F	345	E5	PUSH H		SAVE ORIGINAL STACK POINTER
	20	50	305	C5	PUSH B		SAVE ORIGINAL STACK TOP
	1	1	061	31	LXI SP		INTERRUPT STACK ADDRESS B
	2	2	061	31			
	3	3	010	08			
	4	4	325	D5	PUSH D		SECOND STACK SAVE
	5	5	345	E5	PUSH H		
	6	6	305	C5	PUSH B		
	7	7	061	31	LXI SP		INTERRUPT STACK ADDRESS C
	30	8	045	25			
	1	9	010	08			
	2	A	301	C1	POP B		GET REGISTERS FOR SECOND STACK SAVE
	3	B	321	D1	POP D		
	4	C	341	E1	POP H		
	5	D	061	31	LXI SP		INTERRUPT STACK ADDRESS D
	6	E	035	1D			
	7	F	010	08			

REF	ADDRESS OCTAL	HEX	CODE OCTAL	HEX	MNEMONIC	CALL	COMMENT
	000/140	00 60	345	E5	PUSH H		SECOND STACK SAVE
	1	1	325	D5	PUSH D		
	2	2	305	C5	PUSH B		
	3	3	365	F5	PUSH PSW		
	4	4	052	2A	LHLD		GET EXIT ADDRESS
	5	5	057	2F			
	6	6	010	08			
	7	7	323	D3	OUT		CLEAR FUNCTION LIGHTS, CONNECT CONTROL PANEL
	50	8	007	07	007		
	1	9	323	D3	OUT		
	2	A	017	0F	017		
	3	B	174	7C	MOV A, H		GET HIGH EXIT ADDRESS
	4	C	323	D3	OUT		DISPLAY IT
	5	D	020	10	020		
	6	E	175	7D	MOV A, L		GET LOW EXIT ADDRESS
	7	F	323	D3	OUT		DISPLAY IT
	60	70	021	11	021		
	1	1	227	97	SUB A		A MINUS A = 0
	2	2	323	D3	OUT		DISPLAY IT
	3	3	022	12	022		
	4	4	061	31	LXI SP		TO GET TRAP INSTRUCTION AND DESIGNATOR STORE
	5	5	021	11			
	6	6	010	08			
	7	7	301	C1	POP B		GET INSTRUCTION (B) AND DESIGNATOR (C)
	70	8	353	EB	XCHG		EXIT ADDRESS TO D, E
	1	9	341	E1	POP H		DESIGNATED TRAP ADDRESS TO H, L
	2	A	201	81	ADD C		A WAS ZERO, TEST DESIGNATOR
	3	B	312	CA	JZ		
	4	C	214	8C		LOOK	DESIGNATOR WAS ZERO, (PRAM)
	5	D	000	00			
	6	E	033	1B	DCX D		DECREMENT TO JUSTIFY EXIT ADDRESS
	7	F	172	7A	MOV A,		GET HIGH EXIT ADDRESS

REF	ADDRESS OCTAL	ADDRESS HEX	CODE OCTAL	CODE HEX	MNEMONIC	CALL	COMMENT
	000/200	00 80					
	1	1	274	BC	CMP H		
	2	2	302	C2	JNZ		
	3	3	211	88		FAUT	WAS INCORRECT EXIT, GO TO FAUT
	4	4	000	00			
	5	5	173	7B	MOV A, E		TRY THE LOW BYTE TOO
	6	6	275	BD	CMP L		
	7	7	312	CA	JZ		
	10	8	213	8A		RSTR	WAS CORRECT EXIT, SKIP FAUT
	1	9	000	00			SET FAULT LIGHT
FAUT	2	A	323	D3	OUT		SET FAULT LIGHT
	3	B	010	08	010		H, L = DESIGNATED TRAP EXIT
RSTR	4	C	160	70	MOV M, B		RESTORE THE INSTRUCTION
LOOK	5	D	321	D1	POP D		GET ACCUMULATOR AND FLAG STORE
	6	E	323	D3	OUT		SET FUNCTION LIGHTS TO 111
	7	F	011	09	011		
	20	90	323	D3	OUT		
	1	1	012	0A	012		
	2	2	323	D3	OUT		
	3	3	013	0B	013		
	4	4	323	D3	OUT		
	5	5	004	04	004		WAIT FOR RUN
	6	6	323	D3	OUT		
	7	7	014	0C	014		
	30	8	333	DB	IN		
	1	9	006	06	006		GET SWITCH 6 FOR ESCAPE TO EXRC
	2	A	037	1F	RAR		BIT 0 TO CARRY
	3	B	322	D2	JNC	EXRC	IT WAS ON, GO TO EXRC
	4	C	000	00			
	5	D	000	00			
	6	E	333	DB	IN		
	7	F	001	01	001		
	40	A0	037	1F	RAR		BIT 0 TO

REF	ADDRESS		CODE		MNEMONIC	CALL	COMMENT
	OCTAL	HEX	OCTAL	HEX			
	000/240	00 A0					
	1	1	332	DA	JC		
			353	ED		RNTZ	SWITCH WAS OFF, RE-ENTER PRAM OR DIAG
	2	2	000	00			
	3	3	353	EB	XCHG		ACCUMULATOR AND FLAGS TO H, L
	4	4	315	CD	CALL		
	5	5	267	B7		DSP1	DISPLAY ACCUMULATOR AND FLAGS
	6	6	001	01			
	7	7	341	E1	POP H		GET B, C REGISTER STORE
	50	8	315	CD	CALL		
	1	9	300	C0		DSP2	DISPLAY IT
	2	A	001	01			
	3	B	341	E1	POP H		GET D, E REGISTER STORE
	4	C	315	CD	CALL		
	5	D	311	C9		DSP3	DISPLAY IT
	6	E	001	01			
	7	F	341	E1	POP H		GET H, L REGISTER STORE
	60	B0	315	CD	CALL		
	1	1	322	D2		DSP4	DISPLAY IT
	2	2	001	01			
	3	3	341	E1	POP H		GET STACK TOP STORE
	4	4	315	CD	CALL		
	5	5	333	DB		DSP5	DISPLAY IT
	6	6	001	01			
	7	7	341	E1	POP H		GET STACK POINTER STORE
	70	8	315	CD	CALL		
	1	9	344	E4		DSP6	DISPLAY IT
	2	A	001	01			
	3	B	333	DB	IN		GET SWITCH 2 (MODIFY REGISTERS)
	4	C	002	02	002		
	5	D	037	1F	RAR		BIT 0 TO CARRY
	6	E	332	DA	JC		
	7	F	353	EB		RNT2	SWITCH WAS OFF, MODIFICATION REFUSED

REF	ADDRESS OCTAL	ADDRESS HEX	CODE OCTAL	CODE HEX	MNEMONIC	CALL	COMMENT
	000/300	00 CO	000	00			
	1	1	341	E1	POP H	(RNT2)	DUMMY, SKIP EXIT ADDRESS STORE
INT2	2	2	341	E1	POP H		GET ACCUMULATOR AND CONDITIONS, SECOND STORE
	3	3	315	CD	CALL		
	4	4	267	B7		DSP1	DISPLAY IT
	5	5	001	01			
	6	6	315	CD	CALL		
	7	7	007	07		MODO	ACCEPT MODIFICATION
	10	8	002	02			
	1	9	345	E5	PUSH H		SAVE THE NEW VALUES
	2	A	341	E1	POP H		
	3	B	341	E1	POP H		GET B, C REGISTER STORE AND REPEAT
	4	C	315	CD	CALL		
	5	D	300	C0		DSP2	
	6	E	001	01			
	7	F	315	CD	CALL		
	20	DO	007	07		MODO	
	1	1	002	02			
	2	2	345	E5	PUSH H		
	3	3	341	E1	POP H		GET D, E REGISTER STORE AND REPEAT
	4	4	341	E1	POP H		
	5	5	315	CD	CALL	DSP3	
	6	6	311	C9			
	7	7	001	01			
	30	8	315	CD	CALL	MODO	
	1	9	007	07			
	2	A	002	02			
	3	B	345	E5	PUSH H		GET H, L REGISTER STORE AND REPEAT
	4	C	341	E1	POP H		
	5	D	341	E1	POP H		
	6	E	303	C3	JMP		OOPS! FORGOT TO CALL DSP4 JUMP TO PATCH
	7	F	022	1A		PTCH	

REF	ADDRESS OCTAL	HEX	CODE OCTAL	HEX	MNEMONIC	CALL	COMMENT
	000/340	00 E0					
PTC1	1	1	345	E5	PUSH H	(PTCH)	SAVE THE NEW VALUES
	2	2	341	E1	POP H		
	3	3	341	E1	POP H		GET THE ORIGINAL STACK TOP AND REPEAT
	4	4	315	CD	CALL		
	5	5	333	DB		DSP5	
	6	6	001	01			
	7	7	315	CD	CALL		
	50	8	007	07		MODO	
	1	9	002	02			
RNT2	2	A	345	E5	PUSH H		SAVE THE NEW VALUES
	3	B	052	2A	LHLD		GET THE ORIGINAL STACK POINTER
	4	C	055	2D			
	5	D	010	08			
	6	E	315	CD	CALL		
	7	F	344	E4		DSP6	DISPLAY IT
	60	F0	001	01			
	1	1	315	CD	CALL		
	2	2	007	07		MODO	ACCEPT THE MODIFICATION
	3	3	002	02			
	4	4	061	31	LXI SP		TO RECAPTURE REGISTERS
	5	5	043	23			
	6	6	010	08			
	7	7	361	F1	POP PSW		
	70	8	301	C1	POP B		
	1	9	321	D1	POP D		
	2	A	371	F9	SPHL		H, L WERE THE DESIGNATED STACK POINTER
	3	B	341	E1	POP H		DUMMY TO ADVANCE STACK POINTER
	4	C	052	2A	LHLD		GET THE DESIGNATED STACK TOP STORE
	5	D	053	2B			
	6	E	010	08			
	7	F	345	E5	PUSH H		PUSH IT ON THE STACK

		ADDRESS		CODE				
REF	OCTAL	HEX	OCTAL	HEX	MNEMONIC	CALL	COMMENT	
	001/000	01 00	365	F5	PUSH PSW		SAVE ACCUMULATOR AND CONDITION FLIP-FLOPS
	1	1	072	3A	LDA		GET THE DESIGNATOR
	2	2	021	11			
	3	3	010	08			
	4	4	075	3D	DEC A		
	5	5	302	C2	JNZ		
	6	6	064	34		PRM1	PRAM WAS DESIGNATED, SKIP DIAl
	7	7	001	01			
DIAl	10	8	041	21	LXI H		CUE FOR NEW TRAP ADDRESS
	1	9	001	01			
	2	A	001	01			
	3	B	315	CD	CALL		
	4	C	355	ED		DSP7	DISPLAY IT
	5	D	001	01			
	6	E	315	CD	CALL		
	7	F	007	07		MODO	ENTER A NEW TRAP ADDRESS
	20	10	002	02			
	1	1	041	22	SHLD		SAVE THE TRAP ADDRESS
	2	2	023	13			
	3	3	010	08			
	4	4	174	7C	MOV A, H		SHIFT THE TRAP ADDRESS DISPLAY
	5	5	323	D3	OUT		
	6	6	020	10	020		
	7	7	175	7D	MOV A, L		
	30	8	323	D3	OUT		
	1	9	021	11	021		
	2	A	176	7E	MOV A, M		GET THE INSTRUCTION AT THE TRAP ADDRESS
	3	B	323	D3	OUT		DISPLAY IT
	4	C	022	12	022		
	5	D	323	D3	OUT		WAIT FOR RUN
	6	E	004	04	004		
	7	F	323	D3	OUT		

REF	ADDRESS OCTAL	ADDRESS HEX (01 20)	CODE OCTAL	CODE HEX (OC)	MNEMONIC	CALL	COMMENT
	001/040	01 20	014	OC			
	1	1	333	DB	IN		GET ERASURE SWITCH 5
	2	2	005	05			
	3	3	037	1F	RAR		BIT 0 TO CARRY
	4	4	322	D2			
	5	5	010	08			
	6	6	001	01		DIAl	SWITCH WAS ON, TRY AGAIN
	7	7	176	7E	MOV A, M		GET THE INSTRUCTION AT THE TRAP ADDRESS
	50	8	062	32	STA		SAVE IT
	1	9	022	12			
	2	A	010	08			
	3	B	076	3E	MVI A		PUT A RESTART 7 INSTRUCTION AT THE
	4	C	377	FF			TRAP ADDRESS
	5	D	167	77	MOV M, A		
	6	E	041	21	LXI H		CUE TO ENTER START ADDRESS (DIAG)
	7	F	002	02			
	60	30	002	02			
	1	1	303	C3	JMP		SKIP PRM1
	2	2	067	37		SKP1	
	3	3	001	01			
PRM1	4	4	052	2A	LHLD		GET LAST EXIT ADDRESS (PRAM)
	5	5	057	2F			
	6	6	010	08			
SKP1	7	7	315	CD	CALL		DISPLAY IT, OR 002/002 FOR DIAG
	70	8	355	ED		DSP7	
	1	9	001	01			
	2	A	315	CD	CALL		
	3	B	007	07			ENTER A NEW START ADDRESS, OR CONTINUE
	4	C	002	02		MODO	IF PRAM
	5	D	174	7C	MOV A, H		SHIFT THE START ADDRESS DISPLAY
	6	E	323	D3	OUT		
	7	F	020	10	20		

REF	ADDRESS OCTAL	ADDRESS HEX	CODE OCTAL	CODE HEX	MNEMONIC	CALL	COMMENT
	001/100	01 40	175	7D	MOV A, L		
	1	1	323	D3	OUT		
	2	2	021	11	021		A MINUS A = 0
	3	3	227	97	SUB A		
	4	4	323	D3	OUT		
	5	5	022	12	022		
	6	6	323	D3	OUT		
	7	7	004	04	004		WAIT FOR RUN
	10	8	323	D3	OUT		
	1	9	014	0C	014		
	2	A	333	DB	IN		GET SWITCH 6 FOR LAST CHANCE TO ESCAPE
	3	B	006	06	006		TO EXRC
	4	C	037	1F	RAR		BIT 0 TO CARRY
	5	D	322	D2	JNC		
	6	E	000	00		EXRC	SWITCH WAS ON, GO TO EXRC
	7	F	000	00			
	20	50	315	CD	CALL	CLRO	CLEAR THE FUNCTION LIGHTS
	1	1	016	0E			
	2	2	002	02			
	3	3	323	D3	OUT		DISCONNECT THE CONTROL PANEL
	4	4	007	07	007		
	5	5	361	F1	POP A		RESTORE THE ACCUMULATOR AND CONDITIONS
	6	6	345	E5	PUSH H		ENTER THE NEW START ADDRESS ON STACK
	7	7	052	2A	LHLD		GET DESIGNATED VALUES FOR H, L
	30	8	051	29			
	1	9	010	08			
	2	A	373	FB	EI		ENABLE THE INTERRUPT
	3	B	311	C9	RET		GO TO PROGRAM, END INTR
PRAM	4	C	227	97	SUB A		A MINUS A = 0 FOR DESIGNATOR
	5	D	062	32	STA		SAVE THE DESIGNATOR
	6	E	021	11			
	7	F	010	08			

REF	ADDRESS OCTAL	ADDRESS HEX 01 60	CODE OCTAL	CODE HEX	MNEMONIC	CALL	COMMENT
	001/140	01 60	333	DB	IN		GET SWITCH 2 FOR REGISTER LOADING
	1	1	002	02			
	2	2	037	1F	RAR		BIT 0 TO CARRY
	3	3	322	D2	JNC		
	4	4	302	C2		INT2	SWITCH WAS SET, GO LOAD REGISTERS
	5	5	000	00			
	6	6	303	C3	JMP		ELSE GO DIRECT TO ADDRESS ENTRY
	7	7	353	EB		RNT2	
	50	8	000	00			
DIAG	1	9	076	3E	MV1 A		A = 1 FOR DESIGNATOR
	2	A	001	01			
	3	B	062	32	STA		SAVE IT
	4	C	021	11			
	5	D	010	10			
	6	E	061	31			SET THE STACK POINTER FOR DIAG ENTRY
	7	F	043	23			
	60	70	010	10			
	1	1	333	DB	IN		GET SWITCH 2 FOR REGISTER LOADING
	2	2	002	02			
	3	3	037	1F	RAR		BIT 0 TO CARRY
	4	4	322	D2	JNC		
	5	5	302	C2		INT2	SWITCH WAS SET, GO LOAD REGISTERS
	6	6	000	00			
	7	7	303	C3			ELSE GO DIRECT TO DIAG ENTRY
	70	8	010	08		DIA1	
ALTR	1	9	001	01			
	2	A	041	21	LXI H		ALTR INITIAL ADDRESS
	3	B	000	00			
	4	C	010	08			
ALT1	5	D	104	44	MOV B,H		SAVE THE ADDRESS
	6	E	115	4D	MOV C,L		
	7	F	174	7C	MOV A,H		GET HIGH ADDRESS

REF	ADDRESS OCTAL	ADDRESS HEX	CODE OCTAL	CODE HEX	MNEMONIC	CALL	COMMENT
	001/200	01 80	323	D3	OUT		DISPLAY IT
	1	1	020	10	020		
	2	2	175	7D	MOV A, L		GET THE LOW ADDRESS
	3	3	323	D3	OUT		DISPLAY IT
	4	4	021	11	021		
	5	5	176	7E	MOV A, M		GET WORD AT THE ADDRESS
	6	6	323	D3	OUT		DISPLAY IT
	7	7	022	12	022		
	10	8	333	DB	IN		GET SWITCH 6 FOR ESCAPE TO EXRC
	1	9	006	06	006		
	2	A	037	1F	RAR		BIT 0 TO CARRY
	3	B	322	D2	JNC		
	4	C	000	00		EXRC	SWITCH WAS SET, GO TO EXRC
	5	D	000	00			
	6	E	323	D3	OUT		WAIT FOR RUN
	7	F	004	04	004		
	20	90	333	DB	IN		
	1	1	014	14	014		
	2	2	333	DB	IN		GET NEW ADDRESS AND PUT IT IN H, L
	3	3	020	10	020		
	4	4	147	67	MOV H, A		
	5	5	333	DB	IN		
	6	6	021	11	021		
	7	7	157	6F	MOV L, A		
	30	8	170	78	MOV A, B		GET OLD ADDRESS HIGH BYTE
	1	9	274	BC	CMP H		COMPARE THE NEW
	2	A	302	C2	JNZ		
	3	B	175	7D		ALT1	IT WAS DIFFERENT GO BACK TO TOP
	4	C	001	01	001		
	5	D	171	79	MOV A, C		TRY THE LOW ADDRESS TOO
	6	E	275	BD	CMP L		
	7	F	302	C2	JNZ		

REF	ADDRESS OCTAL	HEX	CODE OCTAL	HEX	MNEMONIC	CALL	COMMENT
	001/240	01 AC	175	7D		ALT1	
	1	1	001	01			
	2	2	333	DB	IN		TEST SWITCH 2 FOR PERMISSION TO
	3	3	002	02	002		CHANGE RAM ENTRY
	4	4	037	1F	RAR		BIT 0 TO CARRY
	5	5	332	DA	JC		
	6	6	253	AB		ALT2	SWITCH WAS OFF, SKIP CHANGE
	7	7	001	01	001		
	50	8	333	DB	IN		ELSE GET NEW VALUE
	1	9	022	12	022		
ALT2	2	A	167	77	MOV M, A		ENTER IT IN RAM
	3	B	333	DB	IN		TEST SWITCH 1 FOR DECREMENT OF ADDRESS
	4	C	001	01	001		
	5	D	037	1F	RAR		BIT 0 TO CARRY
	6	E	322	D2	JNC		
	7	F	263	B3		ALT3	SWITCH WAS ON, DECREMENT ADDRESS
	60	B0	001	01	001		
	1	1	043	23	INX H		ELSE INCREMENT
	2	2	043	23	INX H		
ALT3	3	3	053	2B	DCX H		
	4	4	303	C3	JMP		GO TO TOP FOR NEXT CYCLE
	5	5	175	7D		ALT4	
	6	6	001	01	001		
DSP1	7	7	323	D3	OUT		END EDIT
	70	8	011	09	011		SET FUNCTION LIGHTS TO 001
	1	9	323	D3	OUT		
	2	A	002	02	002		
	3	B	323	D3	OUT		
	4	C	003	03	003		
	5	D	303	C3	JMP		
	6	E	363	F3		SHOW	
	7	F	001	01			

REF	ADDRESS OCTAL	ADDRESS HEX	CODE OCTAL	CODE HEX	MNEMONIC	CALL	COMMENT
DSP2	001/300	01 C0	323	D3	OUT		SET FUNCTION LIGHTS TO 010
	1	1	001	01	001		
	2	2	323	D3	OUT		
	3	3	012	0A	012		
	4	4	323	D3	OUT		
	5	5	003	03	003		
	6	6	303	C3	JMP		
	7	7	363	F3		SHOW	
	10	8	001	01			
DSP3	1	9	323	DB	OUT		SET FUNCTION LIGHTS TO 011
	2	A	011	09	011		
	3	B	323	DB	OUT		
	4	C	012	0A	012		
	5	D	323	DB	OUT		
	6	E	003	03	003		
	7	F	303	C3	JMP		
	20	D0	363	F3		SHOW	
	1	1	001	01			
DSP4	2	2	323	DB	OUT		SET FUNCTION LIGHTS TO 100
	3	3	001	01	001		
	4	4	323	DB	OUT		
	5	5	002	02	002		
	6	6	323	DB	OUT		
	7	7	013	0B	013		
	30	8	303	C3	JMP		
	1	9	363	F3		SHOW	
	2	A	001	01			
DSP5	3	B	323	DB	OUT		SET FUNCTION LIGHTS TO 101
	4	C	011	09	011		
	5	D	323	DB	OUT		
	6	E	002	02	002		
	7	F	323	DB	OUT		

REF	ADDRESS OCTAL	ADDRESS HEX	CODE OCTAL	CODE HEX	MNEMONIC	CALL	COMMENT
	001/340	01 E0	013	0B	013		
	1	1	303	C3	JMP		
	2	2	363	F3		SHOW	
	3	3	001	01			
DSP6	4	4	323	DB	OUT		SET FUNCTION LIGHTS TO 110
	5	5	001	01	001		
	6	6	323	DB	OUT		
	7	7	012	0A	012		
	50	8	323	DB	OUT		
	1	9	013	0B	013		
	2	A	303	C3	JMP		
	3	B	363	F3		SHOW	
	4	C	001	01			
DSP7	5	D	323	DB	OUT		SET FUNCTION LIGHTS TO 111
	6	E	011	09	011		
	7	F	323	DB	OUT		
	60	F0	012	0A	012		
	1	1	323	DB	OUT		
	2	2	013	0B	013		
SHOW	3	3	174	7C	MOV A, H		DISPLAY REGISTERS H, L
	4	4	323	D3	OUT		
	5	5	021	11	021		
	6	6	175	7D	MOV A, L		
	7	7	323	D3	OUT		
	70	8	022	12	022		
	1	9	227	97	227		A MINUS A = 0
	2	A	323	D3	OUT		
	3	B	020	10	020		
	4	C	323	D3	OUT		WAIT FOR RUN
	5	D	004	04	004		
	6	E	323	D3	OUT		
	7	F	014	14	014		

REF	ADDRESS		CODE		MNEMONIC	CALL	COMMENT
	OCTAL	HEX	OCTAL	HEX			
	002/000	02 00					
	0	0	333	DB	IN		GET SWITCH 6 FOR ESCAPE TO EXRC
	1	1	006	06	006		
	2	2	037	1F	RAR		BIT 0 TO CARRY
	3	3	330	D8	RC		SWITCH WAS OFF, RETURN
	4	4	303	C3	JMP		ELSE JUMP TO EXRC
	5	5	000	00			
	6	6	000	00			
MODO	7	7	333	DB	IN		GET THE NEW VALUES TO H, L
	10	8	021	11	021		
	1	9	147	67	MOV H, A		
	2	A	333	DB	IN		
	3	B	022	12	022		
	4	C	157	6F	MOV L, A		
	5	D	311	C9	RET		
CLRO	6	E	323	D3	OUT		CLEAR THE FUNCTION LIGHTS
	7	F	007	07	007		
	20	10	323	D3	OUT		AND CONNECT THE PANEL
	1	11	017	DF	017		
	2	12	227	97	SUB A		A MINUS A = 0
	3	13	323	D3	OUT		CLEAR THE OUTPUT REGISTERS
	4	10	020	10	020		
	5	11	323	D3	OUT		
	6	12	021	11	021		
	7	13	323	D3	OUT		
	30	12	022	12	022		
	1	C9	311	C9	RET		
PTCH	2	A	315	CD	CALL	DSP4	
	3	B	322	D2	322		
	4	C	001	01	001		
	5	D	315	CD	CALL	MODO	
	6	E	007	07	007		
	7	F	002	02	002		

REF	ADDRESS		CODE			CALL	COMMENT
	OCTAL	HEX	OCTAL	HEX	MNEMONIC		
	002/040	02 20	303	C3	JMP		END PATCH END EXRC
	1	1	341	E1		PTC1	
	2	2	000	00			

PROGRAM: EXRC

ENTRY LIST

ENTRY	ADDRESS	
	OCTAL	HEX
PTCH	002/032	02 1A
CLRO	002/016	02 0E
MODO	002/007	02 07
SHOW	001/363	01 F3
DSP7	001/355	01 ED
DSP6	001/344	01 E4
DSP5	001/333	01 DB
DSP4	001/322	01 D2
DSP3	001/311	01 C9
DSP2	001/300	01 C0
DSP1	001/267	01 B7
ALT3	001/263	01 B3
ALT2	001/253	01 AB
ALT1	001/175	01 7D
ALTR	001/172	01 7A
DIAG	001/151	01 69
PRAM	001/134	01 5C
SKP1	001/067	01 37
PRM1	001/064	01 34
DIA1	001/010	01 08
RNT2	000/353	00 EB
INT2	000/302	00 C2
LOOK	000/214	00 8C
RSTR	000/213	00 8B
FAUT	000/211	00 89
INTR	000/070	00 38
POLL	000/034	00 1C
EXC1	000/006	00 06
EXRC	000/000	

RAM MAP

ADDRESS		TITLE
OCTAL	HEX	
010/000	08 00	RAM BASE ADDRESS
010/021	08 11	ROUTINE DESIGNATOR

010/022	08 12	INSTRUCTION STORAGE (DIAG)
010/023	08 13	ADDRESS FOR DESIGNATED
010/024	08 14	EXIT IN DIAG
010/025	08 15	CONDITION FLAGS
010/026	08 16	ACCUMULATOR
010/027	08 17	C-REGISTER
010/030	08 18	B-REGISTER
010/031	08 19	E-REGISTER
010/032	08 1A	D-REGISTER
010/033	08 1B	L-REGISTER
010/034	08 1C	H-REGISTER
010/035	08 1D	ORIGINAL STACK CONTENT
010/036	08 1E	
010/037	08 1F	ORIGINAL STACK POINTER
010/040	08 20	
010/041	08 21	EXIT ADDRESS
010/042	08 22	
010/043	08 23	CONDITION FLAGS, SECOND
		READING
010/044	08 24	ACCUMULATOR
010/045	08 25	C-REGISTER
010/046	08 26	B-REGISTER
010/047	08 27	E-REGISTER
010/050	08 28	D-REGISTER
010/051	08 29	L-REGISTER
010/052	08 2A	H-REGISTER
010/053	08 2B	STACK CONTENT
010/054	08 2C	
010/055	08 2D	STACK POINTER
010/056	08 2E	
010/057	08 2F	EXIT/ENTRY ADDRESS
010/060	08 30	

EXERCISES

The exercises for this chapter comprise suggestions for writing short programs. The programs may be tested with the system constructed for the project above. Additional short programs done as supplemental exercises may be written and tested *ad libidum*.

1. Assume a source delivering one 10 msec pulse/sec. Write a pro-

gram to use this source and the console display registers to form a 24-hour clock with hours, minutes, and seconds displayed in octal or BDC code.

2. Add to the program of exercise A, the provision for manually resetting the clock.

3. Modify the program to accept one $\frac{1}{2}$-sec pulse/sec.

4. Add to the program a classroom-bell timer section that will ring the bell at 07:50:00, 08:00:00, 08:50:00, 09:00:00, etc. The bell should ring in each case for 8 sec; the last class ends at 17:50:00.

5. Write a program to generate and display the sum of the geometric series

$$S_n = \tfrac{1}{2} + \tfrac{1}{4} + \tfrac{1}{8} + \tfrac{1}{16} + \cdots + \frac{1}{2^{n+1}}$$

where n has values from 0–15. Hint: a register of k-bits can be defined to indicate a binary fraction where the full register, 11111 . . . represents the number $(1 - 2^{-k})$ and the lowest bit 2^{-k}.

6. A series of input numbers represents data plus noise. Assuming that the noise is random and that relevant data correlate with a $\frac{1}{2}$-Hz oscillation, write a program to extract data from the noisy signal. The 1 pulse/sec source can be used to provide the reference frequency.

7. Imagine an instrument that requires a complex series of quantitative commands that can be accepted on a single 8-bit buss but that must be distributed within the instrument as prescribed by a 4-bit code on four control lines. Specify the series of commands, and write the program to issue and direct them. Minor equipment modifications may be made in the instrument to simplify the program. What might these be?

APPENDIX

The instruction set of the Intel 8080 microprocessor is presented on the following pages, including the instruction description and the microprocessor codes. The list is drawn from copyrighted publications and is reproduced here by kind permission of the Intel Corporation.

REGISTER CHANGE GROUP

MNEMONIC	BINARY CODE	OCTAL CODE	HEX CODE	DESCRIPTION	CONDITIONS AFFECTED	CYCLES	STATES
MOV r1, r2	01 DDD SSS	1DS	*	Move content of r2 (source) to r1 (destination); r2 is not changed	none	1	5
MOV M,r	01 110 SSS	16S	*	Move content of r (source) to the memory; address in H,L; r not changed	none	2	7
MOV r,M	01 DDD 110	1D6	*	Move content of memory at address H,L to register r (destination) memory is not changed	none	2	7
MVI r, data	00 DDD 110	0D6	*	Move content of the second byte to register r (destination)	none	2	7
MVI M, data	00 110 110	066	36	Move content of the second byte to memory; address in H,L	none	3	10

ARITHMETIC AND LOGICAL INSTRUCTION GROUP

MNEMONIC	BINARY CODE	OCTAL CODE	HEX CODE	DESCRIPTION	CONDITIONS AFFECTED	CYCLES	STATES
INR r	00 DDD 100	0D4	*	Increment and replace register r (destination)	Z, S, P, AC	1	5
DCR r	00 DDD 101	0D5	*	Decrement and replace register r (destination)	Z, S, P, AC		
INR M	00 110 100	064	34	Increment and replace content of memory addressed by H, L	Z, S, P, AC	3	10
DCR M	00 110 101	065	35	Decrement and replace content of memory addressed by H, L	Z, S, P, AC	3	10
ADD r	10 000 SSS	20S	*	Add content of register r to accumulator, place result in accumulator, r is not changed, overflow sets carry	Z, S, P, CY, AC	1	4
ADC r	10 001 SSS	21S	*	Add content of register r with carry, if set, to accumulator; place result in accumulator, overflow sets carry, r is not changed.	Z, S, P, CY, AC	1	4

ARITHMETIC AND LOGICAL INSTRUCTION GROUP (Continued)

MNEMONIC	BINARY CODE	OCTAL CODE	HEX CODE	DESCRIPTION	CONDITIONS AFFECTED	CYCLES	STATES
ADD M	10 000 110	206	86	Add content of memory addressed by H, L to accumulator, place result in accumulator, overflow sets carry, memory is not changed	Z, S, P, CY, AC	2	7
ADC M	10 001 110	216	8F	Add content of memory addressed by H, L with carry, if set, to accumulator, place result in accumulator, overflow sets carry, memory is not changed	Z, S, P, CY, AC	2	7
ADI data	11 000 110	306	C6	Add content of second byte to accumulator, place result in accumulator, overflow sets carry	Z, S, P, CY, AC	2	7
ACI data	11 001 110	316	CF	Add content of second byte to accumulator with carry, if set, place the result in accumulator, overflow sets carry	Z, S, P, CY, AC	2	7
SUB r	10 010 SSS	22S	*	Subtract the content of register r from accumulator, place result in accumulator, underflow sets carry, r is not changed	Z, S, P, CY, AC	1	4
SBB r	10 011 SSS	23S	*	Subtract the content of register r from accumulator, carry, if set; forces adjustment for prior borrow, place result in accumulator, underflow sets carry, r is not changed	Z, S, P, CY, AC	1	4
SUB M	10 010 110	226	96	Subtract content of memory addressed by H, L from accumulator, place result in accumulator, underflow sets carry, memory is not changed	Z, S, P, CY, AC	2	7
SBB M	10 011 110	236	9E	Subtract content of memory addressed by H, L from accumulator, carry, if set; forces adjustment for prior borrow, place result in accumulator, underflow sets carry, memory is not changed	Z, S, P, CY, AC	2	7

ARITHMETIC AND LOGICAL INSTRUCTION GROUP (Continued)

MNEMONIC	BINARY CODE	OCTAL CODE	HEX CODE	DESCRIPTION	CONDITIONS AFFECTED	CYCLES	STATES
SUI data	11 010 110	326	D6	Subtract content of second byte from accumulator, place result in accumulator, underflow sets carry	Z, S, P, CY, AC	2	7
SBI data	11 011 006	336	DF	Subtract content of the second byte from the accumulator, carry, if set; forces adjustment for prior borrow, place result in accumulator, underflow sets carry	Z, S, P, CY, AC	2	7
ANA r	10 100 SSS	24S	*	Form the logical *and* of the register r with the accumulator, place result in accumulator, carry and auxiliary carry are reset, r is not changed	Z, S, P, CY, AC	1	4
XRA r	10 101 SSS	25S	*	Form the logical *exclusive or* of the register r with the accumulator, place result in accumulator, carry and auxiliary carry are reset, r is not changed	Z, S, P, CY, AC	1	4
ORA r	10 110 SSS	26S	*	Form the logical *or* of the register r with the accumulator, place the result in accumulator, carry and auxiliary carry are reset, r is not changed	Z, S, P, CY, AC	1	4
CMP r	10 111 SSS	27S	*	Compare register r with accumulator, r and accumulator are not changed, A = r sets Z flag, A < r sets CY flag	Z, S, P, CY, AC	1	4
ANA M	10 100 110	246	A6	Form the logical *and* of memory content addressed by H, L with the accumulator, place result in accumulator, carry and auxiliary carry are reset, memory content is not changed	Z, S, P, CY, AC	2	7
XRA M	10 101 110	256	AE	Form the logical *exclusive or* of memory content addressed by H, L with accumulator, place result in accumulator, carry and auxiliary carry are reset, memory content is not changed	Z, S, P, CY, AC	2	7

ARITHMETIC AND LOGICAL INSTRUCTION GROUP (Continued)

MNEMONIC	BINARY CODE	OCTAL CODE	HEX CODE	DESCRIPTION	CONDITIONS AFFECTED	CYCLES	STATES
ORA M	10 110 110	266	B6	Form the logical *or* of memory content addressed by H, L with accumulator, place result in accumulator, carry and auxiliary carry are reset, memory content is not changed	Z, S, P, CY, AC	2	7
CMP M	10 111 110	276	BE	Compare content of memory addressed by H, L, memory and accumulator are not changed, A=M sets Z flag, A<M sets CY flag	Z, S, P, CY, AC	2	7
ANI data	11 100 110	346	E6	Form the logical and of the accumulator with the second byte, place the result in the accumulator, carry and auxiliary carry are reset	Z, S, P, CY, AC	2	7
XRI data	11 101 110	356	EE	Form the logical *exclusive or* of the accumulator with the second byte, place the result in the accumulator, carry and auxiliary carry are reset	Z, S, P, CY, AC	2	7
ORI data	11 110 110	366	F6	Form the logical *or* of the accumulator with the second byte, place the result in the accumulator, carry and auxiliary carry are reset	Z, S, P, CY, AC	2	7
CPI data	11 111 110	376	FE	Compare the accumulator with the second byte, accumulator is not changed, A=data sets Z flag, A<data sets CY flag	Z, S, P, CY, AC	2	7
RLC	00 000 111	007	07	Rotate the accumulator left, $A_0 \leftarrow A_7$, $A_{\ell+1} \leftarrow A_\ell$, $CY \leftarrow A_7$	CY	1	4
RRC	00 001 111	017	0F	Rotate the accumulator right, $A_7 \leftarrow A_0$, $A_\ell \leftarrow A_{\ell+1}$, $CY \leftarrow A_0$	CY	1	4
RAL	00 010 111	027	17	Rotate the accumulator left through carry, $A_{\ell+1} \leftarrow A_\ell$, $CY \leftarrow A_7$, $A_0 \leftarrow CY$	CY	1	4

ARITHMETIC AND LOGICAL INSTRUCTION GROUP (Continued)

MNEMONIC	BINARY CODE	OCTAL CODE	HEX CODE	DESCRIPTION	CONDITIONS AFFECTED	CYCLES	STATES
RAR	00 011 111	037	1F	Rotate the accumulator right through carry, $A_\ell \leftarrow A_{\ell+1}, A_7 \leftarrow CY, CY \leftarrow A_0$	CY	1	4
BRANCH GROUP							
JMP addr	11 000 011	303	C3	Jump unconditionally to the address designated in the second and third bytes	none	3	10
JNZ addr	11 000 010	302	C2	Jump to the address designated in the second and third bytes if the Z flag is *not* set			
JZ addr	11 001 010	312	CA	Jump to the address designated in the second and third bytes if the Z flag *is* set	none	3	10
JNC addr	11 010 010	322	D2	Jump to the address designated in the second and third bytes if CY is *not* set	none	3	10
JC addr	11 011 010	332	DA	Jump to the address designated in the second and third byte if CY *is* set	none	3	10
JPO addr	11 100 010	342	E2	Jump to the address designated in the second and third bytes if *parity* condition is *odd*	none	3	10
JPE addr	11 101 010	352	EA	Jump to the address designated in the second and third bytes if *parity* condition is *even*	none	3	10
JP addr	11 110 010	362	F2	Jump to the address designated in the second and third bytes if the *minus* condition is *not* present	none	3	10
JM addr	11 111 010	372	FA	Jump to the address designated in the second and third bytes if the *minus* condition *is* present	none	3	10
CALL addr	11 001 101	315	CD	Call the subroutine at the address designated in the second and third bytes unconditionally, return address is saved in the stack	none	5	17

ARITHMETIC AND LOGICAL INSTRUCTION GROUP (Continued)

MNEMONIC	BINARY CODE	OCTAL CODE	HEX CODE	DESCRIPTION	CONDITIONS AFFECTED	CYCLES	STATES
CNZ addr	11 000 100	304	C4	Call the subroutine at the address designated in the second and third bytes if the Z flag is *not* set, return address saved in the stack	none	3/5	11/17
CZ addr	11 001 100	314	CC	Call the subroutine at the address designated in the second and third bytes if the Z flag *is* set, return address is saved in the stack	none	3/5	11/17
CNC addr	11 010 100	324	D4	Call the subroutine at the address designated in the second and third bytes if CY is *not* set, return address is saved in the stack	none	3/5	11/17
CC addr	11 011 100	334	DC	Call the subroutine at the address designated in the second and third bytes if CY *is* set, return address is saved in the stack	none	3/5	11/17
CPO addr	11 100 100	344	E4	Call the subroutine at the address designated in the second and third bytes if *parity* condition is *odd*, return address is saved in the stack	none	3/5	11/17
CPE addr	11 101 100	354	EC	Call the subroutine at the address designated in the second and third bytes if *parity* condition is *even*, return address is saved in the stack	none	3/5	11/17
CP addr	11 110 100	364	F4	Call the subroutine at the address designated in the second and third bytes if the *minus* condition is *not* set, return address is saved in the stack	none	3/5	11/17
CM addr	11 111 100	374	FC	Call the subroutine at the address designated in the second and third bytes if the *minus* condition *is* set, return address is saved in the stack	none	3/5	11/17

INPUT/OUTPUT GROUP

MNEMONIC	BINARY CODE	OCTAL CODE	HEX CODE	DESCRIPTION	CONDITIONS AFFECTED	CYCLES	STATES
OUT port	11 011 010	323	D3	Place the 8-bit port designator on *both* the high and low 8 address lines, place the content of the accumulator on the data buss, *write* is actuated	none	3	10
IN port	11 011 011	333	DB	Place the 8-bit port designator on *both* the high and low 8 address lines, DABIN is actuated and the content of the data buss is transferred to the accumulator	none	3	10

DIRECT AND INDIRECT MEMORY TRANSFER GROUP

MNEMONIC	BINARY CODE	OCTAL CODE	HEX CODE	DESCRIPTION	CONDITIONS AFFECTED	CYCLES	STATES
STA addr	00 110 010	062	32	Store the content of the accumulator at address designated in the second and third bytes	none	4	13
LDA addr	00 111 010	072	3A	Load the accumulator from the address designated in the second and third bytes	none	4	13
SHLD addr	00 100 010	042	22	Store the content of the L register at the address designated in the second and third bytes; store the content of the H register at this address plus one	none	5	16
LHLD addr	00 101 010	052	2A	Load the L register from the address designated in the second and third bytes; load the H register from this address plus one	none	5	16
STAX B	00 000 010	002	02	Store the accumulator at the address designated by the register pair BC	none	2	7
STAX D	00 010 010	022	12	Store the accumulator at the address designated by the register pair DE	none	2	7
LDAX B	00 001 010	012	0A	Load the accumulator from the address designated by the register pair BC	none	2	7

DIRECT AND INDIRECT MEMORY TRANSFER GROUP (Continued)

MNEMONIC	BINARY CODE	OCTAL CODE	HEX CODE	DESCRIPTION	CONDITIONS AFFECTED	CYCLES	STATES
LDAX D	00 011 010	032	1A	Load the accumulator from the address designated by the register pair DE	none	2	7
				EXTENDED INSTRUCTION GROUP			
LXI B	00 000 001	001	01	Load immediately the C register with byte two and the B register with byte three	none	3	10
LXI D	00 010 001	021	11	Load immediately the E register with byte two and the D register with byte three	none	3	10
LXI H	00 100 001	041	21	Load immediately the L register with byte two and the H register with byte three	none	3	10
LXI SP	00 110 001	061	31	Load immediately the low stack pointer with byte two and the high stack pointer with byte three	none	3	10
INX B	00 000 011	003	03	Increment the content of the register pair B, C; overflow of C increments B	none	1	5
INX D	00 010 011	023	13	Increment the content of the register pair D, E; overflow of E increments D	none	1	5
INX H	00 100 011	043	23	Increment the content of the register pair H, L; overflow of L increments H	none	1	5
INX SP	00 110 011	063	33	Increment the two byte stack pointer, overflow of the low byte increments the high byte	none	1	5
DCX B	00 001 011	013	0B	Decrement the content of the register pair B, C; underflow of C decrements B	none	1	5
DCX D	00 011 011	033	1B	Decrement the content of the register pair D, E; underflow of E decrements D	none	1	5
DCX H	00 101 011	053	2B	Decrement the content of the register pair H, L; underflow of L decrements H	none	1	5

EXTENDED INSTRUCTION GROUP (Continued)

MNEMONIC	BINARY CODE	OCTAL CODE	HEX CODE	DESCRIPTION	CONDITIONS AFFECTED	CYCLES	STATES
DCX SP	00 111 011	073	3B	Decrement the two byte stack pointer; underflow of the low byte decrements the high byte	none	1	5
DAD B	00 001 001	011	09	Add the content of the register pair B,C to the register pair H,L; place the result in H,L; B,C are not changed	CY	3	10
DAD D	00 001 001	031	19	Add the content of the register pair D,E to the register pair H,L; place the result in H,L; D,E are not changed	CY	3	10
DAD H	00 101 001	051	29	Add the register pair H, L to itself, place the result in H, L	CY	3	10
DAD SP	00 111 001	071	39	Add the content of the stack pointer register pair to the register pair H,L; place the result in H,L; the stack pointer is not changed	CY	3	10

STACK MANIPULATION GROUP

MNEMONIC	BINARY CODE	OCTAL CODE	HEX CODE	DESCRIPTION	CONDITIONS AFFECTED	CYCLES	STATES
PUSH B	11 000 101	305	C5	Place the content of the B register at the location designated by SP minus one; place the content of the C register at the location designated by SP minus two; set SP to SP minus two	none	3	11
PUSH D	11 010 101	325	D5	Place the content of the D register at the location designated by SP minus one; place the content of the E register at the location designated by SP minus two; set SP to SP minus two	none	3	11
PUSH H	11 100 101	345	E5	Place the content of the H register at the location designated by SP minus one; place the content of the L register at the location designated by SP minus two; set SP to SP minus two	none	3	11

STACK MANIPULATION GROUP (Continued)

MNEMONIC	BINARY CODE	OCTAL CODE	HEX CODE	DESCRIPTION	CONDITIONS AFFECTED	CYCLES	STATES
PUSH PSW	11 110 101	365	F5	Place the content of the accumulator at the location designated by SP minus one; place the status of the condition flip-flops at the location designated by SP minus two in accordance with the code below; set SP to SP minus two	none	3	11
POP B	11 000 001	301	C1	Place the content of the location designated by SP into register C; place the content of the location designated by SP plus one into register B; set SP to SP plus two	none	3	11
POP D	11 010 001	321	D1	Place the content of the location designated by SP into register E; place the content of the location designated by SP plus one into register D; set SP to SP plus two	none	3	11
POP H	11 100 001	341	E1	Place the content of the location designated by SP into register L; place the content of the location designated by SP plus one into register H; set SP to SP plus two	none	3	11

STATUS CODE STORED

CONDITION	B7	B6	B5	B4	B3	B2	B1	B0
CARRY SET	0	0	0	0	0	0	1	1
PARITY ODD	0	0	0	0	0	1	1	0
AUXILIARY CY SET	0	0	0	1	0	0	1	0
ZERO CONDITION	0	1	0	0	0	0	1	0
SIGN IS MINUS	1	0	0	0	0	0	1	0

multiple status conditions result in the presentation of the inclusive or of these codes

STACK MANIPULATION GROUP (Continued)

MNEMONIC	BINARY CODE	OCTAL CODE	HEX CODE	DESCRIPTION	CONDITIONS AFFECTED	CYCLES	STATES
POP PSW	11 110 001	361	F1	Restore the status of the condition flip-flops in accordance with the word stored at the location designated by SP and the codes shown above; place the content of the location designated by SP plus one into the accumulator; set SP to SP plus two	none	3	11

MACHINE CONTROL INSTRUCTION GROUP

MNEMONIC	BINARY CODE	OCTAL CODE	HEX CODE	DESCRIPTION	CONDITIONS AFFECTED	CYCLES	STATES
PCHL	11 101 001	351	E9	Place the content of the register pair H, L into the program counter; value of H,L is not changed, prior content of the program counter is lost; this instruction is useful to provide an unconditional jump	none	1	5
SPHL	11 111 001	371	F9	Place the content of the register pair H,L into the stack pointer; value of H, L is not changed; prior content of the SP is lost	none	1	5
XTHL	11 100 011	343	E3	Exchange the content of the register pair H,L with the stack top; content of the location designated by SP is exchanged with the content of register L; the content of the location designated by SP plus one is exchanged with the content of the H register; SP is not changed	none	5	18
XCHG	11 101 011	353	EB	Exchange the content of the register pair D,E with the content of the register pair H,L	none	1	4

MACHINE CONTROL INSTRUCTION GROUP (Continued)

MNEMONIC	BINARY CODE	OCTAL CODE	HEX CODE	DESCRIPTION	CONDITIONS AFFECTED	CYCLES	STATES
DAA	00 100 111	047	27	This instruction is designed to adjust the result of arithmetic operations on 8-bit operands consisting of two 4-bit BCD bytes as follows: a) If the low 4 bits of the resulting number amount to more than 1001, or if the AC flag is set, 00000110 is added to the accumulator b) If the high 4 bits of the resulting number amount to more than 1001, or if the CY flag is set, 01100000 is added to the accumulator	Z, S, P, CY, AC	1	4
CMA	00 101 111	057	2F	The content of the accumulator is complemented	none	1	4
STC	00 110 111	067	37	Set the CY flip-flop	CY	1	4
CMC	00 111 111	077	3F	Complement the CY flip flop	CY	1	4
DI	11 110 011	363	F3	Disable interrupt requests	none	1	4
EI	11 111 011	373	FB	Enable interrupt requests	none	1	4
HLT	01 110 110	166	76	Halt the operation of the microprocessor; a restart instruction is required to resume operation	none	1	7
NOP	00 000 000	000	00	No operation; the program counter is incremented	none	1	4

ARITHMETIC AND LOGICAL INSTRUCTION GROUP (Continued)

MNEMONIC	BINARY CODE	OCTAL CODE	HEX CODE	DESCRIPTION	CONDITIONS AFFECTED	CYCLES	STATES
RET	11 001 001	311	C9	Return unconditionally to the address stored at the top of the stack	none	3	10
RNZ	11 000 000	300	C0	Return to the address stored at the top of the stack if the Z flag is *not* set	none	1/3	5/11
RZ	11 001 000	310	C8	Return to the address stored at the top of the stack if the Z flag *is* set	none	1/3	5/11
RNC	11 010 000	320	D0	Return to the address stored at the top of the stack if CY is *not* set	none	1/3	5/11
RC	11 011 000	330	D8	Return to the address stored at the top of the stack if CY *is* set	none	1/3	5/11
RPO	11 100 000	340	E0	Return to the address stored at the top of the stack if *parity* condition is *odd*	none	1/3	5/11
RPE	11 101 000	350	E8	Return to the address stored at the top of the stack if *parity* condition is *even*	none	1/3	5/11
RP	11 110 000	360	F0	Return to the address stored at the top of the stack if the *minus* condition is *not* set	none	1/3	5/11
RM	11 111 000	370	F8	Return to the address stored at the top of the stack if the *minus* condition *is* set	none	1/3	5/11
RST η	11 111 PPP	37P	FP′	Jump to the address designated by OOO/ OPO, (octal); place the content of the program counter plus one on the stack. This a convenient one byte call instruction and it can be a forced start selection. RST η can also be forced on the data buss after the microprocessor accepts an interrupt	none	3	11

VIII

Completing the Automated System

The discussions so far have revolved around the management of digital information, including data processing, that is possible with a microprocessor system. For usage beyond lighting panel lights in elaborate sequences, the microprocessor system must become a subsystem of a larger automated system. In the larger system it may assume a variety of roles; it can be a master or a slave, it can be an open-loop system programmer or a participant in a closed-loop system; it can have many choices of operation, or no choices. In general, it is featured with a combination of roles, being defined to supervise part of an operation and to serve other parts. For any operating role, the microprocessor subsystem must have appropriate communication channels. The microprocessor systems discussed in Chapter VII were furnished with input and output ports and control lines. Other means of communication are also possible. The term *digital interface* is used to describe a collection of methods for digital communication.

The digital interface forms a crucial element in the incorporation of a microprocessor subsystem into an automated system. No set rules can prescribe its best design; however, the nature of its design will have a strong bearing on the specification of the entire system operation and the utlity and convenience of its operation.

In addition to the digital interface, the automated system requires

other devices in order to accommodate the contributions of the microprocessor subsystem and thus to perform the variety of functions required by the basic system problem. From the point of view of the microprocessor subsystem, the digital interface and other such devices
are looked upon as peripherals. The system requirements formulate
the definition of the digital interface. In fact, in the design phase, the
definition of the "peripherals" and their communication requirements, which define the interface, are intertwined with the hope of
maximizing the convenience, simplicity, speed, and economy for the
entire system.

Since an abstract description is valuable only to a point, this chapter
will outline, by example, the embedment of a microprocessor subsystem into a generalized spectrometer, which functions in a measurement cycle to acquire a one-dimensional array of data points. As defined, the system requires commands from an operator, supervises instrument settings relevant to the measurement, acquires and processes
data, and displays results. However, once it starts a measurement
cycle it requires no intervention by the operator in order to complete
the cycle and show the results.

VIII-1 EVOLUTION OF AN AUTOMATED SPECTROMETER DESIGN

The design of an automated system requires that the characteristics
of the system and its function be clearly stated and intimately understood by the designer. In this section it will be assumed that the statement has been made and that it is understood. The focus of the
chapter will be directed to elements of the system, using practical examples to show how the system is built up from its parts, and will include comments on hardware, software, and communication.

The microprocessor subsystem will be treated as the central element of the system. The definition of its characteristics and interfacing
will be progressively stated along with the description of system features.

A. Operator Entries

The first peripheral element to be considered will be the operator's
interface. Means are required for the entry of commands. A popular
input device is a keyboard. The full typewriter keyboard is frequently
used, and the ASCII (American Standard Code for Information Inter-
change) is a universally accepted format for communication.

(ASCII-coded keyboards may be purchased with 6-, 7-, or 8-bit parallel outputs and "data ready" or data strobe lines. Interface to the microprocessor via an input port using sense and reset lines is routine, following the specification of the keyboard chosen.)

For purposes of illustration of the interface function, a less elaborate 10-key entry system will be described in some detail. This keyboard differs from that of the full typewriter only in the smaller number (4) of parallel data lines required to transmit the entries.

Any information entry system must be provided with a method to advise the microprocessor subsystem that new information is ready for transmission. Moreover, the system should be arranged to preclude more than one reading of the input information. A common method that is used to satisfy these conditions is to provide a resettable data-ready line. In operation, actuation of a key sets the data-ready line true, and the input select line from the microprocessor subsystem resets it after acceptance of the information. A usual refinement is to provide that the data-ready event, when set, also disables further key entries until the current entry is accepted.

Figure VIII-1 is a schematic diagram of a 10-key entry system. Encoding of the switch selection is accomplished by using the type 74147 priority encoder. Gates and type D flip-flops are included in the circuit to provide for unambiguous data entry needing no synchronization.

The input acquisition process begins with the ready line low indicating that no entry has been made. If the microprocessor were to sense the line, it would read false, and the data lines would all be low. When one of the spring-loaded switches is actuated, the 74147 generates the appropriate code at its output terminals, setting the corresponding data latches. Switch level zero sets a latch that is independent of the encoder. Setting of any of the five latches is detected by the 74260 five-input inverting **or** gate, initiating two events. First, the output enable terminal of the 74147 encoder is set high. This action locks out any further key entries. Second, the ready flip-flop is set, only if the microprocessor has not engaged the input select at the time.

With the ready line true and the data latches set, the output is available for reading at any time. The data latches are protected from reset by $\bar{Q}$ of the data ready flip-flop, and, of course, no further entries can occur. When the microprocessor actuates input select and reads the data, it sets the second type D flip-flop. This action clears the ready line. Clearing the data latches is deferred unless all of the selection switches have been returned to their spring-loaded normal positions. This arrangement precludes reactivation of the ready flip-flop until an unambiguous new selection has been made.

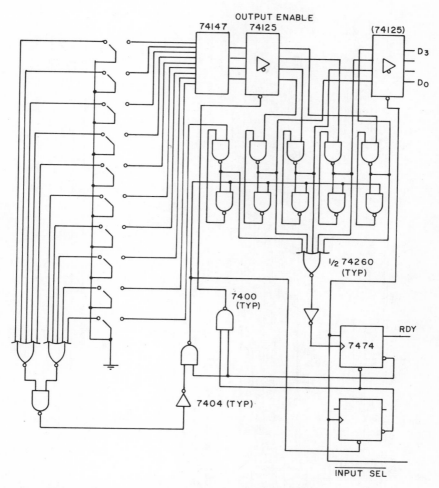

Figure VIII-1 Circuit for a ten-key entry system. Entry of any key actuates a keyboard lockout circuit which is reset when data are read.

In using the keyboard entry system, the microprocessor may be programmed to use the 1-bit data ready signal in two ways, either to wait for an entry and hold up any further operations, or to sense if the data ready is false and skip the reading temporarily in order to perform other tasks, then return to sense the ready line at a later time. Representative software routines to manage these two alternatives are shown in Tables VIII-1 and VIII-2.

REF	ADDRESS OCTAL	ADDRESS HEX	CODE OCTAL	CODE HEX	MNEMONIC	CALL	COMMENT
READ	000/000	00 00	333	DB	IN		THIS ROUTINE WAITS UNCONDITIONALLY FOR A VALID
	1	1	001	01	001		KEY ENTRY BY TESTING A SENSE LINE
	2	2	346	E6	ANI		SETS A CONDITION FLIP-FLOP
	3	3	001	01			
	4	4	312	CA	JZ		THERE WAS NO KEY, GO BACK AND TRY AGAIN
	5	5	000	00		READ	
	6	6	000	00			
	7	7	333	DB	IN		GET THE KEY; HARDWARE PROVISION TO CLEAR
	10	8	021	11	021		THE SENSE LINE UNTIL ANOTHER KEY IS ENTERED
	1	9	323	D3	OUT		DO SOMETHING WITH THE INFORMATION
	2	A	022	12	022		
	3	B	NEXT				GO ON TO OTHER THINGS

REF	ADDRESS OCTAL	ADDRESS HEX	CODE OCTAL	CODE HEX	MNEMONIC	CALL	COMMENT
REAS	000/000	00 00	365	F5	PUSH PSW		THIS SUBROUTINE WILL TRY FOR A KEY ENTRY; IF
	1	1	333	DB	IN		NO KEY WAS ENTERED, IT RETURNS EMPTY HANDED
	2	2	001	01			WITH CARRY CLEARED; OTHERWISE CARRY IS SET
	3	3	346	E6	ANI		SET A CONDITION FLIP-FLOP TO TEST SENSE LINE 1
	4	4	001	01			
	5	5	312	CA	JZ		
	6	6	013	0B		RES1	NO KEY WAS ENTERED, EXIT FOR NOW
	7	7	000	00			
	10	8	333	DB	IN		ELSE GET THE KEY
	11	9	021	11	021		
	12	A	067	37	STC		SET CARRY TO INDICATE ACCEPTANCE OF A KEY
RES1	13	B	063	33	INX SP		RESTORE THE S P TO POINT THE RETURN ADDRESS; FORMER
	14	C	063	33	INX SP		ACCUMULATOR AND CONDITIONS STORED AT SP − 1, SP −
	15	D	311	C9	RET		DONE, RETURNS TO CALLING ROUTINE

2

B. Display

In any system, it is desirable to provide a specific display response to accompany the acceptance of every operator entry. This is an important operator feedback mechanism. The feedback need not be an echo of the specific key or character entered, but some recognizable response should follow each entry. In addition to this communication, a great many other functions of the system will require display.

A wide choice of display devices is open to the designer, such as simple displays made up with LEDs, seven-segment numeral displays, and simple or elaborate pictorial displays.

The displays, in general, will be serviced by the microprocessor. For simple displays such as those involving a few simple lights, no particular burden is placed on the microprocessor system. If the number of individual elements of the display requiring service becomes large, the provision of a sufficient number of output ports will be uneconomical. The aternative of a multiplexing scheme using a single output part with a display refreshment cycle of about $\frac{1}{30}$ sec under the control of the microprocessor is likely to place an inconvenient burden on microprocessor time and will complicate programming.

These difficulties can be avoided by using a self-supporting display having a private memory that can maintain a display of arbitrary complexity. Such a self-supporting display requires only occasional intervention from the microprocessor when an entry is to be changed and otherwise will carry the display quite independently of the microprocessor operation.

For the system under consideration, a display consisting of 16 decimal numerals will be described. Figure VIII-2 is a schematic diagram of the arrangement of such a display. Display information is maintained in a private RAM having 16 words of 4 bits. Each word is a mirror of one of the numerals. The numerals themselves are seven-segment LED devices requiring a decoding step to accommodate 4-bit (BCD) data. To reduce the cost of operation, the decoding is multiplexed to the 16 seven-segment numerals. The inputs of a 7447 seven-segment decoder are connected to the 7489 16-word RAM and accept the RAM data as they are called by RAM address. As the diagram shows, the 7489 outputs are complementary to the data inputs. (If software complementing of the data is inconvenient, hardware inverters could be installed in the display data lines.)

The 7489 RAM input is served by four data lines and four address lines; a total of 8 bits for each word identified. A single output word from the microprocessor thus can be used to convey both the display address and the display word in a single data transfer.

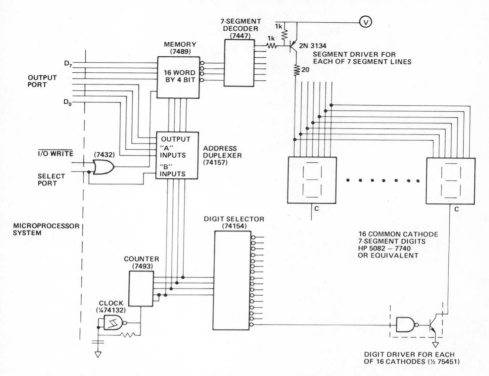

Figure VIII-2 Self-supporting multiplexed display system consisting of sixteen 7-segment numeral displays. Data may be entered in the display asynchronously from an unlatched output port.

In the operation of the display, a 7493 address counter is driven by the clocking circuit at a modest rate of about 10,000 steps/sec. Its output provides a 4-bit address to the 7489. The same 4-bit code is applied to the numeral selector (74154), maintaining a one-to-one correspondence between the selected memory output word and the numeral to which it is directed. Thus the RAM, when loaded with the mirror of the desired display, furnishes the necessary data that are suitably distributed to the numerals. Since higher peak currents are necessary in the pulsed operation, both the numeral encoder and the numeral selector are furnished with power buffers as shown in the figure.

With a display auxiliary constructed along the lines of the circuit in Fig. VIII-2, the burden of display maintenance on the microprocessor subsystem including its software is small, leaving it more freedom for other tasks. The specific display described is relatively simple and inexpensive. With imaginative programming it can satisfy a surprisingly wide range of display needs. More comprehensive display systems could, of course, be devised along the same lines.

C. Instrument Control

A primary use of the microprocessor subsystem is the control of the physical instrument to be automated. In this function, it can relieve both operator attention and instrument complexity. For satisfactory operation, the conventional instrument requires controls and indicators, which are sometimes elaborate and costly. It also requires considerable attention from an operator for tasks that are only indirectly productive. In a microprocessor-operated system, many of the tasks that can be explicitly defined can be carried out automatically. In particular, control of instrument operation is a suitable function to assign to the microprocessor subsystem.

A measurement cycle is ideally carried out by the execution of a standard program of events. The generalized spectrometer, for example, elicits values for a dependent variable upon the programmed variation of an independent variable. The independent variable of the spectrometer may be wavelength, and the program may be to establish a succession of small equal increments of this variable. The physical variable in the instrument, for example, a prism or a grating angle, frequently is *not* linearly related to the wavelength. This does not pose a serious problem in a microprocessor-operated system since the functional or empirical relationship between angle and wavelength can be taken into account in the software of the system.

The task of instrument control in this case reduces to the issuance of a succession of commands from the microprocessor subsystem to the physical instrument via an instrument interface to cause the desired program of events to take place. The format of these commands is necessarily electrical and digital at the microprocessor subsystem output. Suitable devices exist to translate the digital signals to the appropriate physical variable. Analog electrical signals (voltage or current) are often suitable physical variables. For these requirements, digital control words are presented to digital-to-analog converters (DACs). A wide choice of excellent DACs is offered by a number of manufacturers. A brief description of DACs is given in Chapter IX.

Another class of devices provides a direct conversion from digital commands to nonelectrical physical variables. One such device is the stepping motor, which advances its rotor by a known fraction of a turn in response to appropriate exciting pulses presented to its input, at rates up to hundreds of steps per second. Such a stepping motor, with appropriate reduction gearing can, for example, turn the dispersing device of the spectrometer through very small and precisely known increments of angle. In the simplest terms the microprocessor subsystem could control the instrument simply by issuing the correct sequence of pulses to the stepping motor as a function of time to perform a linear scan of wavelength.

In practice, this mode of control might represent an inappropriate preoccupation for the microprocessor, leaving less capacity for other functions. Figure VIII-3 shows a possible alternative to this in which the digital interface includes a specialized instrument controller.

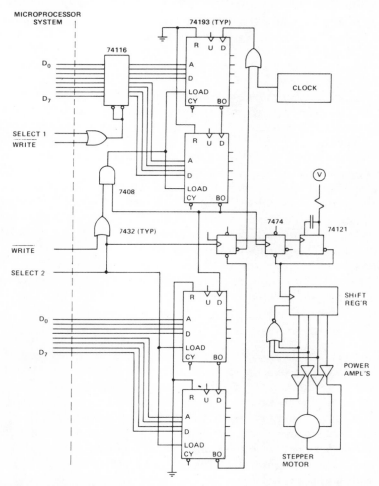

Figure VIII-3 Stepper motor controller having internal provision to control stepping rate and total number of steps.

The required function of the controller is defined to be to advance the independent variable uniformly with time. To accomplish this, time is divided into suitably small uniform intervals τ. For each τ, a known number of motor steps k_m is required to advance the sweep of the independent variable in a linear fashion. Since the k_m may be different for successive intervals and the intervals τ themselves are constant, the rate R_m at which pulses are required varies in accordance with the following formula:

$$R_m = k_m/\tau$$

The controller includes an oscillator operating at a fixed frequency f. Dividing this frequency by an integer N_m will produce a rate R'_m close to R_m if

$$R'_m = f/N_m; \quad N_m = f\tau/k_m$$

Given k_m, the microprocessor computes R_m by the formula above, and for each interval τ both k_m and N_m are issued at output ports as shown in the figure. (N_m is rounded off on the low side making R'_m slightly higher than R_m.)

The control cycle is initiated by a 1-bit control actuation at the beginning of an interval τ. At this point, N_m is loaded into a latch providing the input to a presettable counter (C_1 in the figure), and k_m is loaded into the presettable counter C_2. Counter C_1 counts down until it reaches zero, whereupon a pulse sequence is issued to the stepper motor. C_1 is reloaded and the countdown is resumed. The rate of the pulses is R'_m. The pulses themselves are counted down against the preload in counter C_2. When C_2 reaches zero, the k_m pulses will have been issued, and the time τ will have almost lapsed, leaving just time enough to load the output ports for the next interval. (The remaining time is

$$(k_m/R_m) - (k_m/R'_m)$$

and if this is insufficient, as would be known ahead of time, N_m could be made one unit smaller to furnish the additional time. In fact, the maximum stepping speed of the stepper motor is such that there will always be sufficient time.)

Since the number of steps k_m is by definition an integer, and the microprocessor can count the cumulative steps, there is no cumulative error in the progress of the sweep. Suitable choice of gear reduction and the length of τ allows matching the independent variable control characteristic as precisely as may be desired.

Clearly, there are numerous other ways in which independent variable control could be obtained. The purpose for including a specialized controller is to reduce the throughput requirements levied on the microprocessor subsystem. If even updating the controller, places an excessive burden on the microprocessor, even more of the control process could be taken over by a more elaborate controller. The contrary case, where slow stepping suffices, can be handled directly in the microprocessor subsystem with no more than a 1-bit control line in the interface, the computed time between steps being determined by reference to a real time clock.

A moment's reflection will demonstrate that the specialized controller described is the hardware implementation of an algorithm that could be incorporated in the software for direct microprocessor subsystem control of the stepper motor.

D. Data Acquisition

The results of the instrument operation—values of the dependent variable—are generated by the instrument as physical quantities that are usually expressed in the analog output of some detector. The output may be accumulated at discrete intervals, or it may be continuous. The microprocessor subsystem can manage only digital information presented in discrete elements or samples. Therefore, the output of the instrument detector must be organized into a series of discrete values that can be converted into digital form. This is not a serious limitation even when the instrument output is continuous since the sampling interval can be made as small as necessary.

Conversion of analog electrical signals to digital number expressions is accomplished by analog-to-digital converters that are offered by a number of manufacturers. Nonelectrical physical quantities can be converted to analog electrical form (voltage or current), thereby making it possible to use ADCs for general-purpose analog data acquisition by the microprocessor subsystem. Several representative ADC schemes are described in Chapter IX.

The specific handling of the instrument output is of crucial importance to the quality of the results. Since a sampling scheme is required, great care must be exercised in the choice of sampling methods and sampling intervals in order not to degrade the information present. A typical data acquisition scheme is shown in Fig. VIII-4a. In this illustration, the physical variable is assumed to be an electrical quantity (current). The value of the current may be determined by observing the potential difference it develops in a resistance according to Ohm's law:

$$V = IR$$

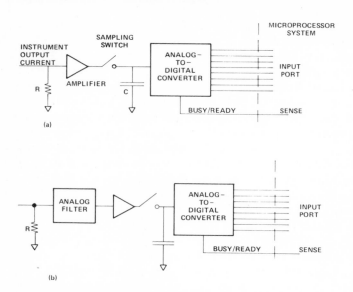

Figure VIII-4 Acquisition schemes to digitize analog electrical signals: (a) direct sampling; (b) sampling via an analog filter to reduce the effect of noise.

A circuit can be devised, as symbolized in the figure by the capacitor and switch, to sample this voltage at a specified time and "hold" the sample for the short interval required for conversion to digital form by an ADC. After conversion, the digital datum is accepted by the microprocessor subsystem at an input port, and at a later time, the sample and hold circuit takes another sample for the process to repeat.

The amplifier in the circuit is primarily present to isolate the holding capacitor from the information source. This is particularly necessary when very small currents are involved, since otherwise the capacitor would cause the response to be unacceptably slow.

It is readily apparent that without further consideration the sampling method could cause a serious degradation of data for two principal reasons. First, the sampling device acquires a sample value of the instrument output during a very short interval. Signal at the instrument output is always accompanied by noise, and instantaneous sampling cannot distinguish noise from signal. Second, significant changes of signal occurring while the sampling switch is open could be missed. The latter problem is conceptually easy to resolve. If the time between samples is short when compared with the minimum time in which significant signal changes occur, information will not be lost.

The situation is not so clear in the matter of noise. In the simple system shown, the signal is actually observed for a very small fraction of the time that it is present. If the analog signal channel is wide band, the signal-to-noise (voltage) could be degraded, at best, to the square root of that fraction. This problem can be avoided if the analog signal is filtered to a narrow band prior to being sampled. The scope of the present discussion does not permit a detailed analysis of signal-to-noise questions. If the signal is accumulated in the analog section and the noise is averaged for times somewhat longer than the interval between samples (as by an analog filter), it is plausible that the sampling process will not seriously degrade the signal-to-noise furnished in the analog output of the instrument. The addition of such a filter is shown in Fig. VIII-4b.

To preclude reading data while a conversion is taking place, the ADC provides a 1-bit BUSY/READY signal on a single line. This line may be queried by the microprocessor subsystem as a sense input, and reading the input port may be delayed until the ADC signals ready.

The data acquisition process includes not only the hardware, described in a simple form above, but also the means to organize the data acquired, which is a function of software design and memory management. It cannot be described in particular terms without reference to a specific problem. However, the capacity of the microprocessor to sort data rapidly can be used to good advantage to organize data tables in a convenient way prior to the actual processing of the data. One example of the planning that can be applied to data management is the use of the memory address structure for assigning data matrix indexes.

Any accumulation of data in memory is, of course, simply a serial string of numbers. However, it may be appropriate to arrange the data in a two-dimensional array such that the row and column numbers classify the individual data. For example, it may be suitable to organize the data into 14 rows of 29 columns. These data could simply be entered serially; but later convenience could be considerably enhanced if a table is begun at a cardinal address XXXXXXX000000000. In the matrix scheme, the last five bits of address, YYYYY may always be used to select the matrix column, omitting the addresses

XXXXXXXXXXX11111,
XXXXXXXXXXX11110,
XXXXXXXXXXX11101.

The row designations begin with XXXXXXX0000YYYYY and continue through XXXXXXX1101YYYYY. Although a few address spaces are skipped (and could in fact be used for other storage), programming can be simplified, and the overall efficiency in the program can be considerably enhanced with such a scheme, when processing is performed a row at a time.

E. Data Processing

One of the more powerful aids that a microprocessor subsystem can furnish to a system is the processing of data from the instrument. This enormous subject merits its own text, and just a few examples will be given here for illustration. Data processing generally involves the application of one or more arithmetic or logical steps. The most elaborate data processing, in the end, can and must be reduced to elementary steps.

One simple example, frequently encountered in applications to instrument, is a base line or background correction to the results of a measurement. Typically, the true data are superimposed on a background signal level that simply may be a known characteristic of the instrument, or a known background of real information that is irrelevant and even confusing to the particular measurement being made. Where the background signal is known (and stored) for each point in a data table, the microprocessor can perform a subtraction and thereby generate a new table of data with the background deleted.

Another process that is often required is the location of turning points in the quantity represented by the data. The simplest algorithm for this process is the successive subtraction of the value of the data point immediately preceding. Changes in algebraic sign of the differences signal the turning points. This process may be applied, for example, to locate peaks in a spectrum.

The presence of any noise accompanying the signal will cause the simple subtraction algorithm to define turning points or peaks that are nonexistent. There are many methods used to minimize false peak detections. The simplest is perhaps to establish a threshold level such that detections triggered by noise are largely distinguishable from those due to real signal variation. More elaborate processing will generally be selected on the basis of the particular problem being treated. Digital filtering of the data prior to application of the turning-point test can be used. A program that would provide an exponential filter, such as that described in Chapter VII, Section VII-4, might be suitable. Even with filtering, it may be necessary to establish threshold criteria to screen the detection of turning points.

Various other methods have also been devised, including the computation of second derivatives to be used in conjunction with the first derivatives found by simple subtractions. The more elaborate programs are often successful only in particular cases, by virtue of taking advantage from some special characteristic of the data for such cases.

Numerical integration and data correlation are processes that are also frequently applied. In addition, many specific computations such as determining mean values and variances, interpolations, functional computations, and a host of other processes may be used in instrument programs, both for reducing data and for instrument control.

F. Display

Because the microprocessor can transfer information at very high rates, it can service a variety of display devices. The chart recorder and the standard laboratory cathode-ray oscilloscope are classical display devices for instruments. Both can easily serve in microprocessor-operated systems with the help of one or more DACs. A variety of digit or character displays and printers are also accessible in a very direct way to the output of the microprocessor with communication in ASCII or other coding. Many commercially available displays and printers require a special interface that provides for bit-serial transmission of data. The standard teletypewriters fall into this category.

Display systems can be almost as diverse as the system problems they illuminate, and a good display concept and design is extremely important to the utility of the system. An example of a simple display system consisting of 16 decimal digits was described above. An even simpler one could be made using just patterns of individual lights turned on and off in recognizable patterns.

A more complex display device using a cathode-ray tube (CRT), which is rapidly coming into general use, is very similar to a television receiver. It generates an image by scanning the entire picture screen with an electron beam that is rapidly switched on and off to form light and dark areas. The tracery of the beam is called a raster. This display device is appealing because it is versatile and can be inexpensive since a conventional television set can be used for the visual output. A display system based on the standard television raster and adaptable to a commercial television set will be described.

The data stream to the television display is a serial string of perhaps one-quarter of a million bits, transferred in $\frac{1}{30}$ sec. This is a large number even by microprocessor standards. However, the perceptual span of the user cannot possibly cope with the potential information content of 250,000 bits. For reasons of economy, it is appropriate to reduce substantially the number of bits used to transfer information. A very large quantity of intelligible information that can be displayed is represented by a screen filled with readable characters—letters, numbers and symbols. The visual resolution of the screen will permit perhaps 32 lines of 32 characters requiring 6 or 7 bits to define each character. This represents a somewhat more than practical maximum for a standard television display using a 7×9 character matrix. Reduction of the total number of characters improves readability. This information may be held in less than 10,000 bits, a much more manageable number than one-quarter million. To be sure, the remaining 240,000 bits must be generated for the operation of the display, but the generation of the other 96% of the total bits used can be automatic in a properly designed system.

To give an example of this concept, Fig. VIII-5 shows how the symbol of the letter R can be made up of 63 bits of information using a 7×9 dissection of points in the symbol. The complete information contained in the symbol R, in the ASCII font containing upper case letters, numbers, and symbols, can be characterized with only 6 bits. The actual formulation of the 63 bits required for the display of the symbol is drawn from an encoding device 7 bits at a time using the 6-bit selection code and a 4-bit line address. The encoding device is actually a $64 \times 9 \times 7$ bit ROM programmed for the display of the

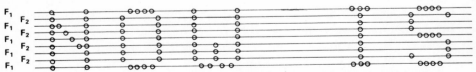

(a) BIT PATTERN FOR THE LETTER "R" GENERATED BY THE SIGNETICS TYPE 2526 CM3941. THE SQUARES MARKED X ARE USED FOR AN ALTERNATE CODE CONVERSION.

(b) RASTER SCAN FOR A LINE OF CHARACTERS SHOWING INTERLACED FIELDS F_1 AND F_2

Figure VIII-5   (a) Bit pattern for the letter "R" generated by the Signetics-type 2526 CM3941. The squares marked X are used for an alternate code conversion. (b) Raster scan for a line of characters showing interlaced fields F_1 and F_2.

Completion of the character row count initiates a field overhead delay of 70 lines. The counter for this delay is arranged as a 5×14 counter for purposes of generating the US NTSC vertical synchronization pattern. The collection of type D flip-flops and gates generates the necessary synchronizing and blanking signals. The horizontal blanking signal must be delayed by one character count due to the fact that the character data are loaded into the shift register at the count of nine. (The character count begins with address zero to the display RAM address duplexer in order that the microprocessor be able to identify the beginning of each line with a cardinal address.) Vertical blanking is accommodated at the normal time for the television raster. No signals are transferred from the shift register while the horizontal and vertical margins are being traversed.

For more general graphic constructions, the character encoding ROM and its character-identifying RAM could be replaced by a larger RAM. This, when loaded by the microprocessor, could then be used to display more general symbols and pictorial representations. The design and programming of such a system, other than simply assigning one bit to every point on the screen is an interesting challenge.

IX

Interface Devices
and Auxiliary Circuits

Some mention was made in Chapter VIII of digital-to-analog (DAC) and analog-to-digital (ADC) converters. These are members of a class of devices that stand between the digital microprocessor subsystem and a generally analog world. To deal with quantities that are often not even electrical in nature, various conversion devices are required. In addition, even where information transfer is digital, it is often useful to provide auxiliary logic circuits that reduce the throughput load in the microprocessor and the complexity of its software. For example, the television controller, described in Chapter VIII, handles an almost mindlessly repetitive task that the microprocessor by itself would be unable to manage. The importance of these devices and auxiliaries warrants a more detailed description of some examples.

IX-1 THE DIGITAL-TO-ANALOG CONVERTER

Digital-to-analog converters, in the main, are devices whose output is an analog current or voltage, of a quantity proportional to the value of a digital number presented to their inputs. Both voltage and current DACs are fundamentally based on programmable current generators

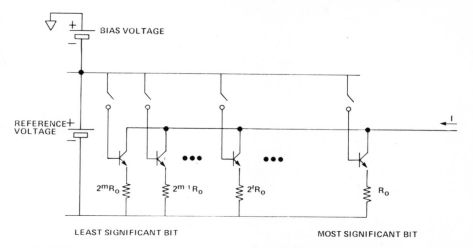

Figure IX-1 Representative scheme for a digital-to-analog converter designed to generate a current proportional to the value of a binary word.

that provide a source or sink of current at a circuit node. Figure IX-1 is the schematic diagram of a generic programmable current sink. In this circuit, each transistor acts like an open switch when its base is disconnected. When a transistor base is connected to the reference voltage, a current I_l flows at its collector such that

$$I_l \cong V_{\mathrm{REF}}/2^l R_0$$

where $2^l R_0$ is the resistance at the emitter. The value is only approximate since a small voltage is required to overcome the barrier of the transistor emitter base junction, and part of the current flowing in the emitter enters via the base. The total output current flowing (within the compliance range of the transistors) is for an $(M + 1)$-digit DAC (approximately)

$$I \cong \frac{V_{\mathrm{ref}}}{R_0} \sum_{l=0}^{l=M} \frac{D_l}{2^l}$$

where D_l is the digit value of the lth place, being either 0 or 1. A bias voltage, shown symbolically in the figure, is usually incorporated to extend the compliance range of the output transistors to include levels below ground potential.

Where a programmable current sink is required, the circuit of Fig. IX-1 can be used directly. If a voltage is required, the circuit may be supplemented by the inclusion of an operational amplifier (Fig. IX-2).

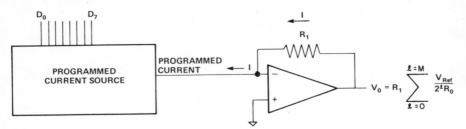

Figure IX-2 Ditial-to-analog converter employing an operational amplifier to deliver a voltage output.

The property of an operational amplifier with a negative feedback resistor R_f, connected as shown, is to adjust its output voltage so that the difference of voltage between its two inputs is (practically) zero. Thus, in the circuit of Fig. IX-2, at the amplifier input, $V(-) = V(+) = 0$, and, since the amplifier input draws (practically) no current, the output voltage is given by

$$V_0 = IR_f - 0$$

which in this case is a positive voltage proportional to I. For negative output voltage, transistors of inverted polarity (PNP) could be used in the DAC to provide a current source rather than a sink. In this case, the operational amplifier output voltage would be negative

$$V_0 = 0 - IR_f$$

Commercial DACs use various types of switches and resistor networks to provide current sources or sinks. Considerable emphasis is necessarily placed on accuracy, linearity, monotonicity, and stability of the result. Units can be specified to a precision of 16 bits or one part in 65,536. DACs with 8- or 10-bit precision can be purchased for relatively low cost, about $20.00. High-precision DACs are considerably more expensive.

IX-2 THE ANALOG-TO-DIGITAL CONVERTER

Analog-to-digital converters are somewhat more complex than DACs. The purpose of their operation is to match an input voltage (or current) with a binary number such that equal increments of the input voltage elicit equal increments of that binary number, and such that an input of zero is matched by a fiducial number, usually zero. Various schemes for matching are used, each having certain advantages. ADC implementations are usually provided with sample and hold circuits either internally or externally (see Fig. VIII-5). This provision precludes the complication of a moving target voltage to be matched. In addition, it allows very precise timing for the sampling process. In the following discussion, the presence of a sample and hold device is tacitly assumed.

One example of an ADC is the so-called *dual-slope converter*. This device converts cyclically, as do most other types of ADC. Its basis for operation is the charge and discharge of a capacitor, where one state of charge, usually zero, can be detected with great precision. Figure IX-3 shows the arrangement of components and the scheme of conversion. The cycle begins with a state of zero charge on the capacitor, assured by the short-circuiting switch S_1. Upon receipt of a start command, the following sequence of events takes place:

1. ADC "busy" line is set true by Q of $U_1(A)$.
2. The transition of Q OF $U_1(A)$ causes a short positive pulse to be formed by the combination of the inverter and the gate connected to it due to the delay in the inverter. This pulse resets the counter chain to zero.

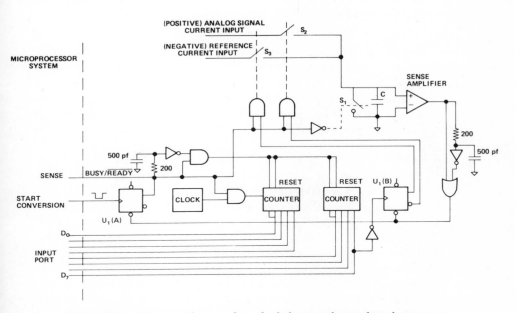

Figure IX-3 Schematic diagram for a dual-slope analog-to-digital converter.

3. At the same time, the clock pulses are admitted to the counter, and counting is begun.

4. In addition, switch S_1 is opened and S_2 is closed, allowing current to flow and charge the capacitor.

5. While the count continues, the analog input current charges the capacitor at a uniform rate, such that its terminal voltage is given by

$$\frac{dV_c}{dt} = \frac{I_{in}}{C}; \quad V_c = \int \frac{I_{in}}{C} dt$$

6. At the time that the counter overflows (all bits zero again) $U_1(B)$ goes from reset to set.

7. When Q of $U_1(B)$ becomes high (and $\overline{Q}$ becomes low), switch S_2 is opened, and switch S_3 is closed.

8. The capacitor now discharges at a fixed rate determined by I_{ref}. This rate is slightly greater (in the discharge sense) than the maximum charging rate encountered during the analog-signal input phase.

9. When the capacitor voltage reaches zero, the condition is detected by the sense amplifier.

10. The output of the sense amplifier resets $U_1(A)$ and $U_1(B)$ completing the cycle. "BUSY" is replaced by "READY," and the counter stops. The output of the counter is the digitally converted value for the analog current in. S_2 and S_3 are opened, and S_1 is closed.

Figure IX-4 shows the capacitor voltage, plotted as a function of time. By similiar triangles, the times, BC are proportional to the peak voltages developed by the input currents during (equal) times AB. The counter measures BC, and hence the count when V_c reaches zero is proportional to the input current. The dual-slope ADC is quite precise using good switches and stable components of nominal value, with no need for precise trimming. It is, however a relatively slow device.

A second example of an ADC is the *successive approximation* type. This ADC makes use of an internal DAC whose output is compared with the input in a succession of trials, beginning with the most significant bit (MSB). Figure IX-5 shows the scheme by which the conversion is made. At the signal to convert, a single pulse is entered into the parallel-output shift register; shown here with 8 bits. The rather complicated looking circuit of gates and type D flip-flops at the bottom of the figure is present to allow an asynchronous arrival of the start pulse. Its operation is first to clear the shift register, which should be clear anyway, and then to clear the storage latches, which, in general, will not be clear. At the same time, it sets the "BUSY" line, indicating that

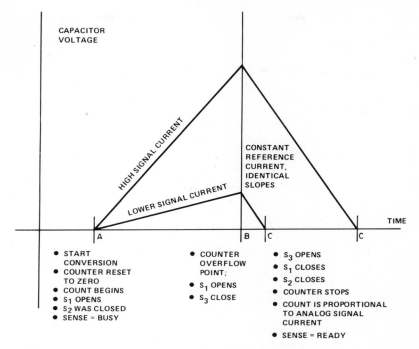

Figure IX-4 Representation of capacitor voltage and events in a dual-slope analog-to-digital conversion cycle.

ambiguous data are present at the data terminals. Following the clearing pulse, which occupies a half clock cycle, the serial input of the shift register is held high long enough to inject a single high state into the shift register. This operation is completed at the end of the second half clock cycle.

After this initialization sequence the single high state is moved down the shift register by successive clock pulses. At each shift register terminal, the upward transition occurring with the arrival of the single high state at that terminal, sets a corresponding latch in the output register. This latch places a test bit in the DAC, and a comparison of the DAC sinking current to the incoming current is made. If the DAC sinking current is higher than the input, the sense amplifier clears the latch for that bit; otherwise the latch remains in the high state. With each successive clock pulse, the same sequence is applied for each successively lower bit until the eighth place, (the least significant bit (LSB), is reached. This bit also is appropriately adjusted in the output register, whereupon the last shift register output is used to

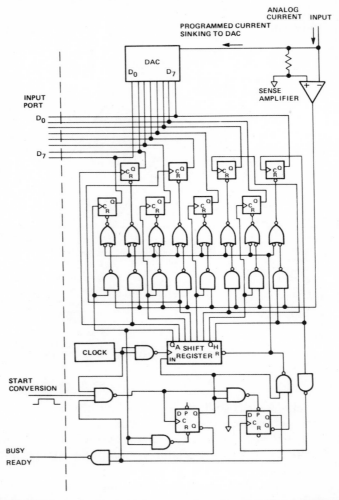

Figure IX-5 Schematic diagram of a successive approximation analog-to-digital converter.

reset the initializing devices and to set the "busy" line low. The data in the output register are unambiguous at this point and can be read at any time.

A third type of ADC, namely, the *tracking* ADC, which is particularly adapted to convert smoothly varying inputs, is sometimes used. This ADC is comprised of an up/down counter, a DAC, and an analog voltage comparison device. The scheme of its operation may be

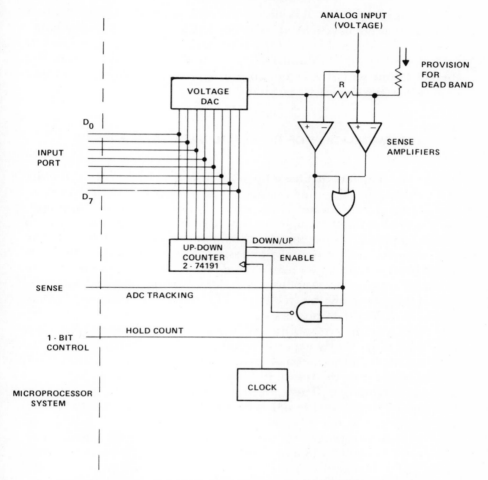

Figure IX-6 Schematic diagram of a tracking analog-to-digital converter.

described by reference to Fig. IX-6. So long as the analog input differs from the DAC output, the counter is able to count, up or down as the case may require, thereby to bring the DAC output closer to the analog input. The analog voltage comparison device is furnished with a dead band slightly greater than the voltage corresponding to the LSB when the DAC output matches the analog input as closely as it can.

When a displacement of the input occurs, the tracking ADC can follow it up to the full clock rate, and, if the displacement is small, it is a faster device than the dual-slope ADC. On the other hand, for large excursions of the input, it is slower than the successive approximation ADC. It does not have a fixed "conversion time." The "ADC tracking" line may be engaged most of the time, and it should be used (or not) with this in mind to inhibit reading. For slowly varying inputs, the digital output will always be close to a measure of the actual input even while the device is tracking.

IX-3 ACCOMMODATION OF BIT-SERIAL DATA TRANSMISSION

The data transfers that have been discussed so far involve primarily the transfer of 1 byte (for example, 8 bits) in parallel. Certain data-transfer requirements and some important devices are more appropriately served with bit-serial transmission over a single pair of lines or a single communications channel. Some of the devices used antedate the extensive use of digital processing. For one example, the telegraph passes information over a single channel with a rather complicated bit-serial code. Another early device using bit-serial transmission is the teletypewriter (teletype). This device has been used extensively in digital data processing systems. It allows a means of entry and display with a versatility to cover almost any requirement. (It is also slow, noisy, fairly expensive and sometimes cranky.)

Of necessity, all serial transmission devices must use some stylized means of ordering the transmitted bits so that they may be sorted out at the receiving end. This ordering is usually arranged to group the bits into bytes of equal length with some means to designate the first bit in a byte. The teletype, for example, creates blocks 11 units long. Its idle state is represented by a closed switch through which a current is impressed on the line. The beginning of a byte block is always signaled by the opening of this switch for one unit of time, after which the switch is closed and opened to communicate a sequence of bits, always concluding with a closed switch for two units of time.

Figure IX-7 shows a few of the teletype signal patterns, plotted to show a closed- or open-switch condition. The time occupied by each bit is approximately 9.1 msec. The first interval is always signaled by an open switch and is appropriately called the start signal. It is followed by seven intervals in which the sequence of open or closed condition constitutes the character code. The ninth interval may be used to denote the parity of the preceding code, signifying whether the sum of the open-switch intervals is odd or even. It is often simply left as a closed-switch interval. The $2^7 = 128$ codes are individually assigned to characters, numbers, symbols, and a number of non-

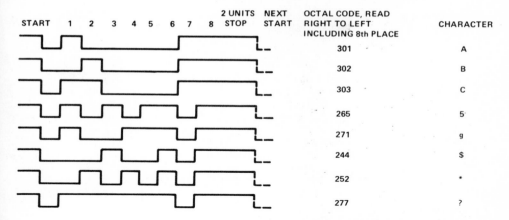

START	1	2	3	4	5	6	7	8	2 UNITS STOP	NEXT START	OCTAL CODE, READ RIGHT TO LEFT INCLUDING 8th PLACE	CHARACTER
											301	A
											302	B
											303	C
											265	5
											271	9
											244	$
											252	*
											277	?

Figure IX-7 Pulse timing sequences for teletypewriter serial codes. Each cycle consists of 11 equal steps occupying a total time of 100 msec.

printing functions in conformance with the ASCII code. The teletype itself uses only alphabet capitals, although codes can be assigned to the lower case alphabet.

The code is adapted to truncations from 7 to 6 bits for designation of characters, numbers, and symbols. This modification was used for the television controller described in Chapter VIII. (When the truncated code is used, the seventh bit must be artificially reconstructed for data transmission to the teletype.)

A detailed description of interface devices for serial/parallel conversion such as the teletype is beyond the scope of this book. The general scheme makes use of shift registers and control circuits patterned after the scheme shown in Fig. IX-8. The two-way transmission circuits in this scheme are two current loops in which current is appropriately interrupted during data transfer.

The currents may be broken either by the interface or by the serial data device. In serial-to-parallel conversion, the interface monitors the receiving current loop via the isolating relay $K1$. The opening of the start interval switch by the serial data device initiates a sequence of clock pulses (nine for the teletype) that advance bit positions in a shift register. The serial input terminal of the shift register is also connected to the contacts of K1, and the open or closed state of the line is thereby impressed serially into the shift register and shifted down the line at each clock pulse. The clock pulses must be timed to the sending rate to better than about 5% for unambiguous data assembly. However, since each sequence of pulses is initiated by the sending

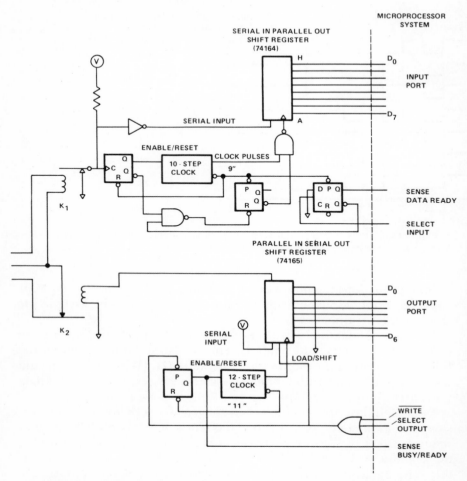

Figure IX-8 Schematic diagram of a scheme for bit serial data transfers adapted to the teletype format.

source, there is no cumulative effect of clock-rate error. When the byte is fully shifted into the register; a data ready state is set to advise the parallel reading device that a new byte is present. The reading process resets the data ready line to prevent repeated reading of the same entry.

For parallel-to-serial conversion, the process described above is reversed. Parallel data are loaded into a shift register and shifted out serially, opening and closing the transmitting current loop, according to the bit pattern, via the isolating relay *K*2. Of course, the first step of this sequence is always to open the current loop.

Design and construction of a serial/parallel interface with standard SSI and MSI devices is straightforward, if somewhat complex and tedious. Happily, there are LSI devices available that perform all of the functions required. These are called universal asynchronous receiver transmitters (UARTs). Examples include the MM5303 by the National Semiconductor Corporation; the S1757 by American Microsystems, Inc.; and the UC1671 by Western Digital Corporation. When serial data transmission is contemplated, the use of one of these or of a similar device is recommended in preference to a design with SSI and MSI devices.

In addition to the teletype, casette tape recorders and some CRT terminals rely on bit-serial data management. Speeds of transmission vary from device to device. Interfacing can be accomodated by UARTs.

IX-4 ELECTROMECHANICAL DEVICES

A great variety of electromechanical devices can be operated and read by microprocessor systems using simple interface arrangements. Many of these involve the transmission of only 1 bit. A few of the devices, including some that have been mentioned before are listed below:

Switches The state of a switch, open or closed, can be monitored via a sense line. The switch can be mechanically operated or it can be a relay contact.

Relays Relays to control larger currents than can be accomodated with ordinary logic outputs can be actuated by 1-bit output lines.

Motors Motors can be started or stopped by the control of 1-bit output lines. Some form of power amplifier is usually required.

Stepping motors A stepping motor requires a pattern of pulses for each increment of shaft rotation. It can be actuated by the appropriate pattern impressed on suitable output lines. The change in shaft position can be accurately prescribed by a count of the pulses issued.

Mechanical encoders   Linear and rotational shaft encoders are provided with digital patterns in a one-to-one correspondence with the position to be encoded. The patterns may be "read" by photo cells or contacts and transmitted via an input port to the microprocessor.

Servo systems   Open- and closed-loop servo systems can be operated by a microprocessor system via input and output ports. In a closed-loop system, the error signal is received in the microprocessor system at an input port and processed in accordance with an appropriate control function; the correction signal is then transmitted to the servo via an output port.

IX-5   ISOLATION DEVICES

It is frequently necessary to isolate a microprocessor system electrically from some of its peripheral devices for reasons other than just the limited power levels that it can accomodate. Two examples typify such isolation requirements. First, the peripheral device to be controlled may be supplied with power at a high voltage level that could be far too great for the integrated circuits to accomodate. Second, peripheral devices such as sensitive detectors and low-level controllers may be susceptible to electrical noise picked up and conveyed by sensing and controlling lines. The desirable or necessary isolation can be provided in several ways and is particularly facilitated by the digital format of the data.

One simple means of isolation is the relay. The relay contacts can be insulated and even electrostatically shielded from the electromagnet that actuates them. The relay can also provide power gain to operate large switches if necessary. It is, however a relatively slow device, and the contacts are prone to bounce for a few milliseconds before complete closure or opening. The relay is certainly a digital device in the sense that, in the long term, its terminals are unambiguously either closed or open; thus, it is well adapted to digital data transfer.

The optical isolator, a more compact and much higher speed device, has been in use for some years in digital systems. In this device the light from a solid-state LED is coupled via an insulating optically transparent medium to a diode photocell or a phototransistor. When the light is on, the photocell or the phototransistor generates an electrically detectable state, thereby providing the means for the transmission of a bit with very good electrical isolation. Although the signal levels are at low power, these devices are very reliable and are not subject to ambiguity equivalent to contact bounce in relays. Moreover, they are capable of switching rates of 10^6/sec or more and thus lend themselves well to the transmission of digital data at microprocessor rates. Electrical isolation to 1000 V is commonly specified, and electrical noise isolation can be very substantial.

X

An Exercise Design for a Microprocessor Automated Instrument System

This last chapter is written to suggest and guide an exercise in the design of a complete digitally automated system whose specific function and structure will be in the mind and eye of the reader. For a digitally automated system of even a modest complexity, the quality of the results, and the utility, convenience, and the economy of operation favor use of one or more microprocessors. The text will outline the steps in the design process and will suggest structural form and parts, by way of example only, as guides in the readers design, and will not attempt to restrain the design in any way. When the text is specific, it is only to avoid a vague or clumsy discussion.

The design process begins with the definition of the objective of the system. An example of a nontrivial system is one that is directed to the analysis of samples of material containing more than one component. Means to perform such an analysis are found in one or more instruments whose application to the analytical problems should be well understood.

In an attempt not to imply too rigid a definition of a system to influence the reader's latitude of choice, the discussion will be structured in a general way. It will refer to an analytical system that uses two distinct instrumental processes, namely, a separatory process and an analytical process. The first process provides a partial or complete separation of the components of the sample, and the second identifies the individual fractions.

The operation of the system is specified by the description of its functions of instrument control, data acquisition, data processing, and display of results. When the problem has been defined and the instrumental means for its address have been chosen, design of the system can proceed. The primary design consideration must be to create the capability to generate valid results. Utility, with timeliness of results, economy, and convenience follow closely as important goals of the design. A well-executed automation design can promote these ends and serve also to unify the system.

X-1 THE OVERALL SYSTEM

The requirements of the system to be designed are to accommodate the individual needs of the instruments and other components which have been selected and to provide for the unity of their combination. In the final system, the instruments and components, themselves, may not be outspokenly visible. However, their function and modes of operation should be apparent in the input and output features of the system.

A. Control

Part of the control that is exercised involves operator-designated inputs to the system, either by detailed specification or mode selection. Automation can reduce the attention required of the operator by placing the details of control under programmed specification, requiring only a mode selection.

In the analytical system being used as an example, the separatory process is likely to require considerable environmental control. Difficult control sequences may be required to optimize each of several separatory procedures in the instrument's repertoire. Environmental control sequences, which would otherwise burden the operator, can conveniently be assigned to a microprocessor system by using suitable peripheral devices and software. Separate control programs, lodged in the software, can be assigned to each of several procedures, subject to call via a single-mode selection on the part of the operator.

Similarly, in the analysis of the separated fractions, several analytical procedures may be used, each requiring a separate control sequence. In the final analysis, the control of the instrument's operating parameters, such as sweep selection and the control of wavelength, frequency, or electric or magnetic fields, may be more important than environmental control. However, the need for control procedures parallels that of the separatory section, and several procedures can be lodged in the microprocessor software in like manner, to be accessed via simple mode selection and operated by microprocessor-controlled peripheral devices.

B. Data Acquisition and Processing

The execution of instrumental procedures results in the generation of new data, often in the form of analog electrical signals. These data must be acquired and processed, to a greater or lesser extent, by the system in order to formulate intelligible results.

As was suggested in earlier chapters, acquisition of the data requires, first of all, a conversion to digital form that will be accepted by a digital processing system. Beyond this requirement, the system design can be advantageously structured, to some degree, in deference to the data processing needs, just as an individual experiment may be designed to put data into a format that facilitates manual processing. Data formats can and should be designed with a view to their convenient management in the automated system. For a simple example of this concept, where possible, quantities should be expressed in binary rather than decimal numbers, and word lengths should be chosen to be easily divisible into byte-sized pieces. It may even be advantageous to structure data tables or matrices to dimensions expressible in integer powers of 2 for convenient addressing, so long as this does not put a strain on the experiment design.

Once acquired, via suitable analog-to-digital conversion, and structured into a suitable format, the data will require more or less processing depending on the nature of the problem and the instruments used. The form of this processing depends on the specifically selected system. The specification of data processing is largely a software specification. It is designed along the same lines as a manual data-reduction program would be, except that it has the very considerable advantage of the speed available with the microprocessor. This advantage can often furnish on-line processed data output. The timeliness of the results provided by on-line processing may even permit an operator to interact with a current procedure.

C. Display

The nature and complexity of the display depends, of course, on the objective and function of the system. Analysis of a sample, for example, must conclude with some sort of listing of the analytical findings. These may be both qualitative and quantitative. They may include probabilistic representations. They may be presented to include cues to the operator to call for additional processing steps or even to select additional analytical procedures to obtain further information.

Part of the display can also serve to monitor a variety of instrument-operating parameters, with particular emphasis on those that deviate from prescribed values. Although the operating system can be provided with automatic responses to these deviations, including aborting or correction of the procedures as the case may warrant, the display of monitor signals provides the operator with a valuable diagnostic tool and an opportunity to override certain decisions when appropriate.

D. Microprocessor Subsystem

The presence of a microprocessor subsystem is implicit in the discussion of this chapter so far. The overall design of this component is relatively straightforward and can follow the structure described in Chapter VII. The details of the organization of memory, buss structures, I/O facility, and the use of interrupts depend intimately on the specifics of the operational system under consideration.

The overall system design necessarily includes the blocking out of microprocessor subsystem details. This preliminary design step may be found to recommend some changes in the overall approach and is, thereby, a help in creating a unified design.

Little can be added here concerning the detailed design of the microprocessor subsystem, since it is fundamentally a general-purpose device. Specification of the particulars of the memory, buss structures, I/O, etc. should be considered an important part of the system design. Exercise 1 at the end of the chapter is structured to guide the overall design of the system. The sections following amplify the considerations pertinent to the design of major parts of the system.

X-2 INSTRUMENT CONTROL

Instrument control falls naturally into two categories, namely, the control of environmental factors, which serves the needs of the instrument and the control of the operational functions of the instrument, which serves the objective of its use. Examples of the former often include control of temperature, humidity, pressure, vacuum, electrical power, and the like; the latter are concerned with instrument control procedures that lead directly to objective results in the form of data.

A. Environmental Control

Control and monitoring of temperature are frequent requirements of the environment of an instrument and will be discussed in
this section as an example of typical environmental control. Simple
maintenance of temperature can be carried out with simple stand-
alone temperature controllers. Even in this case, automated monitoring may be important for authentication of the analytical results.
When programmed temperature control is required, particularly when
the temperature that is programmed interacts in some way with intermediate progress of the instrument operation, the use of the microprocessor is particularly advantageous.

Two approaches to implement temperature control and monitoring
are shown in Figs. X-1a and X-1b. The important elements of either
control scheme are a temperature sensor, a comparison device, and a
servo to drive the heater (or refrigerator) to bring the temperature of
the instrument element to a specifically scheduled value. In the first
scheme illustrated, the servo loop is closed in the controller itself,
comparison and servo drive being exercised without intervention of
the microprocessor, which simply issues the temperature command in
an open-loop sense. In the second scheme, the controller consists
solely of the sensor, the power servo, and the heater. In this case, the
microprocessor system is an active contributor to the closed-loop requirement for temperature control. Comparison of the actual temperature with its scheduled value takes place in the microprocessor, which
then issues power control commands to bring the temperature into
compliance with the prescribed schedule.

Each of these methods has its advantages. In a heavily loaded microprocessor, the added burden of serving the temperature controller
may impose unmanageable demands on its operating time. Notwith-
standing the extra loading of the microprocessor, it is worth considering its use in addressing the temperature-control design problem,
where speed of response and freedom from hunting or oscillation are
considered. If the error sensing and consequent generation of servo
command take place in the microprocessor, it can be programmed to
accommodate the dynamic properties of the thermal system. The
dynamic response of a closed-loop system depends on the filtering imposed on the signal that is fed back for control. In an analog controller,
the feedback filtering is provided by real physical components. A microprocessor used to close the feedback loop can be programmed to
furnish any desired filter characteristics, including those of a class of
filters that cannot be constructed in analog form with real components.
This versatility can lead to advantages in controller stability and
speed via flexibility in the software.

The considerations that have been described in terms of temperature control can also be applied to other areas of environmental control in the instrument. If there are many environmental factors requiring programmable control, and, if the primary microprocessor cannot cope with their service requirements, a separate simple microprocessor system with its own relatively small memory can provide sophisticated control and can process monitor signals before passing them on to the primary microprocessor system.

B. Procedural Control

The control of instrument function via procedures that, in the end, elicit the data to formulate the output often requires an elaborate scheduling of events. The use of digital control lends itself well to sequencing a complicated schedule in an accurate and timely manner. The microprocessor can accommodate the fundamental control requirements for instrument procedures that might otherwise call for difficult hardware design.

One considerable advantage of microprocessor control is found in what might be called software linearization and calibration. This concept is illustrated by an example of the sweep or scan of masses in a magnetic mass spectrometer, wherein the mass scale is proportional to the square root of the magnetic field applied. If the mass scale itself, to be taken as an abcissa, is to be linear, then a control function proportional to the square root of the mass must be generated. Analog square-root generators can be constructed, with some difficulty. However, a microprocessor can generate a square root with ease, and, using the quantity in a DAC can issue a control signal that will result in a linear sweep of mass.

Furthermore, if the control of the dispersing field in a mass spectrometer is via the magnet current, the magnetic field realized will not be strictly in proportion to the current because of saturation effects in its iron components. The correction that is required for the saturation effect is a part of the sweep calibration that can also be accommodated quite simply with digital control using a suitable correction table. The microprocessor may even generate its own correction table by using observations of known masses in a calibrating spectrum.

The interface between the microprocessor and the control of instrument procedures involves a suitable number of input and output ports and the necessary DAC devices. The burden of actual control may be shared between the microprocessor system and the interface element, with the microprocessor system maintaining supervisory control.

A control sequence requiring precise timing of a large number of events could be inconvenient to implement with a microprocessor

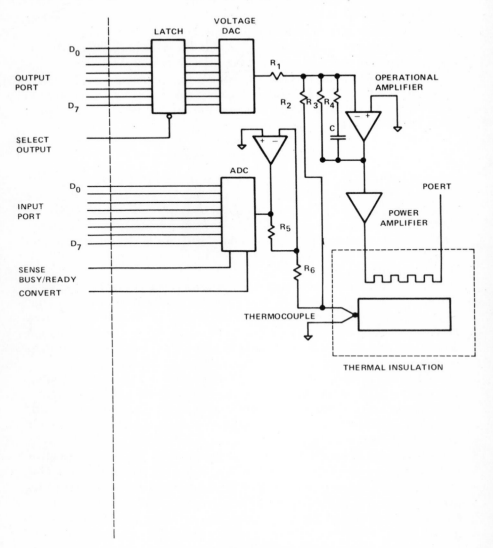

Figure X-1a

Figure X-1 (a) Self-contained temperature controller responsive to a temperature setting word entered from the microprocessor with provision for microprocessor monitoring. (b) Temperature controller scheme in which the control loop is closed via the microprocessor. (See facing page for Fig. X-1b.)

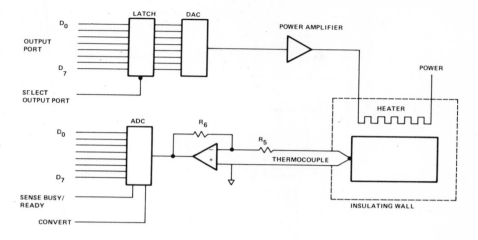

Figure X-1b

that is occupied with other functions. For example, to generate the sweep of an independent coordinate involves the issue of commands for a very large number of individual steps at precise intervals. Although the microprocessor can manage these commands when unburdened, it may be more convenient to lodge the stepping operation in a peripheral controller and require the microprocessor only to specify, for example, the starting point, the step size, the step time, and the total number of steps. This approach is more appropriate if the individual steps themselves require elaboration to control a number of parameters.

One approach to a simple digital controller able to handle and elaborate sequence is shown in Fig. X-2. This device requires only a 1-bit command from the microprocessor to sequence 64 events with an almost arbitrary elaboration of event timing. (The number and complexity of the events to be controlled is limited only by the size of the ROM used in the device.)

The operation of the controller in Fig. X-2 is cyclic and will usually include at least one stopping point. Its operating sequence and timing are governed by an internal clock; events are specified by bits stored in the ROM. In the example illustrated, the ROM stores 64 words of 16 bits. Assignment of functions to the individual bits begins with B_{15}. When this bit makes a transition from low to high, the clock is stopped

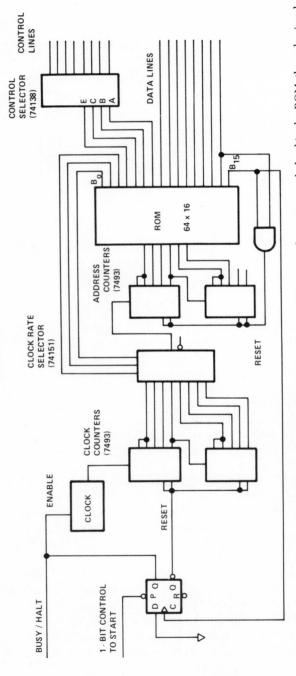

Figure X-2 Digital controller which is largely self-contained. Details of the control program are lodged in the ROM, the only signal required from the microprocessor being a start pulse.

in a high state, and the address counter is static. Words with B_{15} high define either idle or static states. (At least one word with B_{15} low must precede an idle or static state.) A single pulse from the microprocessor restarts the clock to begin an operating sequence. Further assignment of ROM bits is as follows: Bits B_0, B_1, and B_2 are used to select a rate for the advance of the address counter. (With a very fast clock, the selection may have to be stated more than once to take effect.) Bits B_3, B_4, B_5, and B_6 are used to select one of eight control lines. (The extra bit B_6 is required to disable the selection altogether.) Finally bits B_7–B_{14} constitute an 8-bit data buss to distribute control words to various instrumental control devices. If the distribution includes latches, control words of more than 8 bits may be entered from this data buss. The data bits may be used in conjunction with control bits when data transfers are not enabled. This procedure is examplified by the conjunctive use of B_{14} and B_{15} to reset the address clock to address zero. Moreover, discretionary intervention by the microprocessor to halt or modify the sequence could be included in the scheme of Fig. X-2 by using an additional microprocessor output facility. Such an intervention could be made to occur only after completion of a selected sequence by suitable logic and appropriate codes entered in the ROM.

The controller that is described has a very wide latitude of data prescription and timing. The address stepping rate can be changed by binary factors up to 2^8. More than one idle or static state can be introduced, each requiring a restart pulse from the microprocessor. The reader may find it interesting to explore some of the possible control sequences available with the device. If the latitude of operation is insufficient, it may be supplemented by design modification. For example, a presettable address counter could be provided, to be loaded with a 6-bit word from the microprocessor, allowing a restart of the ROM sequence from an arbitrary point. For wider control words or a longer sequence, the ROM itself could be expanded as needed.

Other designs for controllers can, of course, be devised depending on instrumental requirements. For the most elaborate needs, including even interactive control, a subsidiary microprocessor, having its own memory, and program could be used. The operation of a dedicated microprocessor for instrument control can be structured along the lines of the ROM controller illustrated in Fig. X-2. The microprocessor allows the possibility of more elaborate instrumental programming and the additional benefit of software to permit processing of inputs from the instrument to modify the control outputs. Exercises 2 and 3 at the end of the chapter concern the design of environmental and procedural controls.

X-3 DATA ACQUISITION AND PROCESSING

The specification of data acquisition and data processing, of course, depends on the nature of the instrument system designed. Comments made previously may be helpful as a guide to specific designs. A few additional details may be appropriately suggested here. However, most of the design is for the reader to develop.

A. Data Acquisition

The variety of the output form from instruments is considerable, and the acquisition methods used can be almost as varied. Two examples will serve to illustrate a general approach to the design of data acquisition schemes. Of course, the data must be digitized, and the discussion will presuppose an instrumental output comprised of an analog electrical signal suitable to digital conversion by an ADC. It will further assume that the important data represent values of a dependent variable as a response to variations of an independent variable; the dependent variable being a series of peaks whose location, amplitude, and, possibly, shape are of interest.

In the first example, the response peaks may be completely isolated in terms of the independent variable, and their location may be important only as to nominal value. In this case the principal requirement is to determine the amplitude of each peak. Figure X-3a shows two such peaks separated in location as referred to the independent variable. Acquiring the peak values could involve simply making one conversion at exactly the right time. Analog schemes are often useful for capturing the peak values by observing the derivatives of the signal as a function of the independent variable in order to locate the peak center (see Fig. X-3b); for noisy peaks that have known shapes or symmetry, integration of the signal to improve the fidelity of the acquired data can be useful (see Fig. X-3c). These analog signal-conditioning steps can be very helpful in simplifying data acquisition, leaving a requirement only for a single-point conversion for each peak.

The conversion process itself must take account of two particulars, namely, the dynamic range of the signals and the accuracy with which they must be rendered. Analog-to-digital converters with a resolution of 16 binary bits, and an accuracy nearly to match can be obtained at considerable cost. Where large dynamic range is encountered but accuracy and resolution are less critical, the combination of an 8- or 10-bit ADC with a data scaling scheme may be more appropriate than a 16-bit ADC. Figure X-4 schematically shows an integrating detector

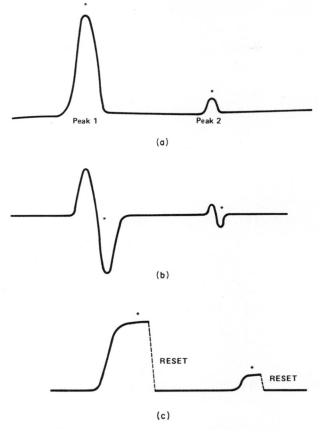

Figure X-3 Acquisition of data from separated peaks.

arrangement with data scaling. Integrators in three ranges are connected to the signal line. Over-range conditions are detected by the sense amplifiers, whose outputs are used to connect the ADC to the appropriate integrator. Range indication and the ADC output are read after the peak has been completely transversed, whereupon all of the integrators are reset to prepare for the next peak.

Where the dynamic range of the input signal permits, the ADC could also be connected directly to the signal line, and a series of ordinate values could be delivered to the microprocessor during the traverse of each peak. The processing described above in application to the analog signal, namely, differentiation or integration, could then be carried out digitally in the microprocessor to elicit the peak values.

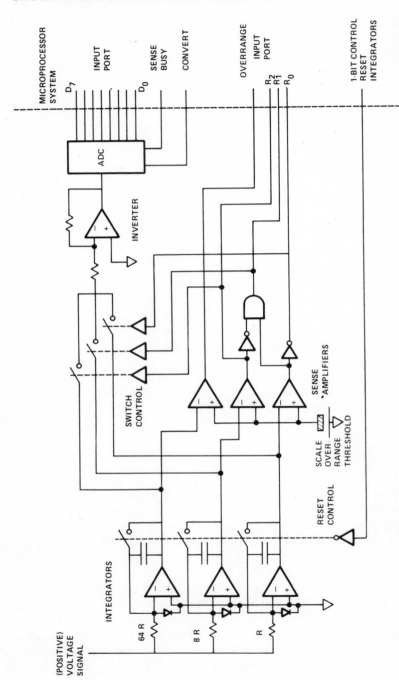

Figure X-4 Multi-range acquisition scheme to accommodate a large dynamic range of input signals with an 8-bit analog-to-digital converter. A complete system would include a scale change lock-out occurring just before conversion to preclude scale ambiguity.

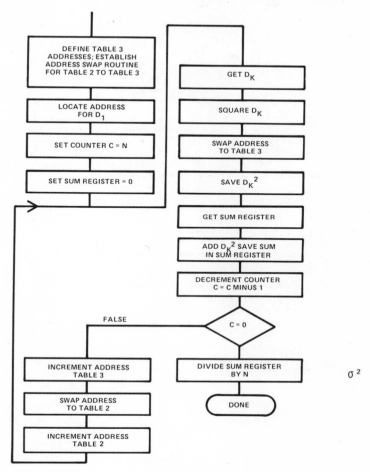

Figure X-7 *Continued.*

may shorten the program. This refinement is left as an exercise for the reader.

PROGRAM LISTING: STAT

PURPOSE: TO COMPUTE THE MEAN VALUE AND THE MEAN SQUARE DEVIATION OF A LIST OF VALUES

ENTRY ADDRESS: 000 (TO BE ADJUSTED)

MEMORY REQUIRED: 289 WORDS ROM, RAM REQUIRE-MENT DEPENDS ON LIST LENGTH

EXTERNAL HARDWARE: NONE

REF	ADDRESS OCTAL	ADDRESS HEX	CODE OCTAL	CODE HEX	MNEMONIC	CALL	COMMENT
STAT	000/000	00 00	061	31	LXI SP		ESTABLISH STORAGE AREA FOR TABLE MANAGEMENT
	1	1	070	38			AND TEMPORARY STORAGE.
	2	2	010	08			
	3	3	305	C5	PUSH B		SAVE COLUMN 3 ADDRESS
	4	4	325	D5	PUSH D		SAVE COLUMN 2 ADDRESS
	5	5	345	E5	PUSH H		SAVE COLUMN 1 ADDRESS
	6	6	365	F5	PUSH PSW		SAVE NUMBER OF DATA POINTS <128 DECIMAL
	7	7	205	85	ADD L		FIND LOW BYTE COLUMN 1 TERMINAL ADDRESS
	10	8	365	F5	PUSH PSW		SAVE IT
2ADD	1	9	016	0E	MVI C		ROUTINE TO ADD 8-BIT DATA FOR DATA AVERAGE
	2	A	000	00			SUM WILL BE SIGNED AND OCCUPY REGISTERS C, D
	3	B	121	51	MOV D, C		
2AD1	4	C	227	97	SUB A		ZERO ACCUMULATOR AND CARRY
	5	D	206	86	ADD M		GET THE VALUE WITH SIGN
	6	E	365	F5	PUSH PSW		TEMPORARY SAVE FOR SIGN MANAGEMENT
	7	F	202	82	ADD D		ADD TO THE SUM
	10	10	127	57	MOV D, A		REVISE SUM
	1	1	171	79	MOV A, C		
	2	2	316	CE	ADD 1		ACCOUNT FOR CARRY
	3	3	000	00			
	4	4	117	4F	MOV C, A		TO HIGH BYTE SUM
	5	5	316	F1	POP PSW		RESTORE AUGEND SIGN
	6	6	362	F2	JNM	2AD2	POSITIVE AUGEND, SKIP SIGN ADJUSTMENT
	7	7	035	1D			
	30	8	000	00			
	1	9	067	37	STC		TO GENERATE A = 377
	2	A	237	9F	SBB A		
	3	B	201	81	ADD C		ADJUST HIGH BYTE FOR ADDED NEGATIVE AUGEND
	4	C	117	4F	MOV C, A		
2AD2	5	D	361	F1	POP PSW		GET TERMINAL ADDRESS
	6	E	365	F5	PUSH PSW		SAVE IT AGAIN
	7	F	043	23	INX H		ADDRESS OF NEXT DATUM

REF	ADDRESS OCTAL	ADDRESS HEX 00 20	CODE OCTAL	CODE HEX	MNEMONIC	CALL	COMMENT
	000/040	00 20	275	BD	CMP L		TABLE DONE?
	1	1	302	C2	JNZ	2AD1	
	2	2	014	0C			GO BACK FOR MORE
	3	3	000	00			
	4	4	361	F1	POP PSW		DISCARD TABLE L TERMINAL ADDRESS
	5	5	361	F1	POP PSW		GET NUMBER OF DATA POINTS
	6	6	365	F5	PUSH PSW		SAVE AGAIN
	7	7	107	47	MOV B, A		SET THE REGISTERS FOR DIVISION; DIVIDEND SUM
	50	8	036	1E	MVI E		IN C, D, E; DIVISOR IN B
	1	9	000	00			
	2	A	315	CD	CALL		
	3	B	223	93		3DIV	SIGNED QUOTIENT WILL BE IN REGISTERS D, E
	4	C	000	00			
	5	D	361	F1	POP PSW		DUMMY, BUT DON'T LOSE IT
	6	E	341	E1	POP H		HEAD OF TABLE 1
	7	F	053	2B	DCX H		AVERAGE OF TABLE 1 WILL BE STORED ABOVE
	60	30	053	2B	DCX H		TABLE 1
	1	1	163	73	MOV M, E		SAVE LOW BYTE
	2	2	043	23	INX H		
	3	3	162	72	MOV M, D		SAVE HIGH BYTE
	4	4	043	23	INX H		RESTORE TABLE ADDRESS
	5	5	102	42	MOV B, D		HIGH BYTE OF AVERAGE, IGNORE TRUNCATION ERROR
	6	6	321	D1	POP D		GET TABLE 2 ADDRESS
	7	7	325	D5	PUSH D		SAVE IT AGAIN
	70	8	345	E5	PUSH H		SAVE TABLE 1 ADDRESS
	1	9	365	F5	PUSH PSW		SAVE NUMBER OF DATA POINTS
	2	A	205	85	ADD L		ESTABLISH TERMINAL ADDRESS FOR TABLE 1
	3	B	365	F5	PUSH PSW		SAVE IT
STT1	4	C	176	7E	MOV A, M		GET A DATUM
	5	D	220	90	SUB B		SUBTRACT THE AVERAGE
	6	E	353	EB	XCHG		SWAP ADDRESSES
	7	F	167	77	MOV M, A		STORE DEVIATION

REF	ADDRESS OCTAL	ADDRESS HEX	CODE OCTAL	CODE HEX	MNEMONIC	CALL	COMMENT
	000/100	00 40	043	23	INX L		ADJUST (BOTH) TABLE ADDRESSES
	1	1	353	EB	XCHG		SWAP ADDRESSES
	2	2	043	23	INX L		
	3	3	361	F1	POP PSW		GET TABLE 1 TERMINAL ADDRESS
	4	4	365	F5	PUSH PSW		SAVE IT AGAIN
	5	5	275	BD	CMP L		TABLE DONE ?
	6	6	302	C2	JNZ	STT1	
	7	7	074	3C			GO BACK FOR MORE
	10	8	000	00			
	1	9	361	F1	POP PSW		DISCARD TABLE 1 TERMINUS
	2	A	361	F1	POP PSW		NUMBER OF DATA POINTS
	3	B	301	C1	POP B		TABLE 1 ADDRESS (TEMPORARY HOLD)
	4	C	341	E1	POP H		TABLE 2 ADDRESS
	5	D	321	D1	POP D		TABLE 3 ADDRESS
	6	E	305	C5	PUSH B		SAVE COLUMN 1 ADDRESS
	7	F	365	F5	PUSH PSW		SAVE NUMBER OF DATA POINTS
	20	50	325	D5	PUSH D		SAVE TABLE 3 ADDRESS
	1	1	205	85	ADD L		ESTABLISH TABLE 2 TERMINAL ADDRESS
	2	2	365	F5	PUSH PSW		SAVE IT
	3	3	345	E5	PUSH H		SAVE TABLE 2 ADDRESS
STT2	4	4	106	46	MOV B, M		SET UP TO SQUARE DEVIATION
	5	5	110	48	MOV C, B		
	6	6	353	EB	XCHG		SWAP ADDRESSES, D, E = TABLE 2 ADDRESS WILL BE LOST
	7	7	315	CD	CALL	MULT	SQUARE THE DEVIATION
	30	8	333	DB			
	1	9	000	00			
	2	A	163	73	MOV M, E		STORE THE SQUARED DEVIATION
	3	B	043	23	INX H		IN TABLE 3, TWO BYTES PER DATA POINT
	4	C	162	72	MOV M, D		
	5	D	043	23	INX H		
	6	E	353	EB	XCHG		TABLE 3 ADDRESS TO C, D
	7	F	341	E1	POP H		RESTORE TABLE 2 ADDRESS

REF	ADDRESS OCTAL	ADDRESS HEX	CODE OCTAL	CODE HEX	MNEMONIC	CALL	COMMENT
	000/140	00 60	361	F1	POP PSW		GET TABLE 2 TERMINAL ADDRESS
	1	1	365	F5	PUSH PSW		SAVE IT AGAIN
	2	2	043	23	INX H		NEXT ADDRESS
	3	3	345	E5	PUSH H		SAVE IT
	4	4	275	BE	CMP L		TABLE DONE ?
	5	5	302	C2	JNZ	STT2	
	6	6	124	54			
	7	7	000	00			
	50	8	341	E1	POP H		TABLE 2 CURRENT ADDRESS, DISCARD
	1	9	361	F1	POP PSW		TABLE 2 TERMINUS DISCARD
	2	A	341	E1	POP H		TABLE 3 ADDRESS, HOLD
	3	B	361	F1	POP PSW		NUMBER OF DATA POINTS
	4	C	365	F5	PUSH PSW		SAVE AGAIN
	5	D	267	B7	ORA A		CLEAR THE CARRY
	6	E	007	07	RLC		2 * NUMBER OF POINTS = LENGTH OF TABLE 3
	7	F	205	85	ADD L		ESTABLISH TABLE 3 TERMINUS
3PAD	60	70	365	F5	PUSH PSW		SAVE IT
	1	1	016	0E	MVI C		SET UP FOR ADDITION OF 2-BYTE POSITIVE DATA
	2	2	000	00			
	3	3	121	51	MOV D, C		ZEROS TO SUM REGISTERS (CD), D, E
3PA1	4	4	131	59	MOV E, C		
	5	5	176	86	MOV A, M		GET LOW BYTE OF SQUARED DEVIATION
	6	6	043	23	INX H		
	7	7	106	46	MOV B, M		AND HIGH BYTE
	70	8	043	23	INX H		
	1	9	203	83	ADD E		ADD TO SUM REGSTERS AND STORE NEW SUM
	2	A	137	5F	MOV E, A		
	3	B	170	78	MOV A, B		
	4	C	212	8A	ADC D		
	5	D	127	57	MOV D, A		
	6	E	171	79	MOV A, C		GET OVERFLOW REGISTER (CD)
	7	F	316	CE	ACI		ADD CARRY IF ANY

REF	ADDRESS OCTAL	ADDRESS HEX	CODE OCTAL	CODE HEX	MNEMONIC	CALL	COMMENT
	000/200	00 80	000	00			
	1	1	117	4F	MOV C, A		HIGH BYTE OF 3-BYTE SUM
	2	2	361	F1	POP PSW		GET TABLE 3 TERMINUS
	3	3	365	F5	PUSH PSW		SAVE IT AGAIN
	4	4	275	BD	CMP L		TABLE DONE ?
	5	5	302	C2	JNZ	3PA1	
	6	6	165	75			GO BACK FOR MORE
	7	7	000	00			
	10	8	361	F1	POP PSW		DISCARD TABLE 3 TERMINUS
	1	9	361	F1	POP PSW		GET NUMBER OF DATA POINTS
	2	A	107	47	MOV B, A		SET UP FOR DIVISION, SUM DEVIATION SQUARED
	3	B	315	CD	CALL	3DIV	IN C, D, E,
	4	C	223	93			MEAN SQUARE DEVIATION IN D, E
	5	D	000	00			
	6	E	341	E1	POP H		GET TABLE 1 ADDRESS
	7	F	053	2B	DCX H		TO AVERAGE VALUE HIGH BYTE ADDRESS
	20	90	106	46	MOV B, M		GET HIGH BUTE
	1	1	064	2B	DCX H		
	2	2	116	4E	MOV C, M		AND LOW BYTE; AVERAGE IN B, C, END STAT
3DIV	3	3	305	C5	PUSH B		SAVE DIVISOR
	4	4	345	E5	PUSH H		SAVE MEMORY POINTER
	5	5	041	21	LXI H		SET TWO COUNTERS
	6	6	031	19			
	7	7	000	00			
3DV1	30	8	315	CD	CALL	C3SG	ADJUST THE SIGN OF DIVIDEND, (DIVISOR IS POSITIVE)
	1	9	301	C1			SAVES THE SIGN IN H
	2	A	000	00			
	3	B	372	FA	JM	3DVI	TRY AGAIN
	4	C	230	98			
	5	D	000	00			
	6	E	345	E5	PUSH H		SAVE THE SIGN INDICATOR
	7	F	170	78	MOV A, B		GET DIVISOR

REF	ADDRESS OCTAL	ADDRESS HEX	CODE OCTAL	CODE HEX	MNEMONIC	CALL	COMMENT
	000/240	00 A0	057	2F	CMA		GENERATE 2'S COMPLEMENT
	1	1	074	3C	INR A		
	2	2	006	06	MVI B		CLEAR B REGISTER FOR PARTIAL DIVISIONS
	3	3	000	00			
3DV2	4	4	365	F5	PUSH PSW		SAVE 2'S COMPLEMENT DIVISOR
	5	5	361	F1	POP PSW		GET 2'S COMPLEMENT DIVISOR
	6	6	365	F5	PUSH PSW		SAVE IT AGAIN
	7	7	200	80	ADD B		TRIAL SUBTRACTION
	40	8	372	FA	JM	3DV3	REMAINDER NEGATIVE, DON'T ADJUST B-REGISTER
	1	9	254	AC			
	2	A	000	00			
3DV3	3	B	107	47	MOV B, A		INSTALL NEW REMAINDER
	4	C	315	CD	CALL	4ASL	SHIFT LEFT 4 REGISTERS (B,C,D,E)
	5	D	316	CE			
	6	E	000	00			
	7	F	055	2D	DCR L		COUNT THE PARTIAL DIVISIONS
	60	B0	302	C2	JNZ	3DV2	NOT DONE, GO BACK FOR MORE
	1	1	245	A5			
	2	2	000	00			
	3	3	361	F1	POP PSW		DISCARD 2'S COMPLEMENT DIVISOR
	4	4	341	E1	POP H		GET SIGN DESIGNATOR
	5	5	346	E6	ANI		SIGN BIT
	6	6	001	01			
	7	7	312	C2	JZ	3DV4	BIT = 0 IMPLIES SIGN WAS POSITIVE, SKIP
	70	8	275	BD			SIGN CHANGER
	1	9	000	00			
	2	A	315	CD	CALL	3CSG	
	3	B	301	C1			
	4	C	000	00			
3DV4	5	D	341	E1	POP H		RESTORE MEMORY POINTER
	6	E	361	F1	POP PSW		GET DIVISOR
	7	F	107	47	MOV B, A		TO B-REGISTER

REF	ADDRESS OCTAL	ADDRESS HEX	CODE OCTAL	CODE HEX	MNEMONIC	CALL	COMMENT
	000/300	00 C0	311	C9	RET		DONE 3 DIV
C3SG	1	1	044	24	INR H		BUMP THE SIGN INDICATOR
	2	2	227	97	SUB A		CLEAR ACCUMULATOR AND CARRY
	3	3	223	93	SUB E		DO A 3-BYTE SUBTRACTION
	4	4	137	5F	MOV E, A		AND REPLACE BYTES IN REGISTERS (C,D,E)
	5	5	076	3E	MVI A		
	6	6	000	00			
	7	7	232	9A	SBB D		
	10	8	127	57	MOV D, A		
	1	9	076	3E	MVI A		
	2	A	000	00			
	3	B	231	99	SBB C		
	4	C	117	4F	MOV C, A		
	5	D	311	C9	RET		DONE C3SG
4ASL	6	E	173	7B	MOV A, E		GET EACH TYE AND ROTATE, BEGINNING WITH
	7	F	027	17	RAL		LOW BYTE; CARRY RETAINS HIGH BIT
	20	D0	137	5F	MOV E, A		OVERFLOW TO NEXT BYTE; HIGH BIT
	1	1	172	7A	MOV A, D		OF B-REGISTER IS LOST.
	2	2	027	17	RAL		
	3	3	127	57	MOV D, A		
	4	4	171	79	MOV A, C		
	5	5	027	17	RAL		
	6	6	117	4F	MOV C, A		
	7	7	170	78	MOV A, B		
	30	8	027	17	RAL		
	1	9	107	47	MOV B, A		
	2	A	311	C9	RET		DONE 4ASL
MULT	3	B	305	C5	PUSH B		SAVE MULTIPLIER, MULTIPLICAND
	4	C	345	E5	PUSH H		SAVE MEMORY POINTERS
	5	D	041	21	LXI H		SET TWO COUNTERS
	6	E	010	08			
	7	F	000	00			

REF	ADDRESS OCTAL	HEX	CODE OCTAL	HEX	MNEMONIC	CALL	COMMENT
MUL1	000/340	00 E0	044	24	INR H		BUMP THE SIGN INDICATOR
	1	1	170	78	MOV A, B		GET MULTIPLIER AND GENERATE ITS 2'S COMPLEMENT
	2	2	057	2F	CMA		
	3	3	074	3C	INR A		
	4	4	107	47	MOV B, A		RETURN IT TO B-REGISTER
	5	5	372	FA	JM	MUL1	IF NEGATIVE, REVERSE THE SIGN
	6	6	340	E0			
	7	7	000	00			
MUL2	50	8	044	24	INR H		BUMP THE SIGN INDICATOR
	1	9	171	79	MOV A, C		GET MULTIPLICAND AND GENERATE ITS 2'S COMPLEMENT
	2	A	057	2F	CMA		
	3	B	074	3C	INR A		
	4	C	117	4F	MOV C, A		RETURN IT TO C-REGISTER
	5	D	372	FA	JM	MUL2	IF NEGATIVE, REVERSE THE SIGN
	6	E	350	E8			
	7	F	000	00			
	60	F0	174	7C	MOV A, H		GET THE SIGN INDICATOR
	1	1	037	1F	RAR		ODD, EVEN (BIT 0) TO CARRY AS INDICATOR
	2	2	365	F5	PUSH PSW		SAVE (CARRY); CARRY SET IMPLIES PRODUCT NEGATIVE
	3	3	021	11	LDX D		CLEAR THE TWO PRODUCT REGISTERS
	4	4	000	00			
	5	5	000	00			
MUL4	6	6	315	CD	CALL	XASL	SHIFT THE PARTIAL PRODUCT ACCUMULATOR,
	7	7	030	18			
	70	8	001	01			STARTING WITH THE TOP BIT
	1	9	170	78	MOV A, B		ENTER B-REGISTER TO GET PARTIAL MULTIPLIER
	2	A	007	07	RLC		SAVE THE REMAINING BIT
	3	B	107	47	MOV B, A,		
	4	C	322	D2	JNC	MUL3	SKIP PARTIAL PRODUCT IF BIT WAS ZERO
	5	D	006	06			
	6	E	001	01			
	7	F	173	7B	MOV A, E		ELSE GET MULTIPLICAND

REF	ADDRESS		CODE		MNEMONIC	CALL	COMMENT
	OCTAL	HEX	OCTAL	HEX			
	001/000	01 00	201	81	ADD C		ADD TO PARTIAL PRODUCT ACCUMULATOR
	1		137	5F	MOV E, A		RESTORE REVISED LOW BYTES
	2		172	7A	MOV A, D		ADD CARRY IF ANY TO HIGH BYTE
	3		316	CE	ACI		
	4		000	00			
	5		127	57	MOV D, A		RESTORE REVISED HIGH BYTE
MUL3	6		055	2D	DCR L		ADJUST THE COUNTER
	7		302	C2	JNZ		
	10		366	F6		MUL4	NOT DONE, GO BACK FOR MORE
	1		000	00			
	2		361	F1	POP PSW		GET THE SIGN DESIGNATOR
	3		322	D2	JNC		
	4		025	15		MUL5	SKIP IF PRODUCT IS POSITIVE
	5		001	01			
	6		227	97	SUB A		ELSE CHANGE THE SIGN OF PRODUCT
	7		147	67	MOV H, A		BY SUBTRACTING 2 BYTES FROM ZERO
	20		223	93	SUB E		AND RESTORE TO REGISTERS C, D
	1		137	5F	MOV E, A		
	2		174	7C	MOV A, H		
	3		232	9A	SBB D		
	4		127	57	MOV D, A		
MUL5	5		341	E1	POP H		RESTORE MEMORY POINTER
	6		301	C1	POP B		RESTORE MULTIPLIER AND MULTIPLICAND
	7		311	C9	RET		DONE MULT
XASL	30		267	B7	ORA A		CLEAR THE CARRY
	1		173	7B	MOV A, E		GET LOW BYTE
	2		027	17	RAL		SHIFT IT LEFT, HIGH BIT TO CARRY
	3		137	5F	MOV E, A		RESTORE SHIFTED LOW BYTE
	4		172	7A	MOV A, D		GET HIGH BYTE
	5		027	17	RAL		SHIFT IT LEFT, CARRY TO LOW BIT, HIGH BIT LOST
	6		127	57	MOV D, A		RESTORE HIGH BYTE
	7		267	B7	ORA A		CLEAR THE CARRY

REF	ADDRESS		CODE		MNEMONIC	CALL	COMMENT
	OCTAL	HEX	OCTAL	HEX			
	001/040	01 20	311	C9	RET		END XASL, END STAT

PROGRAM: STAT

ENTRY LIST:

ENTRY	ADDRESS OCTAL	HEX
XASL	001/030	01 18
MUL5	001/025	01 15
MUL3	001/006	01 06
MUL4	000/366	00 F6
MUL2	000/350	00 E8
MUL1	000/340	00 E0
MULT	000/333	00 DB
4ASL	000/316	00 CE
C3SG	000/301	00 C1
3DV4	000/275	00 BD
3DV3	000/254	00 AC
3DV2	000/245	00 A5
3DV1	000/230	00 98
3DIV	000/223	00 93
3PA1	000/165	00 75
3PAD	000/161	00 71
STT2	000/124	00 54
STT1	000/074	00 3C
2AD2	000/035	00 1D
2ADD	000/011	00 09
STAT	000/000	00 00

RAM UTILIZATION

ADDRESS OCTAL HEX	ASSIGNMENT
000/042 00 22	WORKING AREA FOR TABLE MANAGEMENT AND TEMPORARY STORAGE
.	
.	
.	
OTHER	AS REQUIRED FOR TABLES

Exercises 4, 5, and 6 appearing at the end of the chapter address the topic of data acquisition and processing.

X-4 DISPLAY

Several display devices have been described in earlier chapters. These constitute a very short representation of the possible devices from which display systems can be structured. A variety of so-called digital displays can be found in commercial offerings with costs varying from a few hundred to thousands of dollars.

In addition to digital displays, any number of analog displays may also be added to a microprocessor automated system. For volatile displays, electrical meters and oscilloscopes can be used. For hard copy, analog chart recorders of almost any type can be accommodated. The interface of the digital system to analog displays is a relatively simple matter of using DACs to convert the digital information to a suitable analog form. It should be remarked that although this approach was common about 10 years ago, the present trend in display design is to convert the analog devices themselves to accept data in digital form. For example, chart recorders specifically designed for digital application now frequently use stepping motors for mechanical drive rather than the synchronous motors and analog servos that are appropriate to analog service. Nevertheless, if analog devices are already available in the laboratory, savings can be realized by adapting them with DACs.

Since the specifics of the display are uniquely determined by the system objectives, no further discussion will be presented here regarding display details. Artistry on the part of the system designer in the design of the display system can enhance the utility as well as the esthetics of the system, and the final display design deserves careful consideration.

X-5 SOME ADDITIONAL COMMENTS

The design of a digitally automated system is an iterative process. The outline in the sections above represents a first iteration. When it is complete, possible improvements and simplifications will often be apparent. Some of these may be advantageously incorporated into a second iteration of the design, and within reasonable limits, further design changes can be considered.

At some point, the design must be committed to construction. Further polishing after that point will yield diminishing returns, and a system that works, even lacking the nicest elegance, it very satisfying. Few systems work perfectly immediately after construction. It may take some time to eliminate the "bugs" that frustrate the operation due to error or oversight in both hardware and software design. The consolation for the designer who encounters these sometimes elusive and annoying bugs is that his problems and feelings have been experienced by every system designer. The reward at the end of the trial is a real sense of accomplishment and satisfaction to see a successfully automated operating system that functions in accordance with its conception.

EXERCISES

1. Formulate the overall design of a system including the following:
    a. Definition of the system objective and function.
    b. Specification of the instrumental means to accomplish the objective.
    c. Description of the instrumental procedures for all of the operating modes.
    d. Specification of the operator inputs required for mode selection.
    e. Specification of the instrument control to be accommodated.
    f. Definition of data acquisition requirements and methods.
    g. Specification of instrument data formats and data management requirements.
    h. Outline of data processing to be incorporated in the operating system.
    i. Description of the display and monitoring requirements and specification of the display format.

2. Define and design the environmental controls that are required for the service of instruments and other devices in the system.

3. Define and design the devices that are required for procedural control of the instruments, with suitable attention to the division of control between the supervisory microprocessor and the control devices.

4. Rewrite the listing above to reduce the total number of program words. The reader may reward himself at the rate of $.10 per word saved.

5. Design the data acquisition system needed in the instrument system under consideration, with attention to both hardware components and management of acquired data, anticipating data processing.

6. Define the data processing required for the system. Design flow charts to outline the processing steps. Write the code.

7. Design the display for the system giving consideration to both volatile and hardcopy representation.

Index